Testing Client/Server
Applications

Testing Client/Server Applications

Patricia A. Goglia

To Nigel
with love
from Construction Team

J.K.

QED Publishing Group
Boston • London • Toronto

This book is available at a special discount when you order
multiple copies. For information, contact QED Publishing
Group, POB 812070, Wellesley, MA 02181-0013 or phone
617-237-5656.

Library of Congress Catalog Number: 93-17825
International Standard Book Number: 0-89435-450-7

Printed in the United States of America
93 94 95 10 9 8 7 6 5 4 3 2 1

Library of Congress Cataloging-In-Publication Data

Goglia, Patricia.
    Testing client/server applications / Patricia Goglia.
        p.   cm.
    Includes index.
    ISBN 0-89435-450-7
    1. Client/server computing—Testing.   I. Title.
    QA76.9.C55G64   1993
    004'.36'0287—dc20   93-17825
                                                            CIP

To Rebecca,

for her patience, encouragement, and laughter

Contents

Preface

Client/server computing is not only the wave of the future, but the business solution for today's information systems. The formation of separate client/server computing units by major hardware and software firms is a clear indication of the demand for this technology.

In the client/server environment, the software developers control all aspects of the development, testing, and implementation of their application. They are not governed by the standards and procedures that apply to the mainframe environment. They don't have the controls and restrictions imposed upon their project as do the developers of mainframe-based applications. This autonomy creates both a liberating and challenging development environment.

System design and network preparation are key components in the application development effort. However, the systems testing of that application is critical to the success of the project.

If you thought testing a mainframe-based, online application was difficult, try testing an application for a client/server environment with distributed processing across heterogeneous platforms. A planned and effectively managed systems test is mandatory. The software developers must deliver a reliable, secure system that fulfills the user's requirements for the project to succeed. A haphazard approach to testing will permit application errors to be released throughout the network.

This book describes the activities required in systems testing an application during development and maintenance. It discusses the differences and similarities between the client/server and the mainframe environment in performing these activities.

The book describes in detail how to systems test an application. It discusses when the systems testing activities occur in the system development life cycle. It defines the tasks and deliverables in the planning, design, execution, and maintenance phases of systems testing.

The planning phase section covers the following:

Test strategy

Systems test environment

Staffing requirements and responsibilities

Resource requirements

Selection of testing tools

Systems test deliverables

The design phase section covers designing tests for the following:

Quality/standards compliance

Business requirements

Performance capabilities

Operational capabilities

There are examples to show you how to specify the test conditions and test cases. It explains how to group the test cases to create the minimum test data. Expected results, baseline data, test procedures, testing tools, and test cycles are covered.

The review section is a checklist of issues to address in reviewing the systems test specifications.

The following are examined in the execution phase section:

Execution of the tests
The Activity Log
Incident Reporting
Summary Reporting

The maintenance phase section covers maintaining and controlling systems testing now that the system is in production. It discusses the importance of this task in the client/server environment. The following topics are covered:

Configuration changes
Emergency changes
Business requirements changes
Performance changes
Operational changes
Testing tools changes

The administration section discusses directing the technical aspects of systems testing. It covers management's role in providing the standards, training, and security for the testing process. The administration of systems testing and monitoring of the production system are discussed.

This book is intended primarily for software developers, test practitioners, and managers. DP auditors will find the book valuable for developing testing standards and documentation requirements. End-users will read the book to evaluate the testing techniques used for their systems.

The Client/Server Environment

The term *client / server* seems to be ubiquitous. Most Information Systems managers include client/server in their list of objectives for the next three years. Trade publications tout client/server as the technology for downsizing information systems. Hardware and software vendors stretch the definition of client/server to fit their product.

Client/server is an architecture for information processing systems. The client/server architecture allocates the application processing between a client and a server so that each component performs the tasks for which it is best suited. The client cooperates (acts jointly) with the server to produce the results, hence the term cooperative processing is used in describing client/server. The client/server application software is often distributed to multiple sites. The client/server application system, however, need not be a distributed system in which the application functions are performed in separate sites.

Although the term client/server is relatively new, its concepts are not. Software developers have advocated cooperative processing for years, but until recently, it was not feasible. Major changes have occurred in the hardware industry, particularly in desktop computers. They have increased in processing power and decreased in price. These changes have made client/server appealing.

Management appreciates its cost savings in:

- Development
- Hardware
- Operation

It appeals to users for the following reasons:

- Desktop access to their information
- A familiar interface
- The ability to utilize the information in their desktop software

Software developers like the following features:

- Total control over the development process
- Freedom from the bureaucracy of the mainframe environment
- Faster turnaround time
- Integrated development tools

The client/server architecture contains three components: the client, the server, and the network.

THE CLIENT

The *client* is an intelligent desktop workstation that is used by one user. It has its own operating system and is capable of running desktop software such as a word processor or a spreadsheet, as well as the client/server application.

In client/server-based applications, the functions are processed cooperatively by the client and the server. For example, in an *order entry* system, one of the business functions is to inquire about customer orders. The client presents a screen to the user requesting the customer or order identifier. The client accepts the user's input, submits a request to the server for the order information, and then displays the results. The client provides the interface between the user and the application. Its primary function is presentation services. It accepts user input and displays output. It also contains software to support functions specific to the presentation services. It calculates totals, edits fields, displays contextual help, and provides navigation. It does not perform data retrieval directly; it requests data from the server using a standardized call format called a *Remote Procedure Call* (RPC).

The user interface can be character-based or graphical. Mainframe applications use character-based interfaces where the screens contain characters (letters and symbols). The user navigates through the system in a structured format using hierarchical menus. Many users run desktop software packages that use a *Graphical User Interface* (GUI). The screen images in these packages are composed of individual dots (pixels). The user navigates through the system in a random manner using pointers to select graphical choices. GUIs generally provide the user with a wide range of choices at one time. It would be difficult today to sell a user on a character-based interface. They appear "user-hostile" compared to the desktop GUI applications.

GRAPHICAL USER INTERFACES

Graphical User Interfaces provide the user with a consistent, easy-to-use interface. Many users are already familiar with GUIs from their desktop software. The GUI platform permits the user to have multiple sessions active at one time. They can have a word processing, a spreadsheet, and a client/server application session active concurrently.

The following are some of the GUI elements:

- Windows
- Menus
- Icons
- Pointers
- Scroll bars
- Controls

Figures 1.1 and 1.2 show some these GUI elements.

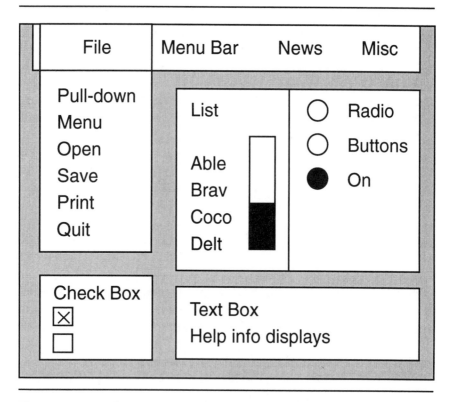

Figure 1.1.   GUI Elements.

Windows

Windows appear as rectangular boxes on the screen and can be various sizes. They can appear next to each other (*tiled windows*) or in some platforms, overlap each other (*cascading windows*). Figures 1.3 and 1.4 show tiled and cascading windows respectively. Windows are used to present information; each can contain a different session or different information for the same session.

There are several types of windows:

- A *dialogue box* is a window that enables the user to communicate with the application. It pops up in the center of the screen, asks the user questions, and accepts the responses. It is called a dialogue box because it conducts a conversation

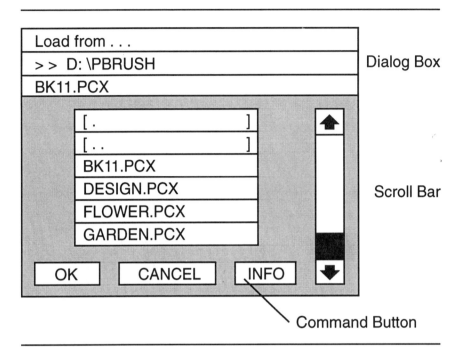

Figure 1.2.   GUI Elements.

with the user. A series of questions and answers may occur until the action is completed.

- A *table* window is used to present multiple rows of information.
- A *text* box is used to present information in text format. The Help function uses this type of box to display information.

Menus

A *menu* is a list of choices from which the user can select. There are several types of menus:

- A *menu bar* appears along the top line of the screen. It contains a series of words, each representing a choice. When the user selects a word, a pull-down menu appears.
- A *pull-down menu* is actually a submenu. It appears when the user selects an item from the menu bar displayed across the top of a screen. It is called a pull-down or drop-down menu

Figure 1.3.   Tiled Windows.

because it is pulled down from the menu bar into the main screen area. The user can select one of the options presented on the menu, and the function is activated.

- A *pop-up menu* appears when the user selects an item on the screen that requires selection and is designed to invoke a menu. The menu displays (pops up) in the main screen area near the item selected. One of the options on the menu can be selected.

Icons

An *icon* is a miniature picture that represents a function available to the user. When the icon is selected, the function is initiated and its screen is displayed.

Pointers

A *pointer* is a symbol that appears on the screen. It can have various shapes (an arrow, blinking box, an underscore). Selections are made by moving it to the desired section of the screen with a *pointing device* such as a *mouse* or a *track ball*.

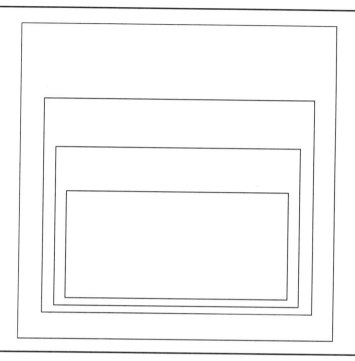

Figure 1.4.   Cascading Windows.

Scroll Bars

A *scroll bar* is used to show more information in the window. When the user moves the pointer up, down, left, or right, the information scrolls in that direction.

Controls

Controls are used in windows to accept input from the users. There are several types of controls:

- *Command buttons* are small rectangular boxes that contain a command indicating an action to perform. Command buttons are used to carry out that action. Two common command buttons in dialog boxes are "OK" and "Cancel." When the user selects the button, that action is performed.
- *Radio buttons* are small circles that appear next to each item

in a list. The user is asked to select one item from the list by pointing to its radio button. The items are mutually exclusive. When the item is selected, the radio button is "turned on" (highlighted). The circle is either filled in with a color or marked in some way, and the option or condition associated with that radio button is set.

- A *list* is a column of words, each indicating an option or condition, from which the user is allowed to select. The items are mutually exclusive. The selected word is highlighted, and its option or condition is set.
- *Check boxes* are small square boxes that appear next to each item in a list. The user is asked to select items from the list. The items are not mutually exclusive; the user can select multiple items from the list. When an item is selected, its check box is marked. The check box is used to toggle (turn on and off) some state or condition. When the check box is marked, the condition is in effect.
- *Sliders* are used when a continual range of settings is required, rather than a set of discrete ones. A slider is an empty track with a slider button inside. The button can be dragged from one end to the other using the pointer. Sliders operate like a tuning knob in a radio. As the button is dragged toward one end of the slider, the setting continually changes in that direction.

THE SERVER

The *server* is a computer on a *Local Area Network* (LAN) that provides services to other network computers. There is nothing special about the hardware that makes it a server. The type of hardware is dictated by its function and the requirements of the application. The server does not interface directly with the user. It receives requests from the clients, processes those requests, and returns the results, if any, to the clients. The client/server application may utilize several servers, each performing a different service. It must have a database server. Figure 1.5 shows the relationship of the client and server. The user interfaces with the client. The client submits requests to the server. The server accesses the database and returns data to the client.

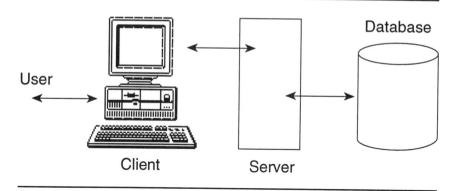

Figure 1.5.   Relationship of Client and Server.

The following are some types of servers:

- *File server*—supports data storage and retrieval for files other than the database. The file server is generally the computer that runs the network operating system software and considered the central node of the LAN.
- *Print server*—supports the printing functions for the application.
- *Fax server*—supports the tasks for sending and receiving facsimile documents.
- *Communications server*—supports WAN communications.
- *Database server*—supports the data requests of the client. The relational database and the SQL data access language have become the standard for client/server processing. A *Database Management System (DBMS)* product executes on the server. It processes the SQL requests from the client and handles the database management functions. It also supports stored procedures or triggers that run on the server.

Stored Procedures

A *stored procedure* is procedural code that resides on the server. It uses SQL commands to access databases. Stored procedures, important features in the client/server application, provide performance enhancements and data integrity:

- They are compiled code and, as such, execute faster than client requests with embedded SQL statements.
- They reside on the server, thereby reducing the network traffic. The client does not have to send each SQL statement over the network. It only sends the single call to the procedure.
- They provide data integrity by centralizing the code. One copy of the code resides on the server. It is shared code that all authorized clients can access. The software developers only need to write, test, and maintain one procedure instead of including the logic performed by the procedure in several client programs.

Triggers

Triggers are a type of stored procedure. They are stored on the server and execute automatically when a predefined event occurs. This event can be an update to a table or the occurrence of a business event. The following events can invoke triggers:

- **A database is updated.**
  A trigger can be invoked that updates an audit table containing the information about the database update. The name and log-on Id of the user who initiated the update can be captured, as well as the date and time of the update.
- **A row is added or changed in a database containing a foreign key.**
  A trigger can be invoked to maintain referential integrity. When a row is added or changed to a database that contains a foreign key (information that is a key in another database), the trigger can verify that the other database does, in fact, contain a row with that key. For example, a *Parts database* contains a column called Manufacturing Unit, which is a foreign key. The Manufacturing Unit specified for the part must exist in the Unit database. A trigger can maintain this relationship. Whenever a new part is inserted, a trigger is invoked to ensure its manufacturing unit exists in the Unit database.
- **A business rule needs to be verified.**
  A trigger can be invoked to enforce business rules. When a condition occurs that requires a business rule to be verified, a trigger can be invoked to do this. For example, if a company

has a business rule that unit price on a purchase order cannot exceed the prior price plus 15%, a trigger can be invoked to verify the unit price. When a purchase order is added, the trigger can be invoked to compare the two prices and notify the client of the results.

THE NETWORK

The *network* provides the connectivity for the system. The clients and the servers are connected to each other by a LAN. The client can also be connected directly or via a communications server to a *Wide Area Network* (WAN). Figure 1.6 shows a client/server architecture. The clients are connected to the database server and a communications server.

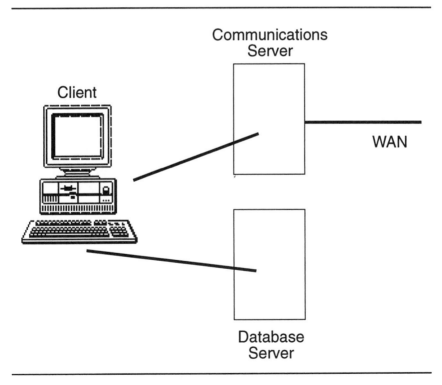

Figure 1.6.   Client/Server Architecture.

Network management is a major challenge in the client/server architecture. There are three separate issues that should be considered:

- Network design
- Network preparation
- Network administration

Network Design

Network design is the initial task in developing an application in a new client/server environment. It includes the following:

- Surveying the physical site
- Creating an inventory of the existing equipment
- Reviewing the existing vendor contracts
- Selecting the network hardware and network software
- Configuring the network
- Documenting the network design
- Specifying personnel requirements

Surveying the Physical Site

The physical site must be surveyed for all network designs. The safety issues, security concerns, fire regulations, and wiring and electrical codes must be considered in designing the network layout. A survey of the premises examines the facilities and the building architecture for these concerns. A site survey may seem like an unnecessary task, but it should be conducted if only to verify that building plans are current and accurate.

Creating an Inventory of Equipment

This is an important and often tedious task. All of the existing equipment must be listed in one consolidated inventory. The hardware, software, telephone facilities, and power supply must be included.

Reviewing the Existing Vendor Contracts

All existing vendor contracts should be reviewed to see if they cover any features that may be required.

Selecting the Network Hardware and Network Software

The user requirements must be reviewed to determine the appropriate network hardware and software for the functions. The network should meet the needs in the specifications. It should be easily expandable to accommodate future requirements.

Configuring the Network

The distribution and location of the nodes must be determined. The configuration should be designed for optimum cost savings.

Documenting the Network Design

The network design should be documented. All equipment and vendor contracts should be listed. The rationale for any decisions should be included in the documentation. It should not only describe how the network was configured, but why it was designed in this manner.

Specifying Personnel Requirements

Network design should also include the personnel required to operate the network. It should specify the qualifications required by that staff. It should also describe the training programs that will be required and outline the network training that each group should receive. This includes IS managers, network administrators, network programmers, and users.

Network Preparation

Network preparation must be performed for both new network installations and new applications on an existing network. The following tasks are included:

- Preparing the site
- Installing the cabling
- Installing the hardware and software
- Defining the network
- Installing any security systems

Preparing the Site

This task involves determining the placement of the cable and the location of the hardware.

Installing the Cable

The cable must be tested prior to its installation and wired according to the design layout. For a new application on an existing network, the existing cabling must be tested. This task is called network certification. The network should be certified before the new application is implemented. This involves testing the wiring for errors.

Installing the Network Hardware and Software

The network hardware and software must be installed and tested.

Defining the Network

A network database contains information on the network—a definition of each node on the network with its type and location. It also identifies all users authorized to access the network.

Installing any Security Systems

Data encryption systems can be installed to secure the network data. The encryption system can be implemented by a hardware or software system. If a hardware encryption system is selected, the physical equipment should be secured and monitored for tampering. If a software encryption system is selected, the software should provide a monitoring facility.

Network Administration

Network administration is an ongoing task. It includes the following:

- Maintaining the equipment
- Controlling errors
- Documenting upgrades
- Maintaining the network database
- Backing up the network software

Maintaining the Equipment

This task includes actual and preventative maintenance of the equipment. It should also include monitoring the equipment for physical tampering.

Controlling Errors

The network administrator is responsible for controlling and correcting errors that occur in the network. This task also includes analyzing the error log for frequency and patterns in the errors.

Documenting Upgrades

The network is documented during the network design. This documentation must be maintained. Any changes to the cabling, network hardware, or software must be included in the documentation. Current copies of the vendor contracts must be made available.

Maintaining the Network Database

The network database must be updated as changes occur. The definition of the nodes must be current. The definition of users authorized to access the network must be maintained.

Backing up the Server and Databases

The network administrator is responsible for backups and restores of the network software.

TESTING THE APPLICATION

The client/server architecture introduces a fundamental change in the way corporate businesses manage information systems. It provides the users and developers with an environment in which they are autonomous. They are not controlled by the standards and procedures that govern the mainframe environment. The software developers have total control over the development, testing, and implementation of their application. They do not compete for machine time as do mainframe-based developers. After the application is installed, the users "own" the system. They can access and manage their own information, and they become the custodians of the system. This freedom, however, does require additional responsibilities. The client/server project must provide its own support and maintain discipline in the environment.

In the mainframe environment, the software is stored in one computer, which is kept in a physically secured computer room. In the client/server environment, the software resides on the client and server computers. It may also be distributed to multiple sites, each site running the application for its own set of information.

Systems testing, in general, is difficult. With distributed systems, the magnitude of this task increases. Software today is still tested in a haphazard fashion. In a client/server architecture, a structured, well-managed systems test is mandatory. An indiscriminate approach to testing will release errors throughout the network. In some respects, client/server applications require more control than mainframe-based systems. The systems testing and management of these applications can prove to be more challenging than its technology and should be planned and organized before the first client/server project is developed.

The major differences between a client/server and a mainframe-based application that affect systems testing occur in the following areas:

- The system development environment
- The infrastructure
- The operational support

The System Development Environment

Client/server processing utilizes new technologies in both the architecture and the software, including the following:

- The cooperative processing architecture
- The distributed processing environment
- The GUI development tools
- The database product
- The testing tools
- The software administration tools
- The network operating systems software

The new technology affects the systems testing of the application. The following items should be considered:

- The staff
- The GUI
- The database server
- The standards

The Staff

The Information Systems staff is not experienced in this new technology. Software development for a client/server application requires database and GUI programming skills. The former mainframe developers are frequently not familiar with the workstation skills required in developing the client software. GUI screens are very different from the character-based screens used in mainframe applications. The PC programmers are generally not trained in the discipline and project control skills required in developing network-based applications. Rigorous testing cannot be used as a substitute for experience and training. However, the inexperience with the new technology does require the systems testing approach to be structured and thorough.

The GUI

Graphical User Interfaces are more difficult to test than character-based applications. GUI programs provide more features than the structured navigation and data entry in non-GUI applications. The user can select a variety of functions from each screen. This exponentially increases the testing work. Each dialogue box, pulldown menu, and button must be tested in combination with the others. The interfaces cannot be tested by sending values directly to the application code. The keystrokes and mouse clicks must be captured or simulated to test the application properly. This feature requires a formal testing plan and often *Computer Aided Software Testing* (CAST) products.

The Database Server

The DBMS products that execute on the server are still evolving. The features in these products vary. The application must—either through the database product or independently—provide for the following:

* Referential integrity
* Data recovery
* Concurrency

The procedures for systems testing the performance capabilities and operational capabilities of the application will vary depending upon the implementation of these features.

Stored procedures and triggers are features in several DBMS products that enable the server to initiate or alter commands. They extend the functions of the server into an active database server. The stored procedures must be tested with each type of input that could be submitted from the client. Each event that causes a trigger to be executed must be tested. Some triggers can invoke other stored procedures or triggers. Some DBMS products permit a stored procedure or a trigger to invoke itself (called recursion). These features require planning and controlled testing.

The Standards

The existing Information Systems design and programming standards may not apply to the client/server environment. Standards must be established and enforced to ensure consistent systems that can be maintained.

The standards should include the requirements for error handling, security checking, screen navigation, and contextual help. It should specify naming convention for both internal (coding) and external (screen labeling) elements; set guidelines for the screen style (colors, layout) to provide consistency within the application and among applications; and promote the use of reusable code. It should distinguish the functions of the client processing from the server processing.

The systems testing team should test the application for *quality/standards compliance*. When the client/server application is to be distributed to multiple sites, quality/standards compliance is essential to the support of the production system. The techniques and tools to perform this testing must be determined by the test team.

The Infrastructure

Infrastructure, as used here, means the physical and procedural structure to support the system. It includes the following elements:

- Hardware and software support
- Security, privacy, and virus prevention
- The central repository
- Testing tools

- Version control
- Project control
- Monitoring the system

In the client/server environment, these elements are managed differently from a mainframe environment. They are not controlled by a central Information Systems department. They may require additional work from the software developers and, therefore, must be included or factored into the scope of the systems testing.

Hardware and Software Support

In the mainframe environment, the software developers are only responsible for developing their application. The hardware is operated and maintained by a separate staff. New releases of the supporting software such as the operating system, the compilers, the database management system, and the utility products are installed and tested by a separate staff dedicated to this function.

In the client/server environment, the same support may not exist. The software developers may be responsible for the backup and restores of their development and testing environments. They may also be responsible for installing and upgrading their supporting software. The new releases of the supporting software may affect the operation of the application. Whether the application is in its development or maintenance phase, the impact of the changes must be tested.

Security

The development and testing environment must be protected. Physical security precautions must be implemented for the client workstations and the servers. Software security must also be implemented to limit access of the software and data to the development project. In addition, the test team must lock the systems test environment so that the software and data are only accessed by authorized personnel.

Guidelines should be established defining the types of data that can be used for testing. It should define the types of information that are considered confidential and, therefore, may not be used in a testing environment where many people have access to it.

In a client/server environment, the production, development, and testing environments are vulnerable to computer viruses. Management must establish procedures for virus prevention, virus detection, and virus recovery. This topic is discussed in greater detail in a later chapter.

The Central Repository

In the mainframe environment, the Information Systems department provides separate environments for the development, systems testing, and production version of an application. Each environment has its own file storage and execution region.

In the client/server environment, this procedure needs to be established. The development, testing, and production environment must be isolated from each other. The systems testing environment, in particular, needs to be controlled.

Testing Tools

New testing tools for client/server environment are released each month. The test team must keep informed on the new developments. The products can significantly ease their workload. The test team must select the appropriate testing tools and maintain them. They must install and upgrade the products and write the procedures to use them.

Version Control

It is necessary to track the version of the software at each node in the client/server environment. Version control is required for the operating system on the client and server computers, the network operating system software at each site, and the application software itself. The supporting software may affect the application, so its version should be verified. All nodes should be executing the same version of the application. Although the software distribution procedures support the initial distribution and the upgrades, the client software must still be verified for version. The user could restore the contents of the hard disk from a backup. An old version of the application software can be restored.

Project Control

The client/server projects are generally smaller than mainframe-based projects. Project controls are still required in the client/server environment. They may, however, need to be implemented differently. The systems test team must control the software that is submitted for testing. They need a turnover procedure to accept software and an incident reporting system to track software that was rejected in executing the systems testing. Although project control is required during initial systems testing, it is critical during maintenance phase systems testing. The application is now in production—the testing of the enhancements must be controlled.

Monitoring the System

During the maintenance phase of the application, the production system is monitored for reliability and performance. In the client/server environment, performance-monitoring software is inadequate. The current technology relies on the design architecture and the initial systems testing of the performance capabilities.

The Operational Support

The Operational Support of a client/server application is an important factor. It functions differently from mainframe-based applications. The application does not execute from a central location and it may not be controlled by a central group. Therefore, the operational capabilities must be thoroughly systems tested. The staff's execution of the procedures as well as the procedures themselves should be tested.

Operational support includes the following:

- Managing the physical site
- Implementing emergency changes
- Providing data backup and restores
- Maintaining security
- Providing a Help Desk facility
- Supporting software distribution

Managing the Physical Site

In the mainframe environment, the computer equipment is kept in a secured room which is specially adapted to support the equipment. The hardware is operated and maintained by a separate trained staff. Application software is stored on these computers. The physical site complies with the firm's security and auditing regulations as well as the local building code ordinances. It is managed by a dedicated staff. This arrangement provides the following:

- Entry is restricted to authorized personnel to prevent theft and vandalism of the equipment.
- The temperature and humidity are controlled to accommodate the equipment.
- The cabling is routed under raised flooring.
- Additional fire alarms and sprinkler systems are installed.
- Preventive maintenance is scheduled.
- Any malfunctions are serviced by an on-call specialist.

In the client/server environment, there is no central computer room. The application software resides on the client and the server. This hardware must be maintained. Each physical site that operates the application must be tested for compliance with operational standards.

Emergency Changes

The procedures to perform emergency changes to the system must be tested. In the mainframe environment the software is centralized. Emergency software changes are controlled by a central support group using standardized procedures. The emergency changes only need to be placed in one environment. In the client/server environment the software is stored on the clients and the servers in one or more sites. When an emergency change to the software is required, it must be applied to all sites in a relatively short period of time. The procedures and the execution of those procedures by the appropriate staff must be tested during the systems test.

Backup/Restore Procedures

The procedures to back up and restore the files and databases must be tested.

Security

The physical security at each site must be tested for compliance with the physical security requirements.

The clients are workstations located on the user's desktops. The data and software on the client is accessible. The software security features of both the network and application must be tested. The data security and privacy features must be tested for compliance with business requirements.

Help Desk

The users in a client/server environment are generally supported by a *Help Desk*. The features of this Help Desk must be tested, and the accuracy and turnaround time provided by this facility must be measured.

Software Distribution

The procedures to distribute the application software must be tested for both the initial distribution and upgrades. Procedures to verify the version level at each site must also be tested.

SUMMARY

The client/server architecture allocates the processing between the client and server to achieve cooperative processing. The client provides the user interface to the application. Graphical User Interfaces (GUIs) are most common. The server receives requests from the clients, processes those requests, and returns the results, if any, to the clients. The database server supports the SQL requests of the client.

The network provides the connectivity for the system. The clients and servers are connected by a Local Area Network

(LAN). The client can also be connected to a Wide Area Network (WAN).

The major differences between a client/server and a mainframe-based application that affect systems testing occur in the following areas:

- The system development environment
- The infrastructure
- The operational support

2

Systems Testing

Information processing has undergone major improvements in the past two decades in both hardware and software. Hardware has decreased in size and price, while providing more and faster processing power. Software has become easier to use, while providing increased capabilities. There is an abundance of products available to assist both end-users and software developers in their work. Software testing, however, has not progressed significantly. It is still largely a manual process conducted as an art rather than a methodology. It is almost an accepted practice to release software that contains defects.

Software vendors use customers as *Beta test sites*. Originally, Beta test sites were marketing focus groups. The vendors used the customers' feedback to determine users' preferences. Today, Beta testing is often used in lieu of complete systems testing, with the theory that the customers will uncover bugs in the software. In fact, the customers only use a small part of the product. When they encounter an error, they either circumvent the problem, bypass that feature, or cease using the product entirely. They don't bother to report the problem to the vendor.

Software that is not thoroughly tested is released for production. This is true for both off-the-shelf software products and custom applications. Software vendors and in-house systems developers release an initial system and then deliver fixes to the code. They continue delivering fixes until they create a new system and stop supporting the old one. The user is then forced to convert to the new system, which again will require fixes.

Software vendors of PC-based products place fixes on electronic bulletin boards so customers can download the fixes. The customers can, alternatively, request the fixes on diskettes, for which a distribution fee is charged. PC newsletters contain columns dedicated to reporting the latest known bugs in a product. They often encourage readers to send in their discoveries. It almost becomes a contest where the users try to find a new way to crash the system.

In-house systems developers generally do not provide any better level of support. They require the users to submit *Incident Reports* specifying the system defects. The Incident Reports are then assigned a priority and the defects are fixed as time and budgets permit.

TESTING—WHY IT'S IMPORTANT

Testing is difficult. It requires knowledge of the application and the system architecture. The majority of the preparation work is tedious. The test conditions, test data, and expected results are generally created manually. System testing is also one of the final activities before the system is released for production. There is always pressure to complete systems testing promptly to meet the deadline. Nevertheless, systems testing is important.

In client/server processing, defective software will release errors throughout the network. When the system is distributed to multiple sites, any errors or omissions in the system will affect several groups of users. Any savings realized in downsizing the application will be negated by costs to correct software errors and reprocess information.

Software developers must deliver reliable and secure systems that satisfy the user's requirements. A key item in successful systems testing is developing a testing methodology rather than relying on the individual style of the test practitioner. The systems testing effort must follow a defined strategy. It must have an objective, a scope, and an approach. Testing is not an art; it is a skill that can be taught.

TESTING—DEFINITIONS

Software development has several levels of testing:

* Unit testing
* Systems testing
* Acceptance testing

Unit Testing

Unit testing verifies that the program works. It is performed by the programmer. It uses the program specifications and the program itself as its source. Program specifications are used to verify that the program contains the logic to perform every function specified. It uses the program to test that the instructions execute correctly. There is no formal documentation required for unit testing. The only deliverable is the unit-tested program.

Systems Testing

Systems testing verifies that the system performs the business functions while meeting the specified performance requirements. It is performed by a team consisting of software technicians and users. It uses the System Requirements document, the System Architectural Design and Detailed Design Documents, and the Information Systems Department standards as its sources. Documentation is recorded and saved for systems testing.

Acceptance Testing

Acceptance testing provides the users with assurance that the system is ready for production use; it is performed by the users. It uses the System Requirements document as its source. There is no formal documentation required for acceptance testing.

Systems testing is the major testing effort of the project. It is the functional testing of the application and is concerned with the following:

- Quality/standards compliance
- Business requirements
- Performance capabilities
- Operational capabilities

Quality/Standards Compliance

The systems test ensures the design and coding of the system adhere to the quality and standards guidelines of the Information Systems department. Formal tests, sometimes using testing tools, are conducted to verify compliance. Although this feature is tested, it is not always included in the systems test. In some organizations this aspect of the system is tested by the software developers prior to systems testing.

Business Requirements

The systems test verifies the system performs the business requirements. The *business requirements* include the normal and exceptional processing, the security and authorization checks, and the auditing controls. It also includes any periodic processing such as year-end and month-end processing. This feature is always included in the systems testing.

Performance Capabilities

The systems test stresses the performance limits of the system. It verifies the system can perform the business functions within the required time frame. *Performance capabilities* includes online response time and overall processing time. This feature is always included in the systems testing.

Operational Capabilities

The systems test verifies the staff can operate the system independently using the operational procedures and instructions. The *operational capabilities* include backup, restore, data recovery, emergency change, and software upgrade procedures. It can also include the Help Desk support facilities. This feature is not always included in the systems test. In some shops, this aspect of the system is tested by a separate group that supports production systems.

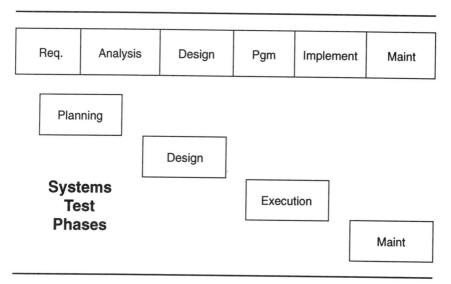

Figure 2.1.   System Development Life Cycle/Systems Testing Life Cycle.

TESTING—WHEN

Testing is generally associated with the execution of programs. The emphasis is on the outcome of the testing, rather than what is tested and how it's tested. Testing is not a one-step activity: execute the test. It requires planning and design. The tests should be reviewed prior to execution to verify their accuracy and completeness. They must be documented and saved for reuse.

Systems testing is the most extensive testing of the system. It requires more manpower and machine processing time than any other testing level. It is therefore the most expensive testing level. It is a critical process in the system development. It verifies that the system performs the business requirements accurately, completely, and within the required performance limits. It must be thorough, controlled, and managed.

Systems testing parallels the development process. It is not isolated in one phase of development as a step that occurs after programming. It has its own life cycle. Figure 2.1 shows the phases of the *System Development Life Cycle* (SDLC) and the phases of the *Systems Testing Life Cycle*. Systems testing begins when the System Requirements document is delivered and continues for the life of the system.

The systems testing phases are as follows:

- **Planning**
  The *planning phase* begins when the System Requirements document is delivered. It establishes the test strategy.
- **Design**
  The *design phase* overlaps with the planning phase. It begins in the design phase of the SDLC, after the systems test objectives and approach are defined.
- **Execution**
  The *execution phase* begins after the design phase is completed and the software has been turned over for systems testing.
- **Maintenance**
  The *maintenance phase* begins when the system is placed into production and continues for the life of the system.

Each phase of systems testing is discussed in a separate chapter. The functions and methodology of each phase are described in detail.

When systems testing is divided into phases with the planning and design phases beginning well before programming starts, several goals are achieved:

- Adequate time is allocated for planning, design, and documenting.
- Sufficient lead time is available to write or acquire testing tools.
- Test conditions are designed from the System Requirements, not the program specifications or the code itself.

The last item is a key goal. The test conditions are designed early in the SDLC. They can be used as examples in design reviews. The users can use the test conditions to verify the requirements are complete. The software developers can use the test conditions to verify the design supports the requirements.

Figure 2.2 shows the work flow for developing and systems testing an application. The software developers use the System Requirements document to design the system and then code programs to implement that design. The test team uses the System Requirements document to design tests to verify that the requirements are satisfied. Systems testing parallels development and uses the same input. It verifies that the system performs the requirements specified in the System Requirements document. It does not verify the code to see that it produces the requirements.

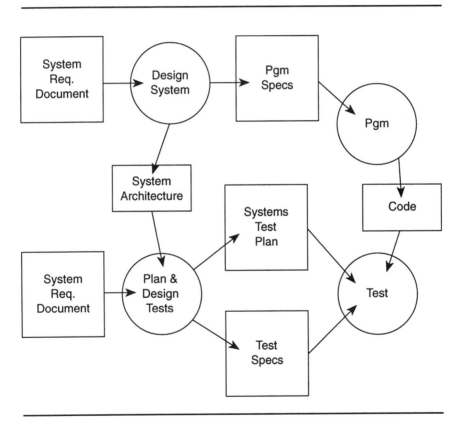

Figure 2.2.   Work-flow for Developing and Systems Testing an Application.

TESTING—DELIVERABLES

Systems testing has deliverables from each phase of its life cycle. In the planning phase of systems testing, the following items are delivered:

- Systems test plan
- Schedule of tasks
- Staffing requirements
- Requests for hardware, software, and network resources
- Requests for disk space, changes/additions to security profiles.

The systems test plan should be saved with the rest of the project documentation.

In the design phase of systems testing, the following items are delivered:

- Systems Test Specifications
- Test data
- Command language files
- Expected results

All of the above items should be saved. The Systems Test Specifications should be saved with the project documentation. The test data, command language files, and expected results must also be saved.

In the execution phase of systems testing, the following items are delivered:

- Systems-tested software
- Actual results of the systems test execution
- Activity Log
- Incident Reports
- User verification and approvals
- Systems Test Summary

The systems-tested software is turned over to the next group. In the initial systems testing, the users are the next group; they receive the system for acceptance testing. The actual results of the systems test execution are reviewed. The results from the final execution should be saved in machine-readable form. A backup of the updated databases and files should be stored in the systems test library. Any output reports or forms created in the execution of systems test should be saved as files. The *Activity Log* can be a handwritten log or a machine-readable file. It should be saved and used in the maintenance phase. The remaining deliverables should be saved with the project documentation.

In the maintenance phase of systems testing the following items are delivered:

- Systems-tested software
- Actual results
- Activity Log entries
- User verification and approvals
- Updated Systems Test Specifications
- Updated test data
- Updated expected results
- Updated command language files

In the maintenance phase of systems testing, the system is in production. The systems-tested software is an upgrade to the existing system and should be moved or distributed to the production environment. The output of the execution should be saved in machine-readable format in the systems test library. The updated test data and command language files replace the current items in the systems test library. The remaining items update the documents stored with the project documentation.

TESTING—TOOLS

Test practitioners utilize testing tools in performing the design, execution, verification, and management of systems testing. Testing tools can be manual or software devices. Manual testing tools are reviews, walk-throughs, and checklists. Software testing tools are programs, utilities, and Computer Aided Software Testing (CAST) products. CAST products are the systems testing counterpart to the software development *CASE* (Computer Aided Software Engineering) products. CAST products provide test practitioners with some of the automated features that

CASE products provide for software developers. There are also some products called *I-CASE* (*Integrated Computer Aided Software Engineering*) products. I-CASE products attempt to combine the CASE and CAST tools into one product. Some products integrate *Upper CASE* (design) and *Lower CASE* (code and test) tools to address the design, coding, and testing of a system. Their testing facilities, however, are more debugging aids than systems testing tools. Testing tools can be commercial packages, shareware, freeware, or custom in-house software.

Shareware is a concept in software distribution, similar to television's public broadcasting system. Shareware is user-supported software. It is copyrighted by the author, but users can copy and share the software freely. They are permitted to use the software to decide whether they like it. If they continue to use it, they are expected to send the author a registration fee. Registered users are authorized to use the product and receive any future upgrades. They may also receive full documentation or technical support. Registration fees vary by author but are always considerably less than commercial packages. Users should register their copy and compensate the authors for their time, effort, and technical knowledge. The shareware concept has provided users with quality software products, including testing tools, at a low cost. The registration fees support continued shareware development.

Freeware is public domain software. The author has placed the software in the public domain. It is not copyrighted and may be copied and used without fees. The author does not provide technical support. In some instances, the author is not even identified.

Shareware and freeware are available through bulletin boards, PC users groups, catalogs, and some retail vendors. The distributors only charge a handling fee. Shareware registration fees are mailed directly to the author.

Testing tools can be categorized into the following groups:

- Debuggers
- Test data generators
- Standards and naming convention compliance tools
- Test design generators
- Test library managers

- Simulators
- Test supervisors
- Screen capture/replay tools
- Test drivers
- Stubs
- File comparators
- Monitors
- Test coverage analyzers
- Test impact analyzers

Debuggers

Debugging tools are used during unit testing to assist the developers in verifying the programs. There are debugging tools that are used to interactively test the execution of the program. There are tools that scan the source code and note inconsistencies and potential coding errors.

Test Data Generators

Test data generators are used to generate test data. They are useful in generating volume data for stress tests of the system's performance limits. They can be used to create random data within specified value ranges. Some test generators can be used to create and edit individual data required to support test cases. They can provide query and reporting features that allow users to select and display specified test data.

Standards and Naming Convention Compliance Tools

Standards and naming convention compliance tools are used to enforce the standards and naming convention of the Information Systems department. They scan source code and report any coding violations. They can be used for quality checking and optimization suggestions and to evaluate the code and suggestion improvements.

Test Design Generators

Test design generators are relatively new testing tools that provide true systems testing design assistance. They generate test cases from the business requirements specifications.

Test Library Managers

Test library managers are used to manage the source library for systems testing. They track and report information on the programs including version level, turnover date, and testing status.

Simulators

Simulators are used to simulate a system configuration or environment. They provid a means of systems testing an application without having to acquire the hardware or software used on the target environment.

Test Supervisors

Test supervisors are tools that automate the execution of the systems test. They automatically submit the test procedures, log the tests, verify results, and report discrepancies. The tools provide a facility to specify the time or interval for submitting the tests and the duration of the tests.

Screen Capture/Replay Tools

Screen capture / replay tools are used to test online (user interface) programs. They capture user input in a file. The file can be compared to previous executions (using a file comparator) or replayed. These tools can be used to collect test data or document test executions. There are testing tools designed specifically for GUI-based program testing. They capture each keystroke and mouse click. This feature is useful in testing GUI-based programs. The sequence of keystrokes is logged and can be referenced or verified at a later time.

Test Drivers

Test drivers are programs that direct the execution of another program. Test drivers are used in the initial testing of the system. They are used in bottom-up designs, where the lower-level programs are ready and the top-level programs are unavailable. The test driver sends data to the lower-level programs.

Stubs

A *stub* is a program that returns a predetermined result to a higher-level program. Stubs are used in the initial testing of a system. They are used in top-down designs, where the top-level programs are ready and the lower-level programs are unavailable. The stub can merely return to the higher-level program or it can send back predetermined data. The data can be a constant value or any one of a range of values depending upon the complexity of the stub coding.

File Comparators

File comparators are utility programs used to compare two files and report the differences. They can be used to compare the actual results of a test execution with prepared expected results. They can compare binary files that contain screen images. The screen images can be captured (using a capture/replay tool) and compared with previous test executions.

Monitors

Monitors are used to measure and report system performance. Monitors can measure memory usage, disk space usage, transaction arrival rates, response time, and database accesses. Memory usage monitoring is useful in testing GUI-based programs for "memory leakage" conditions, where the program fails to release allocated memory when it is through with it.

Test Coverage Analyzers

Test coverage analyzers are tools that provide reports showing the features of the system covered by the test cases. They cross-reference test cases with business requirements and programs and report the following:

- Test cases that test a requirement
- Test cases that test a program
- Requirements tested in each test case
- Programs tested in each test case

Test Impact Analyzers

Test impact analyzers are similar to test coverage analyzers. They provide reports showing the systems test features that are impacted by a change. They cross-reference test cases with business requirements and programs. The tool allows the user to specify a program or business requirement that has changed and provides a report of its impact on the systems test. It is used to determine which test cases must be executed again when a program is modified and which test cases may require changes when a requirement is changed.

SUMMARY

Systems testing is the major testing effort of the project. It is concerned with the following:

- Quality/standards compliance
- Business requirements
- Performance capabilities
- Operational capabilities

Systems testing parallels the System Development Life Cycle (SDLC). It consists of the following phases:

- Planning
- Design
- Execution
- Maintenance

Each phase has its own functions and deliverables.

Testing tools are used by test practitioners to assist them in designing, executing, verifying, and maintaining tests.

3

The Planning Phase

The first phase of systems testing is *planning*. This phase is essential to the success of the systems test and, ultimately, the application. It can and should begin when the requirements phase is complete and the System Requirements document is delivered.

Systems testing, like any other software development activity, must be planned. This statement may seem obvious. However, in most IS departments, systems testing is considered a single-phase activity: executing the test. The test practitioner determines which conditions to test, designs procedures to test these conditions and to verify the results, and then executes the test. This is all considered one activity.

When the planning, design, and execution phases are combined into one activity, it presents several problems:

- **The testing process itself is not planned.**
  The planning that does occur is from an execution point of view. The test practitioner plans what to test and how to test but does not plan an overall test strategy. There is no policy established for accepting software into the systems test environment, suspending testing when the software fails, saving

the test documentation, or testing software changes. The test practitioners are left to improvise procedures during the execution.

- **The emphasis is on the execution of the tests.**
  The activity is considered complete when the systems-tested software is delivered. The test conditions, test procedures, and test data are not considered important deliverables. Therefore, these items are either discarded or poorly documented.

- **The time allocated for the activity is often insufficient.**
  When systems testing is scheduled, the planning, design, and execution of the test are generally all included in one time frame. The tasks are not delineated by phase, so all work is charged to the one activity. Project managers are reluctant to charge an extensive amount of time to one activity, particularly if the activity is viewed as a "post-development" task. The amount of time scheduled is therefore underestimated or understated. The test team is then forced to cut corners in order to meet this schedule, and documentation is frequently the task that suffers. The specifications for the systems tests are not formally recorded and hence unavailable for future testing of modifications and enhancements.

- **The activity is associated with coding and scheduled to begin after coding is completed.**
  The test team is formed shortly before coding is completed. This time frame is too late to prepare a plan for the testing process. Systems test planning should begin when the System Requirements document is delivered. The design phase of systems testing can overlap the planning and begin in the design phase of the software development.

Planning is a separate and distinct phase in which the strategy for the testing activities is established. The strategy must be determined and understood by the project team before any systems tests are designed or executed. The project team must commit themselves to support the strategy. The test team must follow the test strategy to provide consistent and controlled testing of the system.

TEST STRATEGY

The test strategy is formed by the following:

* Identifying the systems test environment
* Defining the objectives and scope of the systems test
* Defining the approach for the systems test
* Determining the staffing requirements and responsibilities for the systems test
* Determining the hardware, software, and network resources required to execute the systems test
* Determining the testing tools required for systems testing
* Determining the deliverables from the systems test
* Identifying the systems test tasks and their sequence

IDENTIFY THE SYSTEMS TEST ENVIRONMENT

The *systems test environment* is the environment in which the systems test is conducted. It consists of a central repository for the application software and the data required to conduct the tests. It is also the set of procedures and controls supporting the testing process.

In the mainframe environment, procedures exist to migrate software from development through several levels of testing to production. The typical mainframe shop supports systems testing with a separate region for executing its tests. The shop provides a central repository for the application software being tested. It provides separate databases that are available for test data. It usually provides a separate version of the DBMS and communications products, with the software defined for the system being tested. Security is installed to restrict access to authorized personnel. The systems test environment is maintained by a separate group or several groups. The test team and software developers request services from them and adhere to their schedule and rules. There is a clear definition of duties and responsibilities. These procedures ensure that the systems testing is isolated from any development and production work.

The client/server environment is not governed by mainframe standards and procedures. The projects are smaller. All aspects of the development, testing, and implementation are handled by the same group. The test team and software developers for the client/server application have more autonomy in this environment. They also have more responsibilities. They must provide their own support and maintain discipline and control in the environment.

A systems test environment must exist for the client/server application, although not in as elaborate a format as the mainframe shop. The environment is tailored to the exclusive needs of this application. The systems test environment provides the central respository for the software being tested. Testing tools and test data reside in this repository, and the source code is migrated to this area.

When the client/server application is designed for distribution on multiple platforms, it must be tested on each platform in which it will run. The central repository is used to prepare the software for all test executions. The test cases, test data, and expected results are the same for each platform. The source code must be controlled so it can be used to generate the executable code for each platform.

The following items should be included in identifying the systems test environment:

- Site
- Security
- Submitting test items
- Software
- The central repository
- Support

The key questions to answer for each item are listed below.

Site
- Where will systems testing execute?
  —What is the geographic location?
  —Is it at the software development site?
  —Is it at an end-user site?
- What other groups use this environment?
  —Will development and systems testing be on the same network?

—Will development and systems testing use the same file server?
- Which workstations will be used for executing the systems test?

Security
- What are the security requirements for the systems test environment?
    —How many people need access to the systems test environment?
    —Which files do these people need to access?

Submitting test items
- What are the procedures to submit software into the systems test environment?
- What are the acceptance standards for software submitted to the systems test environment?
    —What testing is required prior to systems testing?

Software and the central repository
- What software products are required for the systems test environment?
    —Are additional copies of the product required?
    —Can the systems test environment use the development software products?
    —What are the licensing agreements on these products?
- How is the central repository organized?
    —What is stored in it?
    —Who controls it?
    —Where is the test data stored?
    —Where are the test databases stored?
    —Where are the testing tools kept?
    —Where are the source and compiled code stored?
- Does the systems test need to execute on multiple platforms?
    —If so, which platform houses the central repository?

Support
- Who services the hardware?
    —Is there an operations support staff for the hardware?
- Is the systems test environment physically secured?

- Is the file server physically secured?
- Is there a network administrator for the systems test environment?
- What are the backup and restore procedures for the files?
  —What is the frequency of the backups?
  —What can be restored? An individual file? A subdirectory?

DEFINE THE OBJECTIVES AND SCOPE

Systems testing is the major testing effort of the project. It is functional testing. It tests whether the application performs the functions described in the System Requirements document. It is not structural testing and therefore does not and should not test code.

In the mainframe environment, systems testing is an accepted practice. The nature of mainframe projects require a formal systems test.

- The projects are large. There are many people involved. The scope is large, and the development time is long.
- The user involvement is sporadic.
- The design and programming efforts are often performed by different people.
- The programmers may only receive specifications for their individual programs and not have any knowledge of the overall application.
- The programming effort is dispersed among many programmers.
- The programmer codes and unit tests the program in isolation.
- The user is not involved in this phase of the development.

In the client/server environment, systems testing is not an established formal practice in the system development life cycle. The client/server projects are closed loops. There is no need to interface with other projects.

- The projects are small. There are few people involved. The scope is small, and the development time is short.
- The user involvement is integral.
- The design and programming efforts are performed by the same people.

- The programmers consequently have knowledge of the overall application.
- Prototypes are often used to show the approach to the users.
- Rapid development tools are often used in creating the code.
- Each component is thoroughly tested in the development environment.

The systems test still applies in this environment. It may, in fact, be more important. The very factors that make development faster and more responsive to the user lend themselves to creating disconnections in the system.

- The developer and user work together closely.
- The users can make casual verbal requests to change a feature.
- The developers can easily generate and change code.

These factors create an opportunity for on-the-fly changes. When the system is altered without impact analysis, the developers lose control and the design is impaired. The system may no longer accomplish the stated business requirements.

In the planning phase, the objectives and scope of the testing are defined in four major areas: quality/standards compliance of the software, business requirements, performance capabilities, and operational capabilities. The key questions to answer in each area are listed below.

Quality / standards compliance
- Is the software checked for compliance with standards?
- Is there a quality check of the code?
- Is the software checked for ease of maintenance?
- Is the software checked for portability?
- Is the software checked for reusable components?
- Is there a check for conformity of style in messages and help text?
- Is there a check for conformity of style in screen design?
  —Are the navigation, colors, scroll bars, and selection graphics or function keys consistent?
- Is the documentation checked for clarity, completion, and accuracy?

Business requirements

- What business requirements are verified?
  —Which features are tested?
  —Which features are not tested?
- Is exception processing tested?
- Are extremes and abnormalities tested?
- Does the system contain authorization rules?
  —Are the authorization rules tested for compliance?
- Is the adequacy of the security tested?
- Are the manual procedures verified?
- Are Help screens an integral part of the system?
  —Are they tested?
  —Can the Help screen text be updated by the users?
  —Is the update feature tested?
- Are auditing and control procedures tested?
- Are interfaces with other systems tested?
  —What are the boundaries of the systems test?
  —Is the initial conversion of data tested?
  —Is the purging or off-loading of data tested?

Performance capabilities

- Are response times measured for adherence to requirements?
- Is the overall processing time measured for adherence to business requirement?
- Are the performance limits of the software tested?
  —Will the systems test exercise the software in a volume test?

Operational capabilities

- Are backup and restore procedures tested?
- Are recovery procedures tested?
  —Is network recovery tested?
  —Is the data recovery tested?
- Are emergency maintenance procedures tested?

In the client/server environment there are special operational considerations.

- Does the application operate in multiple platforms?

—Is each platform available to the test team for systems test execution?

- Does the application run in an approved site?
  —Does the site comply with physical security requirements?
  —Is access to the site controlled?
  —Is the file server in a secured room?
- Is network security tested?
  —Are unauthorized users rejected by the network?
  —Are unauthorized transactions rejected by the network?
- How will the application software be distributed to each site?
  —For the initial distribution? For upgrades?
- Will the procedures for software distribution be tested?
- Will there be a central Help Desk available for the end-users?
  —Will this feature be tested?
  —Will it test the completeness and accuracy of the information delivered by the Help staff?
  —Will it test the operational hours of the Help Desk?
  —Will it test the turnaround time to resolve issues?
- Is there a virus prevention program in place at each site?
  —Has each site been educated on computer viruses?
  —Do the managers in the area enforce the virus prevention rules?
- Is there a virus recovery program in place?
  —Has each site been trained on procedures to follow if their computer is infected?
  —Has each site been trained to detect a virus infection?

Computer viruses are an important issue in the client/server environment. This subject will be discussed in detail in a later chapter. Management must establish a training program on computer viruses and actively enforce regulations set up to prevent an infection. The systems testing on a client/server application should address these issues. The physical security and operating practices of each site must be evaluated before a client/server application is implemented. The coding standards should include guidelines on security and authorization coding. The test team can then verify the code during quality/standard compliance testing to ensure compliance with these standards. Management, however, must establish an overall policy on virus prevention.

Prior Testing

The prior testing requirements must be defined. The test team must set the standards for acceptance and the procedures for rejection of the software. This must be determined in the planning phase. The test team needs a benchmark for accepting software so software that is not tested or poorly tested does not reach this level.

The *Systems Test Plan* lists all tests and reviews that the software developers are expected to perform before submitting the software for systems testing. This can include design reviews, coding walk-throughs, and unit testing. In a client/server environment, the prior testing requirements for the client and the server must be determined.

When the client software is a graphical user interface-based application, the testing procedures for the GUIs must be specified. In Chapter 1, the characteristics of a graphical user interface were discussed. The GUIs provide the user with an application interface that is easy to use, but they are difficult to test adequately. Unlike character-based interfaces that provide the user with a set number of choices at a given time, GUIs generally provide a wide range of choices to the user at one time. For example, the user can be entering data on a screen and view contextual help, scroll a codes table, pull down a menu, and open a dialogue box. The programmers cannot randomly hit keys and click mouse buttons and consider this a test.

A formal plan needs to be constructed to test the interfaces. The systems test concentrates on verifying the business functions of the client software, and the GUIs must be thoroughly tested prior to this. The Systems Test Plan must indicate who will test the GUIs, what will be tested, and how it will be tested. The testing can be conducted by the software developers prior to systems testing or by the test team as an initial task. There are GUI testing tools available to support the testing effort.

If the database server software utilizes stored procedures and triggers, the testing procedures must be defined. Stored procedures and triggers were discussed in Chapter 1. Stored procedures are procedural code and SQL commands that reside in the server. Triggers are a specific type of stored procedure that executes automatically when a change is made to the database or a predefined event occurs. Triggers are often used to help maintain referential integrity. Some triggers are invoked to enforce business rules. In some systems, procedures and triggers can invoke other procedures and triggers or themselves. The code can get complex and requires careful testing.

A formal test of the server software must be conducted. The systems test will confirm that the database server returns the required data and updates the databases in its verification of the business functions. However, the systems test does not specifically test the server code. The Systems Test Plan must indicate the prior testing requirements for the server. The software developers are responsible for testing the server software. There are testing tools available for debugging the stored procedures and triggers either within the DBMS product or as a separate product.

DEFINE THE APPROACH

In the mainframe environment, the Information Services department "owns" the application software. They develop, test, and install the system. Next, they move into a maintenance mode. A staff is retained to support enhancements and modifications. Any new system requirements are satisfied by the software developers.

In the client/server environment, the Information Services department is considered a resource. They develop, test, and install the system there as well. Next, they turn the system over to the users. The users "own" the application software; they run the system. Any new system requirements are satisfied directly by the users with a support language. This approach to software ownership establishes a "throwaway" attitude toward the systems testing design and supporting test data. Although the users have control over their system, major enhancements and modifications to the system must be done by the software developers. The systems test deliverables must be kept.

Systems testing is an iterative process. The tests are performed many times during the lifetime of the software. The test conditions, test data, and expected results must be predetermined and saved for future use.

In the planning phase, the approach is defined by determining the following:

- How are the test conditions determined?
  —Do any special conditions have to be simulated?
- How is the test data created?
  —How is the baseline data created and loaded in the proper format?
  —Which testing tools, programs, and procedures are used to generate data?
- How are transactions submitted to the system?
  —Which testing tools, test driver programs, and manual entry procedures are used for this?
- How are the expected results of the tests created?
- How are actual results of the tests compared to the predetermined expected results?
  —Which testing tools, programs, and procedures are used for this?
- What is the criteria for approving a test case?
- What are the procedures to report a test case failure?
- What is the criteria for suspending systems testing?
  —Is the test case that failed bypassed?
  —Does testing continue with the next test case?
  —Is testing halted until a correction is made?
  —What corrections can the test team make?
  —What corrections must they send back to the software developers?
- What are the procedures for resuming the testing?
  —Which test cases need to be repeated when the corrected code is submitted again?
  —What are the procedures to report a change or correction to the software?
- What level of support will the test team require for the systems test execution?
  —Will the hardware and network be available for extended hours during the execution?
  —If not, what is the impact on testing?
  —Will the software developers be available to correct rejected items immediately?

—Will the users be available to verify actual results?
- Is performance tested?
- Is security tested as an integral part of business requirements?
  —Is it a separate test?
- Are the test cycles executed in sequence?
  —Can the test cycles be tested independently?
  —If one cycle depends upon the results of a prior cycle, which is not available, can those results be simulated?

DETERMINE STAFFING REQUIREMENTS AND RESPONSIBILITIES

Systems testing is people intensive. The test practitioners, software developers, and users participate in various phases of the activity. The *test practitioners* are the people who plan, design, and execute the systems test. On a small project this activity may be performed by the systems analyst from the software development team. On a large project this activity may be performed by a testing specialist. It's not important who performs the activity, but it is important to recognize that the activity is a separate job function.

The job of test practitioner has its own set of requirements and skills. Management should not assume any data processing person can conduct a systems test. In the mainframe environment, the staff has the advantage of operating under a set of rules and standards for production turnover. They are experienced in the control procedures and the testing efforts required for critical applications. In the client/server environment, the staff may be PC-oriented developers who are unfamiliar with the discipline required to validate an application for use on a network. The selection of test practitioners in this environment should be thorough. There are three items to consider when selecting the test practitioner:

- Personality
- Motivation
- Prior experience

Personality

- **Systems testing is methodical.**
  It requires attention to details. Each test condition must be broken down to test cases and supported with test data. All phases of the systems test must be carefully documented. The results of each executed test case must be validated and reported.
- **Systems testing is a power position.**
  The test practitioner sees everyone's work and records the acceptance or rejection of that work. The task must be accomplished with a professional, nonjudgemental attitude. Systems testing validates systems, not people.
- **Systems testing must be consistent and independent.**
  The test practitioner must execute each test case with the same degree of thoroughness.
- **Systems testing is difficult.**
  It requires control and planning. The test practitioner must plan and maintain the status of each task.
- **Systems testing is stressful.**
  It is often the last activity before implementation. There is a lot of pressure on the project to complete the testing quickly. The test practitioner must work well in a dynamic atmosphere.

Motivation

- **The test practitioner must be motivated.**
  The person should enjoy designing the tests and validating the results.
- **The person should have a commitment to quality.**
  It would be foolish to select a person who enjoys coding a function, testing it, and moving on. Systems testing is iterative. The same test is executed over and over again until the desired results are achieved.

Prior Experience

- **Systems testing is not a natural adjunct to systems analysis or programming.**
  It requires its own set of skills and knowledge. The person must have prior experience or be trained to do this activity.

Responsibilities

The test practitioners must be selected and trained, if necessary. The person or group responsible for each function in the systems test is determined at this time. This assists management in resource allocation and scheduling. It is also a formal assignment of responsibility. The execution phase of the systems testing can be hectic. Without a written assignment of responsibility, a task can be neglected. The following questions should be answered:

- Who designs the tests?
- Who creates the test data?
- Who reviews the design?
- Who executes the tests?
- Who verifies the results?
- Who determines the modules associated with a rejected test case?
- Who modifies the software?
- Who determines the priority of the changes to the software?
- Who tracks the status of rejected software?

It is also important to determine the custodian of the system after it is implemented.

- Who will make changes and enhancements to the system?
- Who will test those changes?

The reliability of the system can deteriorate rapidly if the systems testing process is compromised.

In the mainframe environment, the Information Services department maintains the system. Any changes or enhancements to the system are made by the software developers. It may not be the same staff who originally developed the system, but it will be Information Services personnel. The documentation prepared for the initial systems test is saved and turned over to the maintenance team. They can modify the test cases for any new requirements and have a complete systems test ready for use.

In the client/server environment, the custodian of the system is not always clear. The software developers may not be permanent staff. They could be an outside consulting firm that implements the system and then leaves. They could be staff from another division who are a resource but not dedicated to maintaining the system. Changes and enhancements to the system will be required, and *they* must be tested. The material prepared for the initial systems test must be saved so it can be modified for new requirements and used for continued systems testing.

It's important to know who will maintain the system. The documentation for systems testing can be different depending on who is the custodian. The Information Services staff needs less instruction to maintain the systems test cases. Users need detailed instructions and training.

DETERMINE HARDWARE, SOFTWARE, AND NETWORK REQUIREMENTS

In the planning phase, the hardware, software, and network requirements for systems testing are determined and reserved. Some of these resources must be available during the design phase of systems testing. Software testing tools will be installed and tested during this phase. Test data and expected results must also be prepared before the systems test execution begins.

Any purchasing or requisitioning forms must be approved and submitted in the planning phase. The requirements for the ideal environment and the minimum acceptable environment should be listed. It may not be possible for management to obtain all the resources required.

DETERMINE TESTING TOOLS REQUIREMENTS

Testing tools assist the test practitioner in designing, executing, and verifying the tests. Software testing tools are programs, utilities, and packages. These tools can be commercial products, shareware, freeware, or custom in-house software.

In the planning phase, the requirements for testing tools must be determined and satisfied. The requirements are determined by the following:

- Identifying what needs to be done.
- Investigating what is available to do it.

- Checking the inventory of software already in-house. This includes purchased software products and custom-written programs.
- Checking the software products currently available on the market.
- Determining whether to write your own testing tools.

It is not a trivial task to search the available software for products that fulfill the requirements. This task can require researching a variety of sources. The computer trade publications cover the widely used tools, but for specific needs the search is more difficult. Software directories, trade newsletters, bulletin boards, and computer users groups are sources of information. There are software search companies that provide this service. They can search software product databases to find a match for your requirements and provide a list of the qualifying products. Some search companies also provide detailed information, including demos and review articles.

The results of the investigation should be documented. It is important to record not only the selected tools, but each item investigated. This information will be valuable to future testing efforts.

DETERMINE SYSTEMS TEST DELIVERABLES

In the planning phase of systems testing, the deliverables from each phase of the systems test are determined. The format of the deliverables should also be specified at this time. It is important to state whether the deliverable is a formal printed document, a memo, an online reference file, a form, a checklist, or an approval letter. Do not leave the choice open.

On one project, management required the projects to keep a *Systems Test Activity Log* during the execution of the systems test. They did not specify a format or the items to be recorded. The test teams were left to their own devices. The Activity Logs from each project were different, interesting, and even colorful (figuratively and literally). One project used a word processor, another a spiral notebook, and one project used the back of the Systems Test Specifications document. The spiral notebook was probably the most creative. The team members handwrote their entries in blue ink, black ink, red ink, pencil, and magic markers. It contained doodles in the margins, expressive (if not explicit) comments on the results of the tests, and one page had a grocery shopping list. The person obviously had some waiting time during the execution and jotted down "eggs, light bulbs, milk, peanut butter."

It's important to specify what is to be delivered and how it is to be delivered. The test strategy is determined in the planning phase. The deliverables from this phase are the decisions and findings. They must be recorded in memoranda or a formal document.

The test specifications are created in the design phase. The deliverables from this phase are the Systems Test Specifications, test data, and test procedures. The Systems Test Specifications is a formal document that describes the test conditions, test cycles, test procedures, and expected results. The test data and test procedures are files.

The tests are executed in the execution phase. The deliverables from this phase are the tested software, the outputs produced by the tests, the Activity Log, the verifications, the Incident Reports, and the Summary Report. The outputs are updated databases, transmission files, and reports. The Activity Log is a document used to record the testing activity. The verifications of the test cases are an approval letter or a notation in the Activity Log next to the executed test. Incident Reports are documents used to record any test conditions not satisfied and requiring extensive software changes. The Summary Report is written at the completion of systems testing execution. It is a formal document stating the results of the testing. It summarizes the test team's findings on the application and the testing process itself.

IDENTIFY SYSTEMS TEST TASKS

In the planning phase, the tasks to be performed in the remaining phases are identified. The task list serves as a checklist for the design and execution phases. It must be detailed and specific. The tasks should be listed in the sequence in which they will be performed. Any lead times must also be listed. For example, if the network administrator only establishes security profiles once a week, this should be noted next to the task.

THE DOCUMENTATION

The following documentation is produced during systems testing:

- Descriptions of what to test
- Instructions on how to test
- Records of what happened during the testing

The format of the systems testing documentation should be determined during the planning phase and requires planning. The documentation must be easy to understand by the readers and easy to maintain by the writers.

The format of the systems testing documentation must consider the following:

- The style of the documentation
- The distribution of the documentation
- The maintenance of the documentation
- The design of the documentation
- The naming conventions for the documentation
- The standards within the documentation
- The security and privacy policy for the documentation

Style of the Documentation

The first item to consider in selecting the style of the documentation is the audience.

- Who is going to read this material?
  —Management?
  —Programmers?
  —Users?
- What information do they need?
  —Are they reviewing the actual results of the testing?
  —Are they creating test cases?
  —Are they selecting testing tools?

- How often will they need to refer to the document?
  —One time?
  —Each time the system is modified?
  —Extensively but for a single period of time?
  —Infrequently but for the lifetime of the system?
- When will they need to read this material?
  —Prior to designing the tests?
  —During the execution of the testing?

The documentation should be written with the reader in mind. The physical format of the documentation should suit its purpose. Online documentation should be used for material that needs to be referenced while performing another online task. The Systems Test Plan can be available in both hard copy and online format. The test practitioner may want to refer to information on testing tools when designing test procedures. The Systems Test Summary would not be useful in an online format. It's reviewed by management during progress and planning sessions and not related to an online task. The systems test reviewers need a hard copy of the procedures to follow in performing their review. The online documentation may not be stored on the system where they are executing the testing.

The second item to consider in the style of the documentation is the writer. Systems testing is rigorous in itself. The documentation should assist the test team in performing their task. It should not be an additional burden. The documentation format must be easy to use in creating and maintaining the documents. Many word processors allow graphics and external files to be included in the document. This feature should be utilized when appropriate. The following items should be considered:

- How will the test procedures for data entry and retrieval be presented?
- Will graphics be included in the documentation?

The screen layouts should be shown in any tests where the reviewer must enter or view information. They should be extracted from the design documentation and included where required.

- How will the expected results be presented?
- Will spreadsheets be included in the documentation?

The expected results are created by the test team. This information is often based on a mathematical calculation. The price of finished goods is the sum of the material costs, plus the labor cost, plus the markup and rounding rules. The total on a bill is the sum of the services and disbursements plus any adjustments. A spreadsheet is useful in presenting this information. The expected results will change as the test cases are changed. This occurs in the original design of the systems test as the test cases are refined and during the maintenance phase of the project, when the system requirements are modified. A spreadsheet allows the writer to concentrate on the test data and not the arithmetic.

On one project, we had to use the company standard word processor which did not allow spreadsheets to be included in the document. We spent many frustrating hours modifying the expected results. Each time the test cases changed, we either manually calculated the new results or updated a spreadsheet and then entered those results into our document. This procedure was not only time consuming, it was error prone. We transposed numbers while copying over the figures and introduced errors in our expected results.

- How will the test conditions be presented?
- Will decision tables be included in the documentation?

Decision tables are more effective than narratives in communicating the test conditions. They are easier and faster to read. The word processor should support the line and box drawing required for this presentation.

The third item to consider in the style of the documentation is the language. The writing style should be aimed at the reader. The writers should use semi-formal language. Technical terms are appropriate for the documentation to be used by the technicians. The material written for IS management and end-users should use business terms. The following items should be considered:

Sentence structure
- Sentences should be short and to the point.
- Avoid unnecessary wording.
- Use simple declarative sentences.
- Procedures are how-to documents, and therefore should use the imperative mode (command verbs).
- Use a list or outline format. It's an easy writing style for writers to follow. The documentation will be updated by many different people. This style allows continuity between writers.

White space
- The page layout should contains ample white space.
- It makes the document easy to read.
- It keeps the reader focused on the key words.

Distribution of the Documentation

The distribution of the documentation is concerned with three issues:

- Who receives the documentation
- How the documentation is published
- When the documentation gets distributed

Systems testing documentation consists of the following:

- The Systems Test Plan
- The Systems Test Specifications
- The Activity Log
- The Incident Reports
- The Systems Test Summary

The Systems Test Plan is distributed to IS management, the business user management, and the software developers on the project. Management only receives the document one time, during initial systems testing. The documentation, however, must be updated as the test strategy changes. It should be available online. Any software developers, test practitioners, or test reviewers that join the project should be given this documentation.

The Systems Test Specifications describes the test conditions being tested and the instructions for conducting the tests. Before the execution phase of systems testing, the Systems Test Specifications should be reviewed in a formal meeting. All attendees will be given a copy of the documentation at that time. However, the actual audience for this documentation are the test team and the test reviewers. They should receive copies of the documentation prior to each systems test execution. During the initial systems test execution, the test procedures may need to be distributed several times. If the system is to be installed in multiple sites and the systems testing is executed individually at each installation, the test procedures must be distributed for each site test. Systems testing continues through the maintenance phase. The updated documentation must be distributed again at that time.

The Systems Test Activity Log is not actually distributed to anyone. It is a reference document which will be used in preparing other documents. It serves as a verification of the testing process and may be required by systems auditors. The Activity Log is used by the test team to monitor their work. The contents of the log is never updated, but new entries are added each time a test is executed.

The Incident Reports are not distributed collectively. Individual Incident Reports will be given to software developers, test practitioners, and test reviewers to resolve an issue. The Incident Report Coordinator uses the reports to create a log that generates statistical reports for IS management. The software developers and test team use the Incident Reports to monitor their work. Incident Reports are generated throughout the life of the project. Many Incident Reports will be generated during the initial life of the system; fewer reports are generated for mature systems.

The Systems Test Summary is distributed to IS management. It is only produced one time, after the initial systems test. It is not updated. It is kept with the project documentation as a reference document and a verification of the systems testing process.

The systems testing documentation is used within the company. It is not for public distribution. The documentation can be printed directly from a word processing product. It need not be submitted to a desktop publishing group. The decisions on binding, print fonts, and paper size are a matter of personal choice. It should be consistent with the project documentation.

Maintenance of the Documentation

The systems testing documentation will require updating whenever the system or the testing strategy changes. Some documents will be relatively stable. The Systems Test Specifications document is subject to the most changes. It must be updated whenever the system requirements are changed. The maintenance techniques should be planned.

- **Will an addendum technique, in which changes are appended to the document, be used?**
  In some critical system applications, the auditors require all original documentation to be saved. Any changes made to the system must be shown as an addendum. This helps the auditors review the system. They can concentrate on verifying items that changed since the last audit.
- **Will changes be made in place, overriding the existing documentation?**
  It is easier to read a document that is updated in place. However, there is no one way of knowing what changed.
- **Does the word processor support redlining?**
  Redlining is a revision technique in which a bar line is printed next to the text that has been updated since the last version. Redlining makes it easy to see additions, deletions, and changes in the document.
- **Will the entire document be reprinted, or only the updates?**
  If the document is short, it is easier to reprint the entire document. If the document is long, segmentation should be used and only the changed segment can be printed.

Design of the Documentation

The design of the systems testing documentation involves the following:

- Structuring the document
- Maintaining consistency
- Providing cross-references

Structuring the Document

If the document will be long (more than 25 pages), it should be divided into pieces. This segmentation serves two purposes:

1. It allows pieces to be written by different people concurrently.
2. It allows each section to be printed separately.

One way to do this is to create a *master document*. This document only contains the names of component documents. Most word processors provide control statements that are used to name the other documents that comprise this document.

Figure 3.1 shows a master document for a Systems Test Plan document. This document contains nine control statements, each naming a component document. The comments on each control statement are used to provide an explanation of the component document. Although the component document name (naming conventions are discussed later in this chapter) indicates its position in the master document, its contents are not obvious. The comments are useful in locating a specific section from the printed copy. If the information on testing tools needs to be updated, the

```
LBTP00 Legal Billing Systems Test Plan - Master Document

INCLUDE LBTP10  /* Identification */
INCLUDE LBTP20  /* Systems Test Environment */
INCLUDE LBTP30  /* Objectives and Scope */
INCLUDE LBTP40  /* Approach */
INCLUDE LBTP50  /* Staffing Requirements*/
INCLUDE LBTP60  /* Hardware, Software, Network Requirements */
INCLUDE LBTP70  /* Testing Tools */
INCLUDE LBTP80  /* Systems Test Deliverables */
INCLUDE LBTP90  /* Systems Test Tasks */
```

Figure 3.1.   Systems Test Plan master document.

writer can browse the master document and find that the testing tools text is in the component document named LBTP70.

Maintaining Consistency

The layout of the documentation should be consistent within each section of a document and among the project documents. There are several techniques that can be used to accomplish this:

Standards can be established for page layout, numbering schemes, and terminology.

- The title pages of all the systems testing documentation should be consistent in content and layout.
- The headings and footings used in the documentation should be standardized. The placement of the section names and page numbers should be consistent. Figure 3.2 shows a page layout for the staffing requirements section of the Systems Test Plan.

    In this example the heading contains the project name and page numbers. The page numbers are sequential throughout the document and printed in the heading.

    The footing contains the document name, the section name, and the file name of the component. This document uses a master document that specifies component documents. LBTP50 is the file name of this component document that contains the staffing requirements. The file name is useful in maintaining

---

Legal Billing System   Page 7

5. Staffing Requirements
    The following is a list of the functional responsibilities for the systems testing of the Legal Billing System.

Systems Test Plan   Staffing Requirements   LBTP50

Figure 3.2.   Headings and footings layout.

segmented documents. In the printed copy of the documentation, all components are expanded and printed as one continu-
ous document. When the documentation needs to be modified,
the component document must be identified since it contains the
text. In this example the footing contains the component document name on each page.

- *Boiler-plate text* can be created for common text that appears
  in each document or several times within a document. A
  boilerplate text is a document that can be copied into a document or component document. It can contain the company
  name and address, a proprietary information notice required
  in each document, or a project overview statement. Figure 3.3
  is a boilerplate text with the company's proprietary information notice. It is stored as a separate document (in some word
  processors it is called a library document) and should conform to
  the document naming conventions. This boilerplate text is
  named LBBP04 (see naming conventions later in this chapter).
  Boilerplate text provides consistency and saves writing time.
- *Text templates* can be created and used as a skeleton in writing
  new documents of the same type. Figure 3.4 is a text template
  for the identification section of a Systems Test Plan document.
  The template is a fill-in-the-blanks form. The writers do not
  have to develop a writing style. They merely fill in the appropriate words. In this template the user fills in the developer's
  department name and the end-user group. It contains control
  statements to include two boiler-plate text documents. LBBP08
  is a document that specifies the design architecture and system overview. LBMC00 is a document that names all other
  documentation for this project. This technique will keep the
  Systems Test Plan for all projects consistent.

```
          LBBP04 /* Proprietary Notice */
```

```
AAA Software Services Inc.
This material contains proprietary information. It may not
be copied or reproduced without prior permission.
```

Figure 3.3.   Boiler-plate text.

1.2 Application

    The Legal Billing System is a professional services
billing application. It is part of the corporate accounting
systems. This system was developed by the _____
_____ department of AAA Software Services Inc.
as a program product in its Accounting Packages for
Professional Service Organizations. The end-users of the
system are _____.

Include LBBP08
/* specify design architecture and system overview */

1.3 Document Locator
    This document is stored on the _____ network/
computer. The file name of the master document is :
_____. It is written with word processor
_____. It was printed using the following attributes:
_____.

1.4 Other Documents

    Other documents for this project are stored on the
_____ computer/network at AAA Software Services Inc.
headquarters. They are written with word processor
_____.

Include LBMC00
/* Master control list of project documentation */

Figure 3.4.   Text template for identification section.

Figure 3.5 is a text template for testing tools investigated. It
is a form containing the items that should be specified for each
testing tool that is investigated. Figure 3.6 shows how the template was copied for each testing tool described in the document.

Providing Cross-references

Systems testing documentation is not stand-alone documentation.
It documents the testing of a system and therefore must reference
the other documentation. Each document should contain a section
that lists all the documents for the project. Anyone reviewing the

```
Testing Tool Type/Use:
Source:
Product:
Release:
Vendor:
Description:


Price:
Licensing Agreements:

Date Investigated:
Decision:
Reason:
```

Figure 3.5.   Text template for testing tools investigated.

system can pick up one document and know the total number of documents that exist. In the client/server environment, this cross-reference is essential. The development group may not be the custodians of the system. The development may be performed by an outside consulting firm or the maintenance of the system may be out-sourced. The documentation is a key in these situations.

The document itself should be cross-referenced. A table of contents should be included in the front of the document.

Naming Conventions for the Documentation

Each systems testing document should be identified by a unique document name. This name should be printed on the document and be used as the file name. When the document structure is segmented, the component document names should conform to this naming convention, for example:

The Systems Test Plan document for a Legal Billing System is named LBTP00, where:

LB indicates the system, Legal Billing

TP indicates the document type, Systems Test Plan

00 indicates master document

7.1 Testing Tools Investigated
The following testing tools were investigated for use on
this project.

Testing Tool Type/Use:
Source:
Product:
Release:
Vendor:
Description:

Price:
Licensing Agreements:

Date Investigated:
Decision:
Reason:

Testing Tool Type/Use:
Source:
Product:
Release:
Vendor:
Description:

Price:
Licensing Agreements:

Date Investigated:
Decision:
Reason:

Figure 3.6.   Text template copied into Testing Tools Section.

The staffing requirements section of the Systems Test Plan is named LBTP50, where:

LB indicates the system

TP indicates the document type

50 indicates section 5 of the document

If the staffing requirements section were further broken down into subsections, the last character would be used to denote subsection sequence. For example LBTP51 would be subsection 1 of staffing requirements, and LBTP52 would be subsection 2.

When boiler-plate text is used in the documentation it should also be identified by standard names. The boiler-plate text, by definition, is text that is of a general nature and therefore may be used throughout the project. The naming convention for boiler-plate text documents should identify the project, for example:

The Legal Billing System documents include a boiler-plate text document that specifies the system overview. It is named LBBP05, where:

LB indicates the system

BP indicates the document type, boiler-plate

05 is the sequence number, the fifth boiler-plate text for the project

Standards within the Documentation

Standards are used to provide consistency throughout the documentation. The following items should be considered:

- Naming conventions
- Acronyms and abbreviations
- Numbering and highlighting
- Page numbering

Naming Conventions

The project's data dictionary should be the source for all data names and business terms. The spelling of departments and titles should also be included in the data dictionary or in a reference list to ensure standardization.

Acronyms and Abbreviations

The documentation should capitalize and abbreviate terms in the same manner. Acronyms should be fully written out the first time and used as an acronym thereafter.

Numbering and Highlighting

A numbering style for the documentation should be selected for the sections within the document. The scheme can use numbers or letters, for example:

> The testing tools section of the Systems Test Plan is section 7.

> The testing tools evaluated subsection can be 7.1, and each testing tool evaluated would be 7.1.1, 7.1.2, and so forth.

A standard should be established for highlighting subheadings and denoting items in lists. Subheadings can be in bold print, underlined, capitalized, or numbered. List items can be denoted by bullets, dashes, numbers, or letters.

Page Numbering

A page-numbering scheme should be developed. The pages in the document can be numbered sequentially across all sections, or the pages could be numbered within each section, for example:

> If the staffing requirements in the Systems Test Plan document is section 5, the pages in the section could be numbered 5.1, 5.2, and so forth.

The Security and Privacy Policy for the Documentation

The systems testing documentation must adhere to the security and privacy policy of the company. Any information used in the systems testing process that requires security clearance should not be published in documentation that is intended for general distribution. The security protection for source files of the documentation should correspond to the security level of the people on the distribution list for the printed material, for example:

A document containing all the log-on ids for the system, which will be distributed to branch manager with a high level of security clearance, should not be stored in the general documentation library available to all software developers.

The privacy of the information in the system should also be considered. When the performance capabilities testing uses a subset of production data, both the data and the documentation reporting the results should be restricted, for example:

If the Legal Billing System used production files for performance measurements, any bills generated by the test cases should not be documented in the Systems Test Specifications document available to all project members. The names and addresses of actual clients would be printed on these bills and this information should not be openly distributed.

It is the responsibility of management to establish the security and privacy policy. It is the responsibility of the test team to follow this policy in creating files and distributing printed material.

THE SYSTEMS TEST PLAN

The Systems Test Plan is the deliverable from the planning phase. It contains the decisions and findings made in the planning phase. The Systems Test Plan can be a set of procedures and memoranda, or it can be a formal document. The formal document is recommended. It should be stored with the overall project documentation and updated as the application is modified.

Figure 3.7 is a recommended outline for a Systems Test Plan. Each section in the outline is explained below. Appendix A of this book contains a sample Systems Test Plan.

1. Identification

1.1 Systems Test Plan Title

The Systems Test Plan document has a title page. Figure 3.8 is the title page for the Systems Test Plan for the Legal Billing System developed by the Information Services department of AAA Software Services Inc. Each item on the page is described below.

---

1. Identification
   1.1 Systems Test Plan Title
   1.2 Application
   1.3 Document Locator
   1.4 Other Documents

2. Systems Test Environment
   2.1 Site
   2.2 Security
   2.3 Submitting Test Items
   2.4 Libraries and Directories
   2.5 Backup/Restore Procedure

3. Objectives and Scope
   3.1 Objectives of this Systems Test
   3.2 Scope of this Systems Test
   3.3 Prior Testing

4. Approach
   4.1 Test Design
   4.2 Cycles and Sequence
   4.3 Acceptance/Rejection Criteria
   4.4 Suspending/Resuming the Systems Test
   4.5 Reporting Changes and Correction
   4.6 Support

5. Staffing
   5.1 Systems Test Responsibilities
   5.2 Systems Test Assignment List

6. Hardware, Software, and Network Requirements

7. Testing Tools
   7.1 Testing Tools Evaluated
   7.2 Testing Tools Being Used

8. Systems Test Deliverables

9. Systems Test Tasks

Figure 3.7. Systems Test Plan outline.

1.1.1 Title

This item is the title of the document. It contains the words "Systems Test Plan For" followed by the name of the application.

1.1.2 Company/Organization

This item contains the name of the company or organization and any copyright or proprietary notices that are required.

1.1.3 Prepared By

This item identifies the names and departments of the people who prepared the document.

1.1.4 Date Written

This item is the date the document was originally written.

1.1.5 Modification Date

This item is the date the document was last updated. This item will contain the words "Original Issue" until the first modification.

```
                  SYSTEMS TEST PLAN FOR
                  LEGAL BILLING SYSTEM

                 AAA Software Services Inc.

This material contains proprietary information. It may not
be copied or reproduced without prior permission.

           Prepared by :   Karen Parker
                           Mark Sherwood

           Information Services Department
           AAA Software Services Inc.

           Date written : December 1992
           Modification date : Original issue
```

Figure 3.8.   Systems Test Plan title page.

1.2 Application

This section identifies the application and the system or subsystem to which it belongs. It identifies the business organization for which the system is written and the Information Services department that developed the software. It gives a brief description of the functions of the system. Boiler-plate text can be used to create this item. All documentation that requires an application description can then include this text.

The following completed text would be used in the Legal Billing System:

> The Legal Billing System is a professional services billing application. It is part of the corporate accounting system. This system was developed by the Information Services department of AAA Software Services Inc. as a program product in its Accounting Packages for Professional Service Organizations. The end-users of the system are the management and support staff of the law firm that purchases this product from AAA Software Services Inc.
>
> The Legal Billing System provides law firms with the capability of maintaining and controlling its billing functions. It provides the following features:
>
> - Add and update client information
> - Add and update matter information for these clients
> - Add and maintain attorney assignments to matters
> - Add and maintain service hours (billable and nonbillable) by attorney for each matter
> - Add and maintain disbursements (billable and nonbillable) for each matter
> - Generate bills on a periodic basis and on demand
> - Browse services and disbursements by matter
> - Report billing hours by attorney or matter
> - Generate management reports
>
> This system was designed for a client/server architecture. The application functions are shared between the desktop workstations and other servers. The desktop workstation provides data entry, system navigation, selection specifica-

tion, and data display. The servers provide communications services, file services, database retrieval, and print services. The system will be installed at the customer's site. It supports multiple workstations connected to a LAN. The network software must provide the communication within and between branch offices.

1.3 Document Locator

This section identifies the location of this document and the procedures to update or print the document. It states the LAN or mainframe where the document is stored and its fully qualified file name. It names the software used to create the document. A text template can be used for this item. Each document can fill in the document name.

The following completed text would be used in the Legal Billing System:

> This document is stored on the S: Drive in the Information Services department's LAN at the headquarters of AAA Software Services Inc. The file name of the master document is LBTP00.DOC in the LBDOC directory. It is written with word processor XXX. It was printed using the following attributes: landscape format, continuous form stock paper.

1.4 Other Documents

This section lists the name and location of any other documentation available for the system. It identifies any documents that are sources for this systems test. It serves as a cross-reference.

One way to do this is to create one control document that names all documents produced for the project. It should contain the document title and its file name. Each time a new document is created it is added to this one control document. All documentation could then merely include this component. This would control the cross-referencing of documents and save each group the task of writing and maintaining the information. Each time the individual documents are expanded, the latest version of the control document list could always be included. The following is an example of this control document.

The control document is named LBMC00.DOC. It is listed as the first document in the list.

Document Name   File Name

Master Documentation Control   LBMC00.DOC
System Requirements   LBSR10.DOC
Software Inventory   LBSI00.DOC
System Design   LBSD00.DOC
System Architecture   LBSA00.DOC
Program Specifications Master   LBPS00.DOC
Users Guide   LBUG00.DOC
Installation and Operations Guide   LBOR00.DOC
Systems Test Plan   LBTP00.DOC
Systems Test Specifications   LBRS00.DOC
Systems Test Activity Log   LBTA00.DOC
Systems Test Summary   LBTM00.DOC

---

2. Systems Test Environment

This section describes the systems test environment.

2.1 Site

This section states where systems testing will be executed. It identifies the site, the LAN, and the platform. It lists the hardware and resident software in each execution platform.

The following describes the site for executing the systems test of the Legal Billing System:

Systems testing will be conducted on the LAN in the Information Services department of AAA Software Services Inc. This LAN is also used by the software developers. The test team will have two personal computers attached to this network. This network has a print server that handles printing functions. There are four printers available to the test team: two laser printers, a postscript printer, and a dot matrix printer. The testing of the print drivers is not part of this systems test. However, the Legal Billing System must be capable of printing single-sheet and multipart-form bills. Therefore, both the laser printers and the dot matrix printer will be used in the systems testing. A communications server is used to access the mainframe and the LAN in the annex building. The mainframe access feature may be used in further releases of the product if a module is added to transfer billed matters to an accounts payable system. The current product does not access a mainframe.

The network administrator for the LAN will provide the test team with access to the software development disk packs. These packs contain the software development tools and the testing tools that the test team will need. The firm has a LAN license for these tools, so the test team can use the products under this license agreement. The test team will have its own disk pack. All software that is being systems tested will be moved to the test team's disk pack.

2.2 Security

This section describes the security restrictions for the systems test environment.

The following describes security for the systems testing of the Legal Billing System:

> The Systems Test Environment will have restricted access. The network administrator will set up security so that the systems test team will be the only persons allowed to update any files on this pack. Software developers and project mangers may browse the files.

2.3 Submitting Test Items

This section describes the procedures for submitting items to the systems test team. It contains an example of any form used to do this and gives instructions on how to fill out the form. It identifies the procedures for migrating the software into the systems test central repository.

The following describes the procedures used by the Legal Billing System:

The test team requires a written list of items that are ready for systems testing. For the initial submission to systems testing, the list must be turned in one day prior to systems test execution unless special arrangements have been made with the project leader. The written list is still required for items that are being resubmitted with corrections, but the one-day notice is waived.

Form SYS009 Systems Test Turnover is used for submitting test items. A description of the form can be found in the Information Systems Standards Manual. It explains each field on the form and how to fill it out. This form is stored in the Information Systems forms library. It can be printed or copied to your personal computer. After the form is filled out, it can be sent to the test team in paper format or transmitted to the test team's e-mail (electronic mail) box.

All software will be moved from its current location, specified on the Systems Test Turnover form, to the systems test central repository. Systems testing will use the same development tools as the software developers to generate the systems test version of the application software.

2.4 Libraries and Directories

This section identifies the software files used for the systems test. It describes the central repository and identifies what is stored in it and how it is controlled.

The following is used to describe this information for the Legal Billing System:

The test team uses its disk pack to store the following:

- The application software being tested
- Test data to load the client, matter, services, disbursements, and personnel databases
- Test files to load the codes databases
- Command language files to execute the testing tools
- Expected results for the test executions
- Actual results from test executions
- Backups of the test databases after each test cycle

2.5 Backup/Restore Procedure

This section identifies the procedures for backing up and restoring the systems test environment. It identifies the group responsible for the task and states the schedule for backing up the system.

The Legal Billing System procedures are as follows:

> The network administrator backs up the files on a nightly basis. Backups are run between 2 A.M. and 4 A.M. each night.
> The test team will back up their test databases during test execution. Several test cycles may be run during one day. The test team will control the backups and restores of these files. It will, however, rely on the nightly backups for the other files on its disk pack.

3. Objectives and Scope

3.1 Objectives of This Systems Test

This section states the purpose of the systems test. It lists the goals of each major area of testing.

The following describes this information for the Legal Billing System:

> The systems test verifies the Legal Billing System performs the business requirements specified in the System Requirements document. It also verifies the system reliability and maintenance capabilities.

3.2 Scope of this Systems Test

Features Being Tested

This section states the features being tested.

Features Not Being Tested

This section states the features that are not being tested.

The following business requirements of the Legal Billing System are being tested:

- Add, change, and delete attorney/personnel information
- Add, change, and delete client information

- Add, change, and delete matter information
- Add, change, and delete service hours rendered by attorney for each matter
- Add, change, and delete disbursements incurred for each matter
- Update attorney billing rates by individual attorney and for all attorneys in firm
- Generate bills on a periodic and ad-hoc basis
- Generate management reports
- Inquiry of clients, matters, service hours, attorney billing rates, and disbursement information

The performance capabilities will be tested for adherence to the business requirements.

The following operational capabilities will be tested:

- Restore the systems databases from a backup
- Upgrade the application software

Features Not Being Tested

This section states the features not being tested.

The following business requirements of the Legal Billing System are not being tested:

Print Servers

The systems test team will use only the printers available on the LAN. Any special print drivers that must be developed for customer support are not included in the scope of this testing.

Restrictions

This section states any restrictions to the testing process, for example:

- The network is not available on Sundays from 4 P.M. to midnight. This impacts the schedule during systems testing execution.
- The Database Administration group is not available on weekends. We may need some technical support or system changes during this period. This can impact our schedule.

3.3 Prior Testing

This section states the testing required before systems testing.

The following is an example of the information that may be written here:

> Reviews and walk-throughs will be used throughout the system development process. In addition, the system designers must review the hardware, software, and network traffic that the product must support. The software developers must unit test all software before submitting it to the test team.

4. Approach

4.1 Test Design

This section describes the design techniques for the systems test. It specifies how the test conditions are identified, how the test data is created, and how the expected results are determined. It describes any special conditions that must be simulated to test the features.

The following is the test design information for the Legal Billing Systems:

> The systems test team identifies the test conditions from the System Requirements, the System Design Architecture, and System Design documents. They create test cases for these conditions. They create the test procedures and test data. The test team prepares any special procedures required to verify the results of the tests. This includes procedures to display the actual results and compare them with the expected results.
>
> The users and the test team jointly prepare the expected results for each test case.
>
> The test team, users, network administrators, database administrators, and software developers review the Systems Test Specifications prior to its execution.

4.2 Cycles and Sequence

This section identifies the sequence of testing and any dependencies.

The following cycles and sequences are used in systems testing the Legal Billing System:

Quality/standard compliance testing will be conducted first. After the test items have been submitted to the test team, they will be tested for adherence to Information Systems standards. This is performed by a testing tool that checks the code for key words and format. Another testing tool is used to check the code for quality. It verifies style and complexity. The results of the test must be manually scanned. Some warning messages may be acceptable.

The business requirements testing is divided into test cycles. The test cycle sequence will be determined during the design phase of systems testing. The test cycles, however, will be established in such a way that each cycle can be tested independently. For example, the baseline test data will contain matters that contain service and disbursements charged to them. This will permit the testing of billing software even if the data entry software is not ready or contains critical errors. The Legal Billing System must generate periodic and on-demand bills. The systems testing must simulate end-of-period to test the period-billing features.

Performance capabilities testing will be conducted after the business requirements testing has completed.

Operational capabilities testing can be conducted concurrently with business requirement testing. The sequence will depend upon the availability of the staff, not the design of the testing.

4.3 Acceptance/Rejection Criteria

This section states how test conditions are verified. It identifies the techniques to compare the actual results with the expected results. It states the criteria for accepting and rejecting the results and the procedures to report a rejection to the software developers.

The following describes the acceptance/rejection criteria for the Legal Billing System:

The Systems Test Specifications contains the expected results for each test case. The actual results must agree with the expected results. The systems test reviewers verify the user-viewed results. These results are the items that a user can see: the user interfaces on the screen, the results displayed on the screen from inquiries, and the printed reports. The test team verifies the systems results. Systems results are database records, data files, and data interfaces. When the actual results differ from the expected results, the reviewers generate an Incident Report and notify the test team coordinator. Incident Reports are given to the Incident Report Coordinator for logging.

4.4 Suspending/Resuming the Systems Test

This section identifies the conditions that suspend systems testing. It distinguishes the conditions that can be bypassed and tested later from those that suspend testing. It specifies changes that the test practitioners can make and those that must be returned to the software developers. It identifies the procedures to resume systems testing after a suspension.

The following procedures are used in the Legal Billing System:

A test case fails when its actual results differ from the expected results. A test case that fails is recorded in the Activity Log and reported in an Incident Report. Any dependent test cases are bypassed. The Incident Report is given to the software developers. They must correct the associated software and resubmit it to the test team. The failed test case and its dependent test cases will be retested when the corrected software is resubmitted.

Test data is created so each cycle is independent. If the test cases for Add Service Hours or Change Service Hours functions fail, the test data with those service hours can be loaded from a test data file.

The test team can change any items that they created. This includes command language files, testing tool procedures, control data, baseline data, and test data. They can correct the application command language files, but any correction to the application code must be made by the software developers.

4.5 Reporting Changes and Correction

This section describes the procedure to report a change or correction to the software.

The following procedures are used in the Legal Billing Systems:

Incident Reports are used for both reporting errors and requesting changes or enhancements to the system. Instructions for filling out this form can be found in the Information Systems' *Standards Manual*. All Incident Reports are logged by the Incident Report Coordinator in the Incident Report Log. This log is a spreadsheet that lists all Incident Reports by number. It contains a brief description of each report and its current status. The Incident Log is described in the Information Systems' *Standards Manual*. It is used to track the status of the Incident Reports and generate management reports.

4.6 Support

This section defines the level of support the test practitioners require during systems test execution.

The following describes the support required by the test team for the Legal Billing System systems testing:

The test team requires the following staff to be available during the execution of the systems tests:
   The systems test reviewers—to verify the test cases.
   The software developers—to change or correct software as noted by the systems test reviewers.

4.7 Levels

This section identifies the levels of systems testing that will be performed.

The following describes the levels of testing used by the Legal Billing System test team.

Systems testing will be conducted as three levels.

- Quality/standard compliance testing of the software
  This is the first level. All software submitted to the test team must pass this level of testing before it can proceed.
- Business requirements and operational capabilities testing
  These two components are included in the second level. This level uses controlled test data and verifies functionality.
- Systems performance
  This is the third level. It uses fully loaded databases and measures performance capabilities.

5. Staffing

5.1 Systems Test Responsibilities

This section lists each group and their responsibilities for the systems test.

The following is the staff responsibilities assigned for the Legal Billing System:

Systems Test Team
- Maintain the systems test environment.
- Migrate test items to the systems test environment.
- Generate the systems test version of application software.
- Maintain the status of test items—submitted, accepted, rejected, not available.
- Prepare systems test specifications and test data.
- Prepare expected results.
- Determine the testing tools required.
- Evaluate testing tools.
- Install testing tools and prepare procedures to assist systems test reviewers verify actual results.
- Coordinate the execution of the systems tests.
- Maintain a Systems Test Activity Log.
- Ensure all test cases are verified and reported.
- Document the status of the testing.
- Prepare a summary report for management.

Systems Test Reviewers

- Review the expected results prepared in the Systems Test Specifications prior to systems test execution.
- Verify the actual results of the systems test execution.
- Identify and report any exceptions.
- Submit an Incident Report on each exception.
- Sign off on all approved tests case.

Software Development Team

- Develop and unit test software.
- Submit unit-tested items to test team.
- Modify software as required to resolve Incident Reports.
- Support the test team during the execution phase.

Project Leader

- Assign staff to systems test team.
- Ensure proper security is maintained for systems test environment.
- Review and approve any hardware required for the systems test execution.
- Review and approve any requests for testing tools.
- Arrange availability of the network for the systems test execution.
- Monitor project schedule.
- Monitor software development methodology for adherence to quality and standards requirements.

Incident Report Coordinator

- Review all Incident Reports for completeness.
- Log Incident Reports.
- Analyze Incident Reports to determine the cause of the problem.
- Assign priorities to Incident Reports.
- Track status of Incident Reports.
- Ensure all Incident Reports are closed (via testing or cancellation).
- Update the Incident Reports as their status changes.
- Generate reports for management on the Incident Reports.

5.2 Systems Test Assignment List

This section lists the personnel from each group assigned to the systems test. It contains the name of the group, the person assigned and the date assigned. Systems testing is initially executed during software development. It is executed again each time there is a modification to the production system.

There are two methods for maintaining this section:

- Only keep the current list. Update the section whenever the personnel changes.
- Keep the list of personnel for each iteration of the systems testing. This serves as a permanent record of who participated in the systems testing in each iteration.

The following shows an assignment list using the first method:

The personnel assigned to the systems test team are listed below.

Project Leader

Barbara Grant—Information Services Department

Systems Test Team

Patricia Hall—Information Services Department

Systems Review Team

Patrick Dodge—Sales Department
Mark Sherwood—Information Services Department

Incident Report Coordinator

Sandra Baker—Information Services Department

This list tells us Patricia Hall, Patrick Dodge, Mark Sherwood, and Sandra Baker are on the test team. It does not indicate that Karen Parker, one of the developers of the Systems Test Plan, is no longer on the test team. It does not indicate Barbara Grant was not the project leader during the original systems testing. She was assigned to this position during the maintenance phase.

The next example shows an assignment list using the second method. It shows the assignment list for the same project with all persons who participated in the function listed. When there is high turnover, this list can get long, and it may not be important to know who the players were for each inning.

Project Leader

Larry Barnes—Information Services Department, July 1991–Jan. 1993

Barbara Grant—Information Services Department, Jan. 1993–present

Systems Test Team

Karen Parker—Information Services Department, July 1991–Dec. 1991

Patricia Hall—Information Services Department, Feb. 1992–present

Systems Review Team

Patrick Dodge—Sales Department, Oct. 1992–present

Mark Sherwood—Information Services Department, Jan. 1993–present

Incident Report Coordinator

Patricia Hall—Information Services Department, Oct. 1992–Dec. 1992

Sandra Baker—Information Services Department, Nov. 1992–present

6. Hardware, Software, and Network Requirements

This section identifies the hardware, software, and network requirements for executing the systems test. If the systems test will executed in less than the ideal environment, describe the requirements requested and the actual ones delivered. Explain why this occurred and if there is an effect on the results.

The Legal Billing System is being developed by a software house for sale as a product. The systems test team must test the software using the model environment described in the System Requirements document. When a software product is developed for a specified production site, the systems testing should execute in that type of environment.

The hardware, software, and network requirements for systems testing are the same as those specified in the Systems Requirements document. See the Legal Billing System architecture document LBAD01.DOC for the configurations.

7. Testing Tools

7.1 Testing Tools Evaluated

This section lists the testing tools evaluated for use in systems testing. It describes each testing tool, the selection decision, and reason. This information is useful in subsequent testing.

For each testing tool it lists:

- Source (market or in-house)
- Product name
- Vendor
- Release, version number, or date written
- Platform and minimum configuration
- Licensing agreements
- Date investigated
- Features and constraints
- Decision and reason for selection or rejection

A text template can be used in writing this section. The template can be included for each testing tool. The writer can then fill in the appropriate information.

The following is a completed template describing a testing tool evaluated for the Legal Billing Systems:

- Product: GUI-Capture (market product)
- Vendor: JYZ Company
- Release: 2.1
- Licensing Agreements:
  The product can be purchased with either a single machine, LAN, or site license.
- Price: $$$$ per single users, LAN and site prices higher.

- Date Investigated: Dec. 1992
- Features and constraints
  This product captures screen input, including mouse clicks, and stores it in a file for replay later.
- Decision: Not selected
  There are some capture/replay testing tools that are expected to be released in the second quarter of 1993. Management wants to wait until these products are released before making a purchase decision. The tools will be re-evaluated at that time.

7.2 Testing Tools Being Used

This section describes each testing tool used in the systems test. It lists the following:

- Product or program name
- Vendor or author
- Release, version number, or date written
- Location of the documentation for the product

It describes how the product is used in the systems test. It lists the name and location of any procedures written to execute the testing tool.

The following description is an example of the section. It describes two of the testing tools products used for the Legal Billing System: an in-house product and a market product.

Product: TESTGEN (in-house product)
Author: Information Services department
Documentation for this testing tool is available in the Information Systems library. The test team must write control statements to execute the product for the systems test databases. This testing tool generates test data for databases. The values and ranges of the data can be controlled by control statements.

Product: DB-Standards (market product)
Vendor: Quality Products Company
Release: 3.1

The documentation for this product is in the Information Systems library. The test team must create a list of key words to supplement the vendor supplied list. This testing tool will be used in conducting quality/standards compliance testing.

8. Systems Test Deliverables

This section lists the deliverables required from the Design and Execution Phases of the systems test.

One example of this would be as follows:

The deliverables for the design phase are the following:

- Systems Test Specifications
  This is a document that specifies the tests to be executed. It contains a description of the test cases, the expected results, instructions to perform the tests and verify the results.
- Test data
  This deliverable consists of files that contain the data required by the test cases. The files either load the test databases or create input transactions.
- Expected Results
  This deliverable consists of files that contain the expected outputs. The files can contain reports or images of updated databases. They can be used as input to a testing tool which compares expected and actual results.
- Test Procedures
  This deliverable consists of command language files that execute the test cases or testing tools used in verifying the results.

The following are the deliverables for the execution phase:

- Systems-Tested Software
  This is the tested source code submitted by the software developers and stored in the systems test central repository.
- Actual Results
  This deliverable consists of files that contain the actual outputs. The files can contain reports or images of the updated databases.

- Systems Test Activity Log
  This is a document that contains a record of the details of each test case execution.
- Incident Reports generated during systems test execution
  This deliverable consists of forms used by the reviewers in reporting any inconsistencies or omissions they found in reviewing the actual results of the tests.
- Incident Log
  This is a spreadsheet used to track the status of incident reports.
- Systems Test Summary Report
  This deliverable is a document that contains a summary of the results of the systems test.

9. Systems Test Tasks

This section contains a checklist of the tasks in the design and execution phases of the systems test. The tasks are listed in the sequence required.

This section can either contain a numbered list of tasks or reference a project management report stored in another document. An example of the numbered list is shown below.

1. Determine test conditions.
2. Determine test cases for each test condition.
3. Determine test procedures.
4. Determine expected results.
5. Determine test cycles and their sequence.
6. Write Systems Test Specifications document.
7. Schedule a formal review of Test Specifications.
8. Review Test Specifications in formal review session.
9. Modify Test Specifications, if required, as a result of the review.
10. Create test data.
11. Write command language procedures to load test data.
12. Write command language procedures to assist in executing systems test and reviewing actual results.
13. Write command language procedures to back up and restore test databases.

14. Test command language procedures.

The systems test team is not immune from errors. It does not have the advantage of another team verifying its code. It is annoying to halt systems testing to correct an error in the setup or verification procedures. Test them during the design phase of systems testing. Don't wait until they are being used in the systems test execution to discover an error.

15. Determine whether all items required for testing can be delivered on schedule.

The test team should be informed of changes in the software development schedule. Certain features of the systems may be deferred to a latter release ("de-scoping"). They must be eliminated from the systems test execution. If the feature will be included in a subsequent release, any design work performed for its test conditions and test cases should be saved. The systems test documentation should state the date of this design work and reason for its exclusion. The feature may not be implemented in the later release exactly as it was originally specified.

16. Modify test cycle schedule if test items will not be available.

17. Create any data files required to simulate input for a test cycle.

18. Obtain disk space or tapes required to save actual results.

19. Load test databases with baseline data.

20. Load security and code tables with test data.

21. Initialize data files with any control information required.

22. Arrange systems test execution schedule with network administrator and other departments.

23. Order or arrange for special forms or extra stock paper for volume testing printing.

24. Make special arrangements if required for access to physical premises during after normal business hours.

This may require writing letters to the security staff or arranging for building keys.

25. Make any special arrangements required for physical premise facilities.

Note: This item is important. On two occasions systems testing was scheduled to execute on the weekend during nonstandard business hours.

On one project, in New York City in February, the project leader forgot to arrange with premises for heating. The heat for the building is turned off on weekends. We worked until our hands were too numb to use the keyboard and then went home.

On another project, in Boston in August, the project leader forgot to arrange with premises for the air conditioning to be turned on. It was 90°F without the computers turned on. We went home.

26. Verify all test items required for systems testing have been submitted to the test team.
27. Migrate application software and prepare it for execution.
28. Modify command language files for the execution environment.
29. Set up Activity Log document.
30. Review procedures for entering information into Activity Log with all test team participants.
31. Conduct quality/standards compliance testing.
32. Retest any items that were rejected in the quality/standard compliance testing.
33. Schedule systems test execution announcement meeting.
34. Conduct systems test announcement meeting.
35. Resolve any issues uncovered in the announcement meeting.
36. Conduct business requirements testing.
37. Verify actual results.
38. Resolve any critical Incident Reports generated during systems testing.
39. Conduct performance capabilities testing.
40. Conduct operational capabilities testing.
41. Resolve Incident Reports generated during systems testing.
42. Repeat tests until all required Incident Reports have been resolved.

43. Write Systems Test Summary Report.
44. Modify any systems testing methods and procedures that were inadequate.
45. Modify any systems test cases that were incorrect or inadequate.
50. Update the Systems Test Specifications accordingly.
51. Turn over systems test deliverables to management.
52. Prepare for the maintenance phase of systems testing. This last step is often omitted in schedules. After the systems testing is completed, there is a sigh of relief and a bit of enthusiasm that the task is completed. Systems testing is not over until the product is replaced. It moves into a maintenance along with the rest of the project. After the celebration is over, the next and longest phase of the project begins. The systems test team should prepare for the maintenance phase by ensuring all the documentation is current and all data files have been properly saved. In a client/server architecture, where the systems testing files are stored on a network, it's important to make archival copies of the material. Use tape cartridges and store the tapes in a safe location. Off-site storage is recommended.

SUMMARY

The planning phase of systems testing begins when the System Requirements document is delivered. The testing strategy is established in this phase. It is formed by the following:

- Identifying the systems test environment
- Defining the objectives and scope of the systems test
- Defining the approach for the systems test
- Determining the staffing requirements and responsibilities for the systems test
- Determining the hardware, software, and network resources required to execute the systems test
- Determining the testing tools required for systems testing
- Determining the deliverables from the systems test
- Identifying the systems test tasks and their sequence.

The format of the systems test documentation should be specified in the planning phase. The following items should be considered in planning the format:

- The style of the documentation
- The distribution of the documentation
- The maintenance of the documentation
- The design of the documentation
- The naming conventions for the documentation
- The standards within the documentation

4

The Design Phase

The second phase of systems testing is the *design phase*. The work of this phase should begin during the design phase of software development and be refined as the System Architectural Design and Detailed Design documents are delivered. It can overlap the planning phase of systems testing and begin before the Systems Test Plan is delivered, provided the following elements of the test strategy have been defined:

- The objectives of the systems test
- The approach for satisfying those objectives
- The staff responsible for executing the approach

In the design phase of systems testing, the test team executes the approach by performing the following:

- Define the test conditions and test cases
- Identify and create the test data required for the tests
- Determine the expected results of each test
- Specify the procedures to conduct each test
- Determine the test cycles and their sequence
- Prepare command language files to load the test databases
- Prepare command language files to verify the actual results

- Prepare any special command language files required to conduct the tests

The following are the deliverables from this phase:

- Systems Test Specifications document
- Test data
- Expected results
- Command language files to load data, verify results, and conduct the tests

In the client/server architecture, the graphical user interfaces must be tested using a structured test that covers all the features of the interface. The individual interfaces are tested and debugged by the software developers during development. However, for GUIs, this testing is inadequate. Each interface on the screen must be executed in combination with the other interfaces on that screen. This testing must be conducted prior to the execution of the systems test by either the software developers during development or the test team as an initial test. The test conditions to verify the interaction of the GUIs must be defined early in the System Development Life Cycle. Test cases must be designed and documented. There must be one test case for each possible sequence of these GUIs. For example, a screen with three GUIs (a pull-down menu, a dialogue box, and a text

		TEST CASES			
1	2	3	4	5	6
P	P	D	D	T	T
D	T	P	T	P	D
T	D	T	P	D	P

P = Pull-Down Menu
D = Dialogue Box
T = Text Box

Figure 4.1.   Test cases for the interaction of GUIs.

box) requires six test cases to test all arrangements of these objects. In Figure 4.1 each sequence is listed under a test case and labelled as 1, 2, 3, 4, 5, and 6.

The number of different possible arrangements of n objects, when all objects are selected, can be determined by the formula $n!$ (read as n factorial).

Some examples of factorials:

$1! = 1$
$2! = 2 \times 1 = 2$
$3! = 3 \times 2 \times 1 = 6$
$4! = 4 \times 3 \times 2 \times 1 = 24$
$5! = 5 \times 4 \times 3 \times 2 \times 1 = 120$
$6! = 6 \times 5 \times 4 \times 3 \times 2 \times 1 = 720$
.

.

.

$10! = 10 \times 9 \times 8 \times 7 \times 6 \times 5 \times 4 \times 3 \times 2 \times 1 = 3,628,800$

Factorials increase in size very rapidly. The number of test cases required to test even a simple system is large. Fortunately, there are testing tools available that generate test cases for the specified requirements and track the testing.

There are also GUI testing tools that provide capture/replay facilities. They capture keystrokes and mouse clicks in a file. This file serves as documentation for the test that was performed. In some testing tools, the captured file can be edited to add comments describing each action that was taken. The file can then be saved and played back for subsequent testing. There are some testing tools that also save the screen images and printer output and use them when the file is replayed to compare outputs. The current screen image and printer output are compared against prior outputs, and any differences are reported.

DECISION TABLES

Decision tables are generally associated with program design. However, they are useful in the systems testing tasks. They can be used for both the design and documentation of test conditions.

Decision tables list all conditions that should be tested for a requirement and the corresponding actions to be taken. They provide a structure for defining test conditions. When the test practitioners prepare a decision table, they are forced to consider all combinations of conditions and their appropriate actions. This process helps them to develop all the variations and avoid any omissions. It also helps them to determine any test conditions that are irrelevant and can be excluded.

Decision tables are graphical representations of a problem. They provide a clear and concise method of presenting conditional logic. They can show the test practitioners—in one picture—all the information they need to know about a specific test. Decision tables are easier and faster to read than narratives. They are also more effective in communicating the information. The test practitioners do not need to read long paragraphs with complicated "IF" statements. The writing styles used by the test practitioners, in documenting the test conditions, can vary. The wording within the documentation may be ambiguous. Decision tables have a predefined format and thereby provide a standard and effective format for communicating the logic.

Figure 4.2 shows the basic layout of a decision table. Decision tables contain the following sections:

- Title
- Conditions
- Responses
- Rules
- Actions
- Effects

The Title section contains a name or number used to uniquely identify this decision table. It should follow the naming conventions being used for the project or within the systems testing documentation.

The Conditions section contains all the conditions that are being examined for this requirement. The conditions are presented in a question format, and each is listed separately. The questions in this section are constructed so that their answers will be a binary response. That is, the question can only be an-

Title	
	Rules
Conditions	Responses
Actions	Effects

Figure 4.2.   Decision table layout.

swered by one of two possible answers: "Yes" and "No" (or "True" and "False"). A decision table containing only binary responses is called a limited-entry decision table. This type of decision table is used in creating and documenting test cases.

The Responses section contains the responses to the questions listed in the Conditions section. All combinations of these responses are developed and then simplified. The decision table can show either the original fully expanded responses or the finalized version.

The Rules identify each variation of responses within the table. They are sequentially numbered.

The Actions section contains a list of all actions that can result from the conditions. The actions are presented as imperative statements. They state an action that will take place for the above conditions.

The Effects section indicates which actions will be taken for each rule developed in the Responses section. The indicator used in this table is an "X". One indicator appears under each rule to indicate the action taken for the responses of this rule.

Figure 4.3 is an example of a decision table used to describe the tests for a requirement to reprice a company's product line. The conditions for determining which products increase in price are expressed in the "IF" statement below:

IF the product is active (currently being manufactured)
    and
    the product is printed in the company's catalog
    and
    the product's current price is less than $1000
THEN
    Increase the price by 10%

The information in each section of this decision table is described below.

The Title section contains a number and a description, 5-401 and Repricing Catalog Products, respectively.
    The Conditions section contains three conditions listed in the form of questions:
    "Is this an active product?"
    "Is the product printed in the catalog?"
    "Is the current price less than $1000?"

The Responses section contains the responses to these questions. In this table the response symbols are "Y" (Yes) and "N" (No). The responses are listed under each rule.
    The Rules section identifies and numbers the Rules as 1 through 4.
    The Actions section lists two actions that can be result from these conditions: "Increase price by 10%" and "Don't increase price".
    The Effects section indicates the action taken for rule 1 is "Increase price by 10%." The action taken for rules 2, 3, and 4 is "Don't increase price."

When a condition does not need to be tested for one of the rules, it is skipped and its response in the Response section is left blank. In this example, when a product is not active (the company is not manufacturing the item this year), there is no need to increase its price. Therefore, when the answer to the first condition, "Is this an active product?," is "N," condition 2 and condition 3 don't need to be tested. They are irrelevant to the action and

5-401 Repricing Catalog Products

		1	2	3	4
1.	Is this an active product?	Y	Y	Y	N
2.	Is the product printed in the catalog?	Y	Y	N	
3.	Is the current price < $1000?	Y	N		
Increase price by 10%		X			
Don't increase price			X	X	X

Figure 4.3. Decision table for repricing example 5-401.

can be eliminated. The Responses columns under rule 4 for these two conditions are left blank.

The decision table in Figure 4.3 has conditions with an "AND" logical relationship. All three conditions must be satisfied ("Y") for the price to increase.

The product must be active
AND
it must be printed in the catalog
AND
its current price must be less than $1000

There are two actions the system can perform:

Increase price by 10%
or
Don't increase price

In rule 1, the responses to condition 1, condition 2, and condition 3 are "Y." The product is active, it is printed in the catalog, and its current price is less than $1000. The action is "Increase price by 10%."

In rule 2, the responses to condition 1 and condition 2 are "Y." The product is active and it is printed in the catalog. The third condition must be tested. Its response is "N"—it is not less than $1000. The action is "Don't increase price."

In rule 3, the response to condition 1 is "Y"—the product is active. Condition 2 must be tested. The response to condition 2 is "N"—the product is not in the catalog. The third condition doesn't need to be tested. The action is determined, "Don't increase price."

In rule 4, the response to condition 1 is "N"—the product is not active. The first condition is the only condition that needs to be tested. The action is now determined. Since all three conditions must be "Y" to increase price, the first "N" encountered determines the action is "Don't increase price."

When the maximum rules resulting from n conditions are specified in a decision table, the table must provide 2^n rules where the exponent n is the number of conditions, for example:

A decision table with three conditions would have a maximum of 8 rules, $2^3 = 8$ rules.

A decision table with four conditions would have a maximum of 16 rules, $2^4 = 16$ rules.

The maximum rules in the decision table for the repricing example in Figure 4.3 would be $2^3 = 8$ rules. Figure 4.4 shows these rules.

5-401 Repricing Catalog Products

	1	2	3	4	5	6	7	8
1. Is this an active product?	Y	Y	Y	Y	N	N	N	N
2. Is the product printed in the catalog?	Y	Y	N	N	Y	Y	N	N
3. Is the current price < $1000?	Y	N	Y	N	Y	N	Y	N

Increase price by 10%	X							
Don't increase price		X	X	X	X	X	X	X

Figure 4.4. Maximum rules.

When the maximum rules are defined, the responses to condition 1 will always be 50% "Y" and 50% "N." All the "Y" responses should be grouped together, followed by all the "N" responses. The responses to condition 2 will have a pattern of 25% "Y" responses, followed by 25% "N" responses, followed by 25% "Y" responses and 25% "N" responses. The responses should be entered with the "Y," "Y," "N," "N" responses for the condition 1 "Y" responses first followed by the "Y," "Y," "N," "N" responses for the condition 1 "N" responses. This pattern continues for condition 3. The responses to condition 3 will have a pattern of 12.5% of the total responses. The responses should be entered as "Y," "N," "Y," "N," "Y," "N," "Y," "N." Figure 4.4 shows this pattern. This layout provides a visual check of the design. It enables the designer to spot any duplications or omissions.

The maximum rules only apply when there is no logical relationship between the conditions. The conditions have a logical relationship when the response to one condition affects the relevance of subsequent conditions. A decision table should only contain conditions that have a logical relationship. If the conditions are not logically related, they do not belong in the same table. In Figure 4.4 all conditions were tested. The table does not consider the logical relationships that exist. Some of the conditions in this table don't need to be tested.

To determine which tests can be eliminated, compare the responses in each rule. When two rules have the same effect and their responses only differ by one answer, eliminate the test where the responses differ. When the pattern previously described was used in filling out the decision table, the last tested condition is the one that differs. Rules 3 and 4 have the same effect; their action is "Don't increase price." Their responses to condition 1 and condition 2 are the same. Condition 3 can therefore be eliminated for both rules 3 and 4. The same situation exists for rules 5 and 6 and rules 7 and 8. Figure 4.5 shows the table with the unnecessary tests eliminated and their responses left blank.

The rules in this table now need to be analyzed for redundancies. Any rules that are now the same (their responses and effects are equal) can be combined. Rules 3 and 4 are identical and therefore can be combined. The same situation is true for rules 5 and 6

5-401 Repricing Catalog Products

	1	2	3	4	5	6	7	8
1. Is this an active product?	Y	Y	Y	Y	N	N	N	N
2. Is the product printed in the catalog?	Y	Y	N	N	Y	Y	N	N
3. Is the current price < $1000?	Y	N						
Increase price by 10%	X							
Don't increase price		X	X	X	X	X	X	X

Figure 4.5.   Eliminate unnecessary tests.

and rules 7 and 8. Figure 4.6 shows the simplified table. The rules have not been renumbered for clarity in this example. The lower of the two numbers was retained.

The table should be examined again for unnecessary tests. Rules 5 and 7 have the same effect. Their action is "Don't increase price." Their responses to condition 1 are the same, and neither rule tests condition 3. Condition 2 is the last tested condition and can therefore be eliminated. Figure 4.7 shows the table with the unnecessary test eliminated.

5-401 Repricing Catalog Products

	1	2	3	5	7
1. Is this an active product?	Y	Y	Y	N	N
2. Is the product printed in the catalog?	Y	Y	N	Y	N
3. Is the current price < $1000?	Y	N			
Increase price by 10%	X				
Don't increase price		X	X	X	X

Figure 4.6.   Combined rules.

5-401 Repricing Catalog Products

	1	2	3	5	7
1. Is this an active product?	Y	Y	Y	N	N
2. Is the product printed in the catalog?	Y	Y	N		
3. Is the current price < $1000?	Y	N			
Increase price by 10%	X				
Don't increase price		X	X	X	X

Figure 4.7. Further eliminated tests.

The rules should be examined again for redundancies. Rules 5 and 7 are now identical and should be combined. Figure 4.8 contains only relevant rules, and after the rules are renumbered, it will be the same as the original example shown in Figure 4.3

Decision tables with logical relationships generally go through several designs before they are finalized. The testing of conditions are eliminated, and the rules are combined. The process explained above is useful in developing the rules for complex requirements. Experienced test practitioners may not need to go through all of

5-401 Repricing Catalog Products

	1	2	3	5
1. Is this an active product?	Y	Y	Y	N
2. Is the product printed in the catalog?	Y	Y	N	
3. Is the current price < $1000?	Y	N		
Increase price by 10%	X			
Don't increase price		X	X	X

Figure 4.8. Further Combined rules.

the steps shown. They may be able to produce a simplified version of the decision table directly from the conditions. However, it is important to understand the process before any shortcuts are taken. Furthermore, the decision tables are generally of more use as an analysis aid when they are left in their fully expanded version. The analyst can easily scan the table ensuring every possible combination of conditions has been considered and handled.

The number of rules required for the systems testing decision tables can be calculated as followed:

Number of Rules $= n + 1$
where n is the number of conditions.

In the repricing example, there are three conditions, so four rules are required. This is the number derived by the process used above. The Repricing Decision Table is correct. Although the number of rules can be determined by the formula $n + 1$, the contents of the table must still be validated. The process used to derive the rules is valuable in checking the accuracy of the table.

A decision table in which the conditions have an "AND" logical relationship will have the pattern shown in Figure 4.9.

A decision table in which the conditions have an "OR" logical relationship will have the pattern shown in Figure 4.10.

There are testing tools available that check decision tables.

AND			
	1	2	3
1. Condition 1	Y	Y	N
2. Condition 2	Y	N	Y
Action accept	X		
Action reject		X	X

Figure 4.9. Conditions with "AND" logical relationship.

OR

	1	2	3
1. Condition 1	Y	N	N
2. Condition 2	N	Y	N
Action accept	X	X	
Action reject			X

Figure 4.10. Conditions with "OR" logical relationship.

They scan the table for omissions, redundancies, and contradictions. These tools will sort the Condition Entry responses so that for a given path, all "Yes" responses are grouped together and all "No" responses are grouped together. However, the testing tools are only tools for the test practitioners to use in checking their work. They do not validate the logic within the decision table. This is the responsibility of the test practitioner on the systems test team. Decision tables are not only a useful technique, they are also the input to some test-case-generating tools. These testing tool products generate test cases and supporting test data from the information supplied in a decision table.

A spreadsheet can be used to record the decision tables. The spreadsheet can then be included in the appropriate section of the Systems Test Specifications document.

THE MAJOR AREAS OF THE SYSTEMS TESTING

The Systems Test Plan defines the objectives and scope of systems testing in the four major areas:

- Quality/standards compliance
- Business requirements
- Performance capabilities
- Operational capabilities

In the design phase, tests are developed for each of these areas and recorded in the Systems Test Specifications.

QUALITY/STANDARDS COMPLIANCE TESTING

Quality standards compliance testing verifies the system was developed in accordance with the standards established by the Information Services department. It confirms that the application code and documentation meet the specified quality guidelines. The type of testing performed in this area varies with the policy of the management. The system should have been tested for compliance with standards and methodology in prior phases of the SDLC. The design and coding reviews should have included compliance testing. Management determines whether quality/standards compliance testing is included in the systems testing. When it is included, the specific objectives and the testing tools to be used are defined in the Systems Test Plan.

Quality/standards compliance testing is specified as follows:

• Define the test conditions to satisfy the objectives
• Determine the expected results
• Specify the procedures to conduct these tests

Define Test Conditions

The Standards Manual is the source document for defining the conditions to test in quality/standards compliance testing. It contains the rules and guidelines that the software developers should follow in developing an application system. The following example lists two objectives of compliance testing and their test conditions:

Objective

1. To determine the completeness and accuracy of the systems documentation

Test Conditions

1.1 Are all objects in the system listed in the software inventory list?

1.2 Do program specifications exist for each program in the system?

1.3 Does each program specification contain all components, as specified in *Standards Manual*?

Figure 4.11 is the decision table for the systems documentation testing objectives.

Objective

2. To ensure the application code adheres to coding guidelines and naming standards

Test Conditions

2.1 Does the application code include reusable objects whenever available?

2.2 Does the application code use the standard for database calls (not issue any direct database commands)?

2.3 Does the application code adhere to naming conventions?

1-101 Systems Documentation

	1	2	3	4
1.1 Are all objects in the system listed in the software inventory list?	Y	Y	Y	N
1.2 Do program specifications exist for each program in the system?	Y	Y	N	
1.3 Does each program specification contain all components as specified in the *Standards Manual*?	Y	N		
Approve Documentation	X			
Reject Documentation		X	X	X

Figure 4.11.   Quality/standards compliance testing decision table 1-101.

2-101 Coding And Naming Conventions				
	1	2	3	4
2.1 Does the application code include reusable objects whenever available?	Y	Y	Y	N
2.2 Does the application code use the standard for database calls?	Y	Y	N	
2.3 Does the application code adhere to naming conventions?	Y	N		
Approve Code	X			
Reject Code		X	X	X

Figure 4.12.   Quality/standards compliance testing decision table 1-201.

Figure 4.12 is the decision table for the coding and naming conventions objectives.

Determine Expected Results

The expected results for quality/standards compliance testing is actually the action entries in the decision table. In the examples above, there are only two actions: approve code and its documentation, or reject code and its documentation. In some instance, the expected results of quality/standards compliance testing must indicate an acceptance level. This is the minimum "passing grade" for the test. For example, there may be a condition, "Does the application code generate any diagnostic messages when prepared for execution?" The acceptance level may be to accept warning messages. Another example would be a condition, "Does the program specifications contain all components?" The acceptance level may be to accept the program without unit test plans. These situations require a third action, "Approve, but issue a warning to software developers."

Specify Procedures

The test procedures are the instructions for executing the tests. For compliance testing, they specify the tasks required to conduct the tests for each test condition.

Any test case that uses a testing tool to perform the test or verify the results should either reference the testing tool's documentation or list the instructions for using the tool. The command language file (a CLIST, JOB, or BAT file) required to execute the testing tool is prepared and tested in the design phase. The following example lists the test procedures for testing the conditions stated above.

Test procedures to

1. Determine the completeness and accuracy of the systems documentation.

    1.1 Compare the list of items submitted to the test team with the software inventory list. Both lists must match.
    Log any mismatches in the Systems Test Activity Log. These items are rejected. They must be returned to the software developers for investigation.

    1.2 Compare the programs listed in the software inventory list with the specifications in the program specification library. Both lists must match.
    Log any mismatches in the Systems Test Activity Log. These items are rejected. They must be returned to the software developers for investigation.

    1.3 Verify that each program specification contains all components as specified in the *Standards Manual*.
    Reject any program that does not have complete program specifications. The programs are returned to the software developers. The program documentation must be completed. Log all programs that pass the documentation test. The software is accepted by the test team for further systems testing.

Test procedure to

2. Ensure that the application code adheres to coding guidelines and naming standards.

2.1, 2.2, 2.3

For each program submitted to the test team for systems testing, execute the in-house testing tool, "Standard Check." This testing tool checks the code for standards violations. It performs the tests for test conditions 2.1, 2.2, and 2.3. Standard Check is described in the Systems Development manual.

Execute "Standard Check" by entering the following on the screen:

STDCKV followed by a space and the program name.

The testing tool will examine the program and display a pass or fail message on the screen. A report is generated for any program that fails the test.

BUSINESS REQUIREMENTS TESTING

Business requirements testing verifies that the system satisfies the business requirements specified in the System Requirements document. This area is always tested in the systems test and constitutes the major testing effort. Its objectives are defined in the Systems Test Plan. Business requirements testing is specified as follows:

- Define the test conditions for each requirement
- Identify the test data
- Determine the expected results
- Specify the procedures to conduct these tests

Define Test Conditions

The System Requirements document is the source for defining the conditions to test in business requirements testing. This document contains a formal definition of the requirements for the system. It is used by the software developers to design the system and should be used by the test team to develop the test conditions. The document defines the business requirements in general terms. They must be broken down so any complex or multiple requirements are individually defined. This task is accomplished during the functional decomposition process. In this process, the requirements of the system are decomposed into increasingly smaller functions until all the activities to be performed in the system are listed.

The initial step in the functional decomposition creates an itemized requirements list. Each requirement is clearly stated so that no ambiguity or inconsistencies exist. This itemized requirements list must be validated by the users to ensure the requirements, as specified, are what the users want. The itemized requirements are presented to the users in a review session. Business requirements are tested in every phase of the life cycle; this is the first test. The approved requirements list is used by the software developers and the test team.

The test team uses the list to develop test conditions for the functionality of each requirement. Program specifications and application code should not be used to define test conditions. When the test team constructs test conditions using program specifications, the systems test can verify a system that does not produce the business requirements. The systems testing can produce the expected results, but those results were developed by using program specifications that may have missing or incorrect business requirements. The test will only confirm the program and data definitions are correct, not the business requirements.

On one project, the business requirements for pricing components manufactured by a subsidiary of the company were unclear. The software developers didn't clarify the information. Instead, they made assumptions. The test team was also confused about the requirements so they used the program specifications to develop the test conditions. The systems testing verified the functions (constructed from the program specifications). The system was implemented and these components were incorrectly priced. The system did not perform the business requirements.

When programs are delivered to the test team, they have presumably been tested and perform the instructions correctly. Systems testing should not be duplicating that effort. This area of systems testing verifies the functionality, not the code. The test conditions are identified from the System Requirements document and can be designed without knowledge of the programming language and the systems architecture.

The following is partial list of the business requirements for the Legal Billing System.

Maintain personnel information

Maintain client information

Maintain matter information

Maintain billing rates

Maintain services rendered for matters

Maintain disbursements incurred for matters

The itemized list of the requirement to maintain billing rates is as follows:

Maintain billing rates

Add billing rate for personnel

Change billing rate for personnel

Delete billing rate for personnel

Change billing rates for all billable personnel

Test conditions are developed for each of the itemized business requirements.

Define Test Cases

The test cases are the actual tests required to execute the test conditions. The initial test cases are constructed from the System Requirements document. They are refined and expanded during the systems development process to include specific implementation features. Additional test cases are developed as the System Architectural Design and Detailed Design documents are delivered.

The systems test must cover all variations the system can perform for a test condition. The test cases should be constructed so each variable will be executed. They should also be designed to detect whether any requirements errors exist. Requirement errors are omissions and misinterpretations of the requirements either by the analyst in preparing the specification or the programmer in writing the code. A separate test case is required for each variable so its effect can be isolated for testing. This enables the test team to identify the source of any test failure.

For the Legal Billing System, the business requirement to

change billing rates for all billable personnel has the following specifications:

IF the employee is a paralegal
OR
    the current billing rate < $300/hour
OR
    the last rate increase was > 1 year ago
THEN
    Increase billing rate by x%

The conditions for this requirement have an "OR" logical relationship. If any one of the conditions are satisfied ("Y"), the billing rate is increased. Figure 4.13 presents this information in a decision table. There are three conditions: "Is the employee a paralegal?," Is the current billing rate < $300/hour?," and "Was the billing rate updated > 1 year ago?" There are two actions: "Increase billing rate by x%" and "Don't increase billing rate."

This decision table was designed using the process previously described. For an "OR" logical relationship, the first "Y" response determines the action to be taken: "Increase billing rate by x%." Four rules are required to test this requirement. In order to test for missing business requirements, each variable must be isolated.

4-401 Change Billing Rates for all Personnel

	1	2	3	4
1. Is the employee a paralegal?	Y	N	N	N
2. Is the current billing rate < $300/hour?		Y	N	N
3. Was billing rate updated > 1 year ago?			Y	N
Increase billing rate by x%	X	X	X	
Don't increase billing rate				X

Figure 4.13. Change billing rates.

4-401 Change Billing Rates for all Personnel

	1	2	3	4
1. Is the employee a paralegal?	Y	N	N	N
2. Is the current billing rate < $300/hour?	N	Y	N	N
3. Was billing rate updated > 1 year ago?	N	N	Y	N
Increase billing rate by x%	X	X	X	
Don't increase billing rate				X

Figure 4.14. Change billing rates—modified table.

Only one "Y" response should exist in each rule. The decision table must be modified to ensure that the variables are isolated. All responses that were left blank because the testing of the condition was unnecessary must be changed. The response must be set to "N." The modified decision table is shown in Figure 4.14.

Rule 1 isolates the paralegal variable. Only condition 1 has a response of "Y." This rule tests the paralegal condition by itself to verify this condition is correctly specified.

> If the system omitted the condition the billing rate would not be increased. The test would fail.

Rule 2 isolates the "Less than $300/hour" variable. Only condition 2 has a "Y" response.

Rule 3 isolates the "Billing rate updated more than 1 year ago" variable. Only condition 3 has a "Y" response.

Rule 4 has all conditions set to "N." This rule verifies that the system correctly specifies the requirements. It verifies that the system does not use another variable in performing this function.

The business requirements testing is not testing the code. It should not be checking whether the code computes 1 year ago correctly. It should test whether the system specified the 1 year ago condition in performing the change billing rate functionality.

The business requirement to "add a services rendered" record has the following specifications:

IF the matter is open
AND
    the service hours rendered are less than 16
AND
    the personnel rendering the service is employed by the company
THEN
    add the service record

The conditions for this requirement have an "AND" logical relationship. All of the conditions must be satisfied—"Y"—for the service to be added. Figure 4.15 presents this information in a decision table. There are three conditions: "Is the matter open?," "Are the service hours rendered less than 16?," and " Is the personnel rendering the service employed by the company?" There are two actions: "Add service record" and "Don't add record."

For an "AND" logical relationship, the first "N" response determines the action to be taken, "Don't add record." Four rules are required to test this requirement. Only one "N" response should exist in each rule. The decision table must be modified. All re-

---

6-601 Add Service Record

	1	2	3	4
1. Is the matter open?	Y	Y	Y	N
2. Are the service hours rendered < 16?	Y	Y	N	
3. Is the personnel rendering the service employed by the company?	Y	N		
Add service record	X			
Don't add record		X	X	X

Figure 4.15. Add service record.

6-601 Add Service Record

	1	2	3	4
1. Is the matter open?	Y	Y	Y	N
2. Are the service hours rendered < 16?	Y	Y	N	Y
3. Is the personnel rendering the service employed by the company?	Y	N	Y	Y
Add service record	X			
Don't add record		X	X	X

Figure 4.16. Add service record—modified table.

sponses that were left blank must be set to "Y." The modified decision table is shown in Figure 4.16.

Rule 1 has all conditions set to "Y." This rule verifies that the system correctly specifies the requirements. It verifies that the system does not omit a condition in performing this function.

Rule 2 isolates the personnel employed by company variable. Only condition 3 has an "N" response. If the system omitted this condition, the rule would be considered satisfied and the service record would be added. The test would fail.

Rule 3 isolates the service hours variable. Only condition 2 has an "N" response.

Rule 4 isolates the matter-status variable. Only condition 1 has a response of "N." This rule tests the matter-status condition by itself to verify this condition is correctly specified.

The test cases should be constructed using the extreme or limit values for a variable. In the billing rate example, where the current billing rate must be under $300, values of $299.99 and $300.00 would test the limits of this variable. If the system incorrectly set the current billing rate to under $100, a value of $10.00 would confirm the requirement was included but would not confirm its accuracy.

When an error is detected, the test fails and the associated software must be corrected. When the software is resubmitted, all test cases for that test condition must be executed again. An error in one test case can mask an error in another test case.

In the add service record example, if the system omitted the matter-status (open) requirement and incorrectly set the service hours rendered requirement to under 10 hours, rule 1 is the only test case that would fail. The other test cases would still produce the correct result.

> The missing matter-status requirement causes the matter-status response in rule 4 to be incorrectly set to "Y," but it will not be detected.
> The service hours rendered error masks the matter-status error.
> When the service hours rendered error is corrected, and all test cases are rerun, the matter-status error in rule 4 will be uncovered.

The design of the test cases is a demanding task. It requires planning and time to construct the correct number of test cases that test all the actions. The test cases can be constructed manually or generated by a testing tool. There are testing tools, called test design generators, that can construct the test cases required to test a condition. The conditions are defined to the tool by a set of parameters.

The test cases must be documented and saved so they can be used again when the system is modified. The decision tables can be used to document each test case. However, an overall cross-reference is required. When a business requirement changes, the test team needs to know which test cases need to change.

A test case/requirements matrix is useful in tracing the test cases for a requirement. Figure 4.17 is an example of such a matrix. The test cases, identified by test case number, are listed along the Y-axis. The requirements, identified by requirement number and an abbreviation, are listed along the X-axis. The requirements tested by a test case are marked. When a requirement changes, all test cases associated with that requirement can be readily identified. Test coverage analyzers and test impact analyzers are testing tools that automate this task. They provide cross-reference reports that associate the test cases with the requirements.

TEST CASE/REQUIREMENTS MATRIX

				REQUIREMENT			
	1	2	3	4	5	6	7
TEST CASE	CLN	PRSN	MTRS	RTS	SVC	DSB	BLL
1-1-01	X						
1-1-02	X						
1-2-01	X						
1-2-02	X						
1-3-01	X						
1-3-02	X						
1-3-03	X						
2-1-01		X					
2-1-02		X					
2-1-03		X	X		X		
2-1-04		X	X				
2-2-01		X					
2-2-02		X					
2-2-03		X	X				

Figure 4.17.   Test case/requirements matrix.

In the Legal Billing System, data integrity rules are implemented by a stored procedure. The following presents the data integrity rules.

- This system provides a personnel and a matter database.
- The personnel database contains information about the company's employees. It contains termination date, which is updated when an employee terminates employment with the company.
- The matter database contains information about open matters for which the company renders and bills services and disbursements. It contains an attorney-in-charge identifier that indicates the attorney responsible for this matter.

- The attorney-in-charge must be currently employed by the company (the termination date must be null). When an attorney-in-charge terminates employment with the company, the attorney cannot be assigned as an attorney-in-charge on any matters. All matters where that attorney is the attorney-in-charge must be reassigned.

The stored procedure is triggered when the termination date in the personnel database is updated. The test cases for the requirement to terminate an employee should verify this stored procedure performs the specified requirements. The test conditions are shown in two decision tables shown in Figure 4.18. The test procedures must include instructions for verifying, both the personnel and matter databases.

Legal Billing System: Terminate employee
Test Conditions

1-501 Terminate Employee	1	2	3
1. Is the person employed by the company?	Y	N	
Terminate, Go to Table 1-502	X		
Reject		X	
1-502 Change attorney-in-charge			
2. Is the person an attorney?	Y	Y	N
3. Is the person attorney-in-charge on an open matter?	Y	N	
Change attorney-in-charge to office	X		
No changes required		X	X

Figure 4.18. Terminate employee—test conditions.

1. Is the person currently employed by company?
2. Is the person an attorney?
3. Is the attorney an attorney-in-charge on any open matters?

The first decision table tests the condition, "Is the person currently employed by the company?" Its actions are "Terminate employee and go to next Table" and "Reject." The second decision table tests the second and third conditions. Its actions are "Change the attorney-in-charge to the office account" and "Don't change any records."

Identify Test Data

The test cases are grouped together to identify the supporting or baseline data required to execute the tests. For example, a test case to add an attorney to the personnel database would require data in all the codes databases used to verify the input. The branch office, legal speciality, and employee classification Codes databases would need entries. The test team identifies the data requirements for each test case and attempts to satisfy it with the minimum data.

A test case/database matrix is useful in designing the test data. Figure 4.19 is an example of this matrix. A detailed sample is also included in Appendix A. The test cases, identified by test case number, are listed along the Y-axis, and the databases, identified by an abbreviation, are listed along the X-axis. The databases used by a test case are marked with either a single character indicating its use or a specific code indicating its access method (Insert, Replace, Delete). This matrix presents a visual cross-reference that can be used for impact analysis during the maintenance phase. When a database changes, all test cases affected by that change can be readily identified.

The decision tables used in creating the test cases are used along with the test case/database matrix to create the values required in the test data files. The values required for each rule in the decision table must be determined. Figure 4.20 shows the data values for the requirement to "add a service record."

Test data is created in the design phase. The data can be created by a testing tool, extracted from production, individually

TEST CASE/DATABASE MATRIX

| | DATABASE | | | | | | | |
| | 1 | 2 | 3 | 4 | 5 | 6 | 7 | 8 |
TEST CASE	CLN	PRSN	MTRS	RTS	SVC	DSB	BLL	CDE
1-1-01	I							R
1-1-02	R							R
1-2-01	U							R
1-2-02	R							R
1-3-01	D		R				R	
1-3-02	R							
1-3-03	R		R				R	
2-1-01		I						R
2-1-02		R						R
2-1-03		U	U					R
2-1-04		U	R					R
2-2-01		U						R
2-2-02		R			U			R
2-2-03		R	U					R

Figure 4.19.   Test case/database matrix.

entered, or generated by a program. Any command language files required to create, load, back up, or restore the test data should be written and tested in the design phase.

Baseline data are the initial values required to execute the tests. It should be saved so it can be restored for subsequent testing. It should be stored as separate files. Data that is added and modified during the execution of the tests should not be merged with the baseline file. Any backup files created during the execution of the tests should be discrete files. The baseline data should be described in the Systems Test Specifications. The document could either include a copy of the baseline data or contain instructions for printing it from the files.

6-601 Add Service Record

	1	2	3	4
1. Is the matter open?	Y	Y	Y	N
2. Are the service hours rendered < 16?	Y	Y	N	Y
3. Is the person rendering the service employed by the company?	Y	N	Y	Y
Add service record	X			
Don't add record		X	X	X

Rule 1	Matter Number : 0004 Service Hours : 15.9 Attorney Number : 0001	Added Service record Number 0019
Rule 2	Matter Number : 0004 Service Hours : 15.9 Attorney Number : 0002	Not Added
Rule 3	Matter Number : 0004 Service Hours : 16.0 Attorney Number : 0001	Not Added
Rule 4	Matter Number : 0005 Service Hours : 16.0 Attorney Number : 0001	Not Added

Figure 4.20.   Add service record—data values.

Determine Expected Results

The expected results for the business requirements testing are divided into two categories: user-viewed results and systems results. The user-viewed results are the results the user sees as each test case is executed. They are the messages, actions, and data shown on the screen or printed in a report. These results should be determined and described in the test procedures. The systems results are the updated databases and files created as a result of executing the test case. The results should be determined and either described or actually created. After all test cases for a business objective are executed, the contents of the databases and files are verified. The procedure should confirm all adds, changes, and deletes that were expected to occur as a result of the test cases did in fact occur. If a file is created with the expected results, a procedure can be used to compare it with the actual results.

Specify Procedures

Test procedures are written for each test case. The procedures describe the setup, execution, verification, and exit processes required to execute the test. They should include instructions for both the manual and automated steps. The procedures should describe the following:

- **The setup steps required prior to execution**
  This would include instructions for data preparation, input balancing, database restores, and file initialization.
- **The execution steps to execute the test case**
  This would include the log-on procedures required to access the system in the systems test environment. This section could be written as boiler-plate text. In a client/server architecture where the systems testing will be executed in multiple sites, these instructions may vary with the site. The appropriate boiler-plate could be included in the distributed version of the test procedures.

  The system navigation required to get to the function being tested should also be included. General instructions on how to use the mouse or the keyboard should *not* be included here. When these instructions are part of the system (in a Help function), they are actually tested as part of that feature of the system.

  A screen image of the screen should be included in any tests that require the user to enter information or make selections from a system menu or list.
- **The verification steps required to verify the results**
- **The exit steps required after the tests are executed**

All command language files required to back up, restore, or print databases must be created and tested in the design phase.

Any testing tools required to execute or verify the tests must be prepared. The instructions for using them must also be included in the test procedures.

The test procedures are created in a skeleton format when the test conditions are defined. They are refined as the system develops and the test team receives detailed design specifications.

The following is one example of a test procedure for a test case used to verify the change customer information requirement. These test case procedures describe the user-viewed results. The test cycle procedures describe the systems results. The backup, restore, and file compare procedures are performed for the test cycle and therefore described in those procedures. This is a simple test case with only one condition: "Is the customer active?"

There are two rules.

In rule 1 the customer is not active and therefore cannot be updated.

In rule 2 the customer is active and the information is updated.

Test Procedures and Expected Results

Test Case : 1-102   Change Customer Information

System Status: The test procedures for the test cycle in which this test case is executed will contain the instructions to restore the system to the correct status. The system will have baseline customer information. Any changes made as a result of this test case have been cleared by that restore procedure.

1. Log-on on to the Order Entry System using the log-on Id assigned to you by the test team.

    This function is a general system function. The system does not require supervisor level authority to change customer information. The log-on Id used for this test case has general order entry capabilities. It does not have authority to perform supervisor functions.

2. Select the "Customer" option from the menu bar.

3. Select Customer No. SB0004.
    Type in the number in the field provided.
    The Customer screen should display with the information for customer Sally Jones.
    A screen image with the exact information should be included in the document at this point. A skeleton screen image should be stored as separate document that could be used to fill in appropriate expected results. The document could then be included in this document. This will make maintenance of the documentation easier. The screens will change during the lifetime of the software. It is easier to update the Systems Test Specifications by only replacing the screen image documents with the updated screens, then to update each imbedded screen image.
4. This customer account is closed. No changes are allowed. The screen image should contain the full message that would appear in the production system.
5. Select customer David Bremer from the list box.
    The Customer screen should display with the information for this customer. His customer number is SB0005. This customer account is open. Change the "Receive Catalog" information from monthly to quarterly.
    The change is accepted. The information is updated.
6. Log the test case in the Systems Test Activity Log.

PERFORMANCE CAPABILITIES TESTING

Performance capabilities testing verifies that the system operates within the performance measures specified in the System Requirements document. This area is always tested in the systems test. It's conducted after the business requirements testing has verified the functionality. Its objectives are defined in the Systems Test Plan. Performance capabilities testing is specified as follows:

- Define the test conditions for each objective
- Identify the test data
- Determine the expected results
- Specify the procedures to conduct these tests

Define Test Conditions

The System Requirements document is the source for defining the conditions to test in performance capabilities testing. It contains the performance requirements for the system. The following example lists an objective of performance capabilities testing and its test conditions:

Objective

To verify that the system can satisfy the performance requirements with the normal volume of transactions.

Test Condition

Can transactions be entered into the network from multiple workstations with each user receiving a response within the required time ($.n$ seconds)?

Identify Test Data

For some performance capabilities test conditions, the databases must be fully loaded files. The test data for these conditions need not be individually created. Performance capabilities testing does not examine the results of each input, but rather it measures the performance of the system in processing the data. The test data can be created by a testing tool that generates test data, or it can be extracted from the production system and formatted for this system.

When testing the network performance, the transactions must be submitted to the network from several workstations, in competition with other work. The test cases can be those previously identified for the business requirements testing. Each test case could be entered many times with different data. The Systems Test Plan identifies the testing tools that can be used for this area.

Determine Expected Results

The expected results for performance capabilities testing are the minimum "passing grade" for the test. For example, the response time for a transaction must not exceed $.n$ seconds.

Specify Procedures

For performance capabilities testing, the test procedures specify the instructions for conducting each test case. It should indicate any prior arrangements that must be made before executing the tests. For example, schedule the network to operate during off-hours, or obtain permission for a volume test to be performed.

OPERATIONAL CAPABILITIES TESTING

Operational capabilities testing verifies the system can operate in a production environment. After the system is implemented, the users and the operations staff must be able to operate the system independently of the software developers. The operational capabilities testing must be conducted prior to implementation. It confirms the operational procedures and the execution of those procedures. This testing verifies the operational procedures are adequate and satisfy the standards established by the Information Services department. It then verifies the procedures can be executed by the operations staff and produce accurate results.

In a client/server environment, where the system is distributed to multiple sites, the operational procedures must be tested for and at each site. The procedures may be performed locally and, therefore, the staff would be different at each site. The procedures may be different for each site. The site itself must be tested for security compliance prior to implementation. The procedures to distribute the software must also be confirmed.

The type of testing performed in this area varies with the policy of the management. Management decides who is responsible for the operational capabilities testing and what will be tested.

When operational capabilities testing is included in the systems testing, the specific objectives and the testing tools to be used are defined in the Systems Test Plan.

Operational capabilities testing is specified as follows:

- Define the test conditions for each objective.
- Determine the expected results.
- Specify the procedures to conduct these tests.

Define Test Conditions

The Standards Manual and the System Requirements are the source documents for defining the conditions to test in operational capabilities testing. The Standards Manual contains the standards and guidelines for developing operational procedures. It contains the rules and specifications with which a physical site must comply. The System Requirements document contains the user requirements for operation of the system. It identifies the functions and hours required from a Help Desk facility. The following example lists an objective of operational capabilities testing and its test conditions:

Objective

1. To verify that the operational procedures to restore the master databases can be executed by the operations staff

Test Conditions

1.1 Do operational procedures for restoring the master databases exist for each site?

1.2 Are the operational procedures complete, accurate, and in compliance with the guidelines in the Standards Manual?

1.3 Can the operations staff use the procedures to restore the master databases without any assistance from the software developers?

1.4 Can the master databases be restored from a backup file?

Figure 4.21 is the decision table for the operational procedures testing objectives.

Determine Expected Results

Operational capabilities testing are checklists. The expected results of conditions are that the conditions were satisfied. For example, a test condition for physical site security compliance would be "Are the backup files stored in a secure location?" The expected result is compliance with this condition. The exception to this is

7-101 Operational Procedures

	1	2	3	4	5
1.1 Do operational procedures for restoring the master databases exist for each site?	Y	Y	Y	Y	N
1.2 Are the operational procedures complete, accurate, and in compliance with the guidelines in the Standards Manual?	Y	Y	Y	N	
1.3 Can the operations staff use the procedures to restore the master databases without any assistance from the software developers?	Y	Y	N		
1.4 Can the master databases be restored from a backup file?	Y	N			
Approve procedures	X				
Reject procedures		X	X	X	X

Figure 4.21.   Operational capabilities testing decision table 7-101.

the expected result from the tests to verify the operations of the Help Desk. The test conditions may include the turnaround time to resolve an issue or the quality of an answer. For each of these conditions, the expected result is the minimum "passing grade" for the test. For example, the turnaround time to resolve an issue must not exceed three hours.

Specify Procedures

For operational capabilities testing, the test procedures specify the instructions to conduct each test case. It should indicate any prior arrangements that must be made before executing the tests.

TEST CYCLES

A test cycle is a suite of ordered test cases that will test a logical portion of the system.

Define Test Cycles

The test team creates test cycles to divide the testing into manageable work units by grouping the test cases into test cycles. The cycles should parallel the business flow. They are created in a way that allows one cycle to build on a prior cycle. The Systems Test Plan defines the method used for building test cycles. It indicates whether the test cycles will build on one another or the test data should be constructed so any cycle can be started independently. The method indicates the amount of test data required, not the number or order of the test cycles.

A systems test may be divided into ten test cycles. Cycle 1 could build the data required to run Test Cycle 2, or test data could be created separately for Test Cycle 1 and Test Cycle 2. The systems test will contain ten cycles with either method.

Define Test Cycles Sequence

The test team determines the sequence in which the test cycles are to be executed. When several test cycles can run concurrently they are assigned the same sequence number. The sequence numbers, not the test cycle numbers, are used to indicate the execution order. The systems test is modified as the system is modified. Additional test cycles may need to be added. A test cycle numbering scheme should not be used to indicate sequence. It would be inflexible and create test cycles labeled 2A and 2B. A new cycle should be given the next available number, and the test cycle sequence can be used to define its execution order.

Specify Test Procedures

Test procedures are written for each test cycle. The procedures describe the setup, execution, verification, and exit processes required to test the cycle. The systems results are described for the test cycle. The steps in the test procedures identify the test cases executed in this test cycle and their execution sequence. The test procedures can either, list the test cases or reference a test case/ test cycle matrix.

An example of a test case/test cycle matrix is shown in Figure

TEST CASE/TEST CYCLE MATRIX

	TEST CYCLE						
TEST CASE	1	2	3	4	5	6	7
1-1-01	X						
1-1-02	X						
1-2-01	X						
1-2-02	X						
1-3-01	X						
1-3-02	X						
1-3-03	X						
2-1-01		X					
2-1-02		X					
2-1-03		X	X		X		
2-1-04		X	X				
2-2-01		X					
2-2-02		X					
2-2-03		X	X				

Figure 4.22.   Test case/test cycle matrix.

4.22. Test cases are listed along the Y-axis, and test cycles are listed along the X-axis. Each test cycle in which the test case participates is marked.

A test case may participate in more than one test cycle. It may be used again to test another requirement or condition. The test case may be executed again with different data or the same data. The test procedures to execute the test cases are described once in the business requirements section and referenced in any test cycles where they are used.

The following is an example of the test procedures for a business requirements test cycle.

Test Cycle 1: Maintain master databases

Test Cycle Description:
This cycle executes the test cases that verify all functionality for the following requirements:

Maintain client information

Maintain matter information

Maintain personnel information

Test Procedures

1. Restore the master databases from the backup file by executing the command language file CYC01RSK.
2. Log the execution of the restore in the Activity Log.
3. Execute the test cases for this test cycle. See test case/test cycle matrix for test case numbers. The test procedures for each test case are located in the business requirements section. Log each test case execution in the Activity Log.
4. Print the contents of the master databases by executing the command language file CYC01PT. The updated master databases are the systems-results for this test cycle.
5. The systems-results must be compared to the expected results. The expected results were created as a file. To compare the two files, execute command language file CYC01V. It executes a program that compares the files and notes any discrepancies. The results of the comparison are displayed on the screen and printed in a report.
6. Log the results of the comparison in the Activity Log. If any discrepancies were noted, complete an Incident Report and notify the test team coordinator.
7. Back up the updated master databases by executing command language file CYC01BK.
8. Log the execution of the backup in the Activity Log.

THE SYSTEMS TEST SPECIFICATIONS

The Systems Test Specifications is a formal document describing the individual tests in the systems test and the instructions for executing them. It is a permanent document that is stored with the project documentation. Figure 4.23 is a recommended outline

SYSTEMS TEST SPECIFICATIONS

1. Identification
   1.1 Systems Test Specifications Title
   1.2 Contents
   1.3 Document Locator
   1.4 Other Documents

2. Quality/Standards Compliance
   2.1 Test Conditions
   2.2 Test Procedures and Expected Results

3. Test Cycles
   3.1 Test Cycle Descriptions
   3.2 Test Cycle Sequence
   3.3 Test Cycle Procedures and Expected Results
       3.3.1 Test Cycle 1 Procedures and Expected Results
       . . . .

4. Business Requirements
   4.1 Itemized Requirement *n*
       4.1.1 Test Conditions - Test Cases *n*-001
       4.1.2 Test Procedures and Expected Results
       . . . .
       4.1.n Test Conditions - Test Cases *n-nnn*

5. Performance Capabilities
   5.1 Test Conditions
   5.2 Test Procedures and Expected Results

6. Operational Capabilities
   6.1 Test Conditions
   6.2 Test Procedures and Expected Results
       . . . .

7. Baseline Data

8. Cross-References
   8.1 File Location
   8.2 Test Case/Requirements Matrix
   8.3 Test Case/Database Matrix
   8.4 Test Case/Test Cycle Matrix
   8.5 Test Case/Object Matrix

Figure 4.23. Systems Test Specifications outline.

for the Systems Test Specifications. Each section of the document is described below. Appendix A of this book contains a sample Systems Test Specifications.

1. Identification

This section identifies the document and supplies background information.

1.1 Systems Test Specifications Title

The Systems Test Specifications document has a title page. Figure 4.24 is the title page for the Systems Test Specifications for the Legal Billing System. Each item on the page is described below.

1.1.1 Title

This item contains the words "Systems Test Specifications for" followed by the name of the application.

1.1.2 Prepared By

This item identifies the names and departments of the people who prepared the document.

```
             SYSTEMS TEST SPECIFICATIONS FOR
                  LEGAL BILLING SYSTEM

                AAA Software Services Inc.
This material contains proprietary information. It may not
be copied or reproduced without prior permission.

             Prepared by :   Karen Parker
                             Mark Sherwood

             Information Services Department
             AAA Software Services Inc.

             Date written : December 1992
             Modification date : Original issue
```

Figure 4.24.   Systems Test Specifications title page.

1.1.3 Date Written

This item contains the date the document was originally written.

1.1.4 Modification Date

This item is the date the document was last updated. This item will contain the words "Original Issue" until the first modification.

1.2 Contents

This item is the contents of the Systems Test Specifications. This document will vary depending on the individual project. The tables of contents can be used as quick references for the following:

The number of test cycles

This is described in section 3 "Test Cycle Procedures and Expected Results." There should be one entry in this section of the contents for each test cycle in the systems test.

The number of business requirements test conditions and test cases

This is described in section 4 "Business Requirements." There should be one entry in this section of the contents for each test condition. For each test condition, there should be at least one test case entry.

The following is the contents of the Systems Test Specifications for the Legal Billing System.

CONTENTS

1. Identification
2. Quality/Standards Compliance
   2.1 Test Conditions
   2.2 Test Procedures and Expected Results
3. Test Cycles
   3.1 Test Cycle Descriptions
   3.2 Test Cycle Sequence
   3.3 Test Cycle Procedures and Expected Results
      3.3.1   Test Cycle 1 Maintain Client, Matter, Personnel Information

1.3 Document Locator

This item identifies the location of this document and the procedures to update or print it. It states the LAN or mainframe where the document is stored and its fully qualified dataset name. It names the software used to create the document. A text template can be used for this item. The Systems Test Specifications document can copy a text template for this section and fill in the appropriate words.

1.4 Other Documents

This item lists the name and location of any other relevant documentation available for this system. It serves as a cross-reference. A control document is created for the Legal Billing System which lists all documents created for the project. This document is included in that master document.

2. Quality/Standards Compliance

2.1 Test Conditions

This section lists the objectives of quality/standards compliance testing and the test conditions to satisfy those objectives. There should be a complete description for each objective and its test conditions. A decision table can be used for presenting the conditions, the actions, the responses to the conditions grouped as rules, and the actions taken for each rule. The decision table should be included in this section of the document.

2.2 Test Procedures and Expected Results

This section specifies the procedures for executing the quality/standards compliance tests. It specifies the expected results for each test condition.

The information for the Legal Billing System was shown earlier in this chapter. This section contains all the test conditions and test procedures and expected results descriptions required to support the testing of each quality/standards compliance testing objective.

3. Test Cycles

3.1 Test Cycle Descriptions

This section describes the test cycles for the systems test.

The following list contains the name and description of the test cycles for the Legal Billing System.

Cycle Number	Name	Description
1	Maintain Client, Matter, and Personnel Information	Add, change, and delete client information in the databases
		Add, change, delete, and close matter information in databases
		Add, change, delete, and terminate personnel information in databases
2	Maintain Codes	Add, change, delete, inactivate information in codes databases
3	Maintain Billing Rates	Change billing rates for personnel
4	Maintain Service Hours	Add, change, and delete service hours rendered by personnel for matters
5	Maintain Disbursements	Add, change, and delete disbursements incurred for matters
6	Generate Bills	Generate office preliminary reports and client's matter bills on a cyclical and ad-hoc basis
7	Generate Management Reports	Produce reports for standard management reporting and ad-hoc queries
8	Measure System Performance	Measure response time when volume data is entered into the network for a combination of transactions
9	Verify Operational Procedures	Restore databases. Upgrade software.

3.2 Test Cycle Sequence

This section lists the test cycles with their sequence number. This is the sequence in which the cycles will be executed. When test cycles can be executed concurrently, they are assigned the same sequence number.

The following list contains the sequence of execution of the test cycles of the Legal Billing System. Test cycles with the same sequence number can be executed concurrently. Test Cycles 1 and 2 can be executed concurrently. Test Cycles 3, 4, and 5 can be executed concurrently. Test Cycles 8 and 9 can be executed concurrently. The output from Test Cycles 1 and 2 are used for Test Cycles 3, 4, and 5. However, the test data has been built to load the expected results of Test Cycles 1 and 2 if this portion of the system were unable to produce the required output.

Sequence	Cycle Number	Cycle Name
01	1	Maintain Client, Matter, Personnel Information
01	2	Maintain Codes Information
02	3	Maintain Billing Rates
02	4	Maintain Service Hours
02	5	Maintain Disbursements
03	6	Generate Bills
04	7	Generate Management Reports
05	8	Measure Performance
05	9	Verify Operational Procedures

3.3 Test Cycle Procedures and Expected Results

This section contains the procedures and expected results for each test cycle. It describes the following:

- The setup steps for the test cycle
- The test cases executed in this cycle
- The verification steps for the test cycles. For business require-

ments testing, this includes steps to verify the contents of the databases and files.

- The exit steps for the test cycle

The following are the test procedures and expected results for Test Cycle 3, Maintain Billing Rates of the Legal Billing System.

3.3.3 Test Procedures for Test Cycle 3 Maintain Billing Rates

This procedure describes the steps required to execute Test Cycle 3, Maintain Billing Rates. The steps must be performed in the sequence indicated, unless otherwise noted.

Status of the System

This cycle relies on the output of Test Cycle 1.

1. Execute LBTC03 to restore the files from the Test Cycle 1 backup files.
   LBTC03 is a batch command file that executes programs to restore the system to its status before any billing rates where modified. This procedure restores all system files from a backup.

NOTE:

The files are normally backed up after Test Cycle 1 executes. However, if a problem occurred with the results of Test Cycle 1 or the software for that portion of the system was not available for systems testing, a special procedure was run to load the expected results of Test Cycle 1 and then a backup was created.

2. Log the restore in the Systems Test Activity Log.
3. Execute the test cases for Test Cycle 3, Maintain Billing Rates.
   The test cases are listed in the test case/test cycle matrix. Each test case is described in the Business Requirements Section 4, Subsection 4.3. The test condition—test cases and the test procedures and expected results are located in this subsection. The test cases should be executed in the order presented.
4. Log the results of each test case in the Systems Test Activity Log.

Log the date and time the execution of the test cases were completed.

5. Execute LBTC05 to produce a report that lists all billing rate records.

 LBTC05 is a batch command file that executes an in-house testing tool. It produces a report listing the contents of the billing rate database at the end of Test Cycle 3. It is an auditing requirement to save the actual results from systems testing. Therefore, the output of this step must be saved to document the testing.

6. Log the execution of the billing rate report in the Systems Test Activity Log.

7. Execute LBTC06 to produce a report that lists the expected results Test Cycle 3.

 The expected results were created as a file. LBTC06 is a batch file that executes a testing tool that prints the contents of this file.

8. Log the execution of the expected results billing rate report in the Systems Test Activity Log.

9. Execute LBTC07 to compare the expected and actual results.

 LBTC07 is a batch command file that executes a testing tool that compares the two files.

 Verify the actual results are the same as the database expected results.

10. Log the results of the comparison in the Systems Test Activity Log. If any discrepancies were noted, complete an Incident Report and notify the test team.

11. Execute LBTC04 to back up the files.

 LBTC04 is a batch command file that executes programs to back up the files after Test Cycle 3 test cases are completed. All files for the system are backed up.

12. Log the backup in the Systems Test Activity Log.

4. Business Requirements

This section lists the business requirements that will be tested in this systems test. There is one subsection for each business requirement with the following:

4.1 Test Condition—Test Cases

This item identifies the test conditions for a business requirement and the test cases for each test condition.

4.2 Test Procedures and Expected Results

This item contains the procedures and the expected results for each test case identified in the subsection. It describes the steps required to execute the test case and shows its user-viewed expected results.

The information for the Legal Billing System was shown earlier in this chapter. This section contains all the test conditions and test procedures and expected results descriptions required to support the testing of the business requirements.

5. Performance Capabilities

5.1 Test Conditions

This section lists the objectives of performance capabilities testing and the test conditions to satisfy those objectives. There should be a complete description for each objective and its test conditions. A decision table can be used for presenting the conditions, the actions, the responses to the conditions, and the actions taken for each rule. The decision table should be included in this section of the document.

5.2 Test Procedures and Expected Results

This section specifies the procedures for executing the performance capabilities test cases. It specifies the expected results for each test case.

The information for the Legal Billing System was shown earlier in this chapter. This section contains all the test conditions and test procedures and expected results descriptions required to support the testing of the performance capabilities testing objectives.

6. Operational Capabilities

6.1 Test Conditions

This section lists the objectives of operational capabilities testing and the test conditions to satisfy those objectives. There should be a complete description for each objective and its test conditions. A decision table can be used for presenting the conditions, the actions, the responses to the conditions, and the actions taken for each rule. The decision table should be included in this section of the document.

6.2 Test Procedures and Expected Results

This section specifies the procedures for executing the operational capabilities test cases. It specifies the expected results for each test.

The information for the Legal Billing System was shown earlier in this chapter. This section contains all the test conditions and test procedures and expected results descriptions required to support the testing of each operational capabilities testing objective.

7. Baseline Data

This section identifies the baseline data required to execute the systems test. It describes the data for each database and file that requires initial data to support the testing.

The baseline data should be stored in files that are used to load this data into the appropriate system database or file. There are several ways to present this information.

The information in each file could be entered, in ASCII format, in a separate document that can be included in the Systems Test Specifications document. This method is easy to use for initial systems testing but difficult to maintain. We used this method on one project. A clerical support person entered the baseline data for each file. This enabled the test team to concentrate on the technical aspects of the test design. The baseline data was modified many times during the initial design and later during the maintenance phase of the project. The documents with the baseline data were never updated on a timely basis, if at all.

A report can be created from each file, listing all the information in that file in ASCII format with appropriate column headings. Each report could then be included in this document. This method is easy to generate. However, when the baseline data file is modified, the report that is being included may not be updated. Therefore any subsequent issues of this document would not contain accurate information.

The Systems Test Specifications document need not list the baseline data. It could, instead, list the names of the files that contain this data. Anyone interested in the information could then browse these files or generate reports that list their contents. This method documents the source of the data. It is easy to implement and requires no maintenance. The latest baseline files are accessed directly. This method can be used when the baseline data files are stored on a system which is available to all persons interested in its contents. There are several items that should be considered before selecting this method.

- The baseline data files may be on a mainframe computer or on a network that is not accessible to the workstations.
- The baseline data files may not be in ASCII format.
- The file size could be too large to browse.
- The reader may not have a technical background, or at least be unfamiliar with the technology used in creating these files. This can often happen in a client/server architecture where the system is a replacement for a mainframe application.

One solution to the above situation is have the documentation list procedures for displaying or printing the baseline files.

A procedure can be developed for printing the entire Systems Test Specifications document or only the baseline data section. This procedure would generate the baseline data reports from their respective files creating new baseline report documents. The document can then be expanded and printed by the word processing software. This method requires some technical planning but is well worth the initial effort.

In the contents of the Systems Test Specifications document presented earlier in this chapter, is listed the baseline data files for the Legal Billing System that are described in this section.

These files are listed in alphabetical order. This was a decision made by the test team. The baseline data files are included in the Systems Test Specifications using the last method stated above. A preprocessor generates reports from the baseline data files, which are then included in this document. This section is fairly long. The report for each baseline file begins on a new page. We found it easier to locate the file descriptions when they were listed alphabetically. We often printed only the baseline data section of the document. It did not contain a table of contents listing the page number of the baseline data files. We would scan the section for the file we wanted relying on the alphabetical sequencing.

8. Cross-References

The section contains the following five items:

- File location
- Test case/test cycle matrix
- Test case/requirements matrix
- Test case/database matrix
- Test case/object matrix

Each of these items should be a separate document that can be included in the Systems Test Specifications master document. These items are cross-reference documents and, therefore, will be referenced frequently. As separate documents they can be easily maintained and printed.

8.1 File Location

This section identifies all files required for systems testing. It specifies the file name and its location. The following types of files would be identified:

- Command Language Files
  The command language files are any BAT files, *CLIST*s, or JOBs required to prepare, execute, or verify the systems testing.
- Test Data Files
  The test data files are the files required to load or initialize the system for systems testing.

- Expected Results Files
  The expected results files contain expected results in a file format. The files can be all the records a database should contain after a test cycle is executed. They can contain an image of a report that should be created in a test. These files are useful in comparing expected and actual results.
- Actual Results Files
  The actual results files are files created during the execution of the tests. They can contain database records, transaction records, or reports.
- Backup Files
  The files are backed up after they are initially loaded and after the execution of each test cycle. Separate files should be kept for each type of backup. This procedure will allow the system to be restored to any system status. If Test Cycle 3 needed to be executed again the appropriate backup file could be used for the restore procedure.

The file location document is similar to the master documentation control document. It is one central file that lists the name and location of all files used in systems testing. It should contain the file name and file location. It could also include a description of file contents. Alternatively, the file names could be grouped by category: command language files in one group, followed by test data files, followed by expected results files, and so forth. Each time a new systems testing file is created, its name is added to this file control document. The following is an example of this file location control document.

File Location	
File Name	Location
Command Language Files	
LBTC01.BAT	All command files are stored
LBTC02.BAT	on S:\LEGAL\SYSTST\BAT
LBTC03.BAT	
LBTC04.BAT	
LBTC05.BAT	

        LBTC06.BAT
        LBTC07.BAT
        LBTC08.BAT

Test Data Files
        LBDTCLN.DAT   All test data files are
        LBDTMAT.DAT   stored on S:\LEGAL\SYSTST\TSD
        LBDTPER.DAT
        LBDTSVC.DAT
        LBDTDSB.DAT
        LBDTRTE.DAT

Expected Results Files
        LBER01C.DAT   All expected results files
        LBER01M.DAT   are stored on
        LBER01P.DAT   S:\LEGAL\SYSTST\EXPCT
        LBER02X.DAT
        LBER03S.DAT
        LBER04D.DAT

Actual Results Files
                                    All actual results files are
                                    stored on S:\LEGAL\SYSTST\ACT

Backup Files
        LBBKINIT.DAT   All backup files are stored
        LBBK01.BAK   on S:\LEGAL\SYSTST\BKUP
        LBBK02.BAK
        LBBK03.BAK
        LBBK04.BAK
        LBBK05.BAK
        LBBK06.BAK
        LBBK07.BAK
        LBBK08.BAK
        LBBK02.BAK

8.2 Test Case/Requirements Matrix

This section contains a matrix listing the test cases and the requirements they test. This matrix shows the test cases that verify a business requirement.

An example of a test case/requirements matrix for the Legal Billing System was shown earlier in this chapter.

8.3 Test Case/Database Matrix

This section contains a matrix listing the test cases and the databases they use.

An example of a test case/database matrix for the Legal Billing System was shown earlier in this chapter.

8.4 Test Case/Test Cycle Matrix

This section contains a matrix listing the test cases and the test cycle where they are used.

An example of a test case/test cycle matrix for the Legal Billing System was shown earlier in this chapter.

8.5 Test Case/Object Matrix

This section contains a matrix listing the test cases and the objects they use. This matrix is useful in verifying that all software required for the test case was delivered. It is also useful during the maintenance phase to reference all test cases that execute an object that has been modified. When an object is changed, all test cases that execute the object can be readily identified.

This information can be presented in several ways. Figure 4.25 is a matrix with the test cases, identified by test case number listed along the Y-axis and the objects, identified by object identifier name, listed along the X-axis. The objects tested by a test case are marked with an "X." For systems with many objects, this matrix can become cumbersome. It can be created in a spreadsheet, but the sheet will be very wide. After the test case is located, the entire row must be scanned to determine its objects. It is difficult to read and even more difficult to maintain.

Figure 4.26 is a cross-reference report. It lists the objects used by each test case in an outline format. This format can be many pages long, but it is easy to read. The test case can be sorted in any sequence and its objects are listed directly below it.

A test case/object matrix is difficult to generate and maintain manually. It is a tedious and time-consuming task. There are testing tools, test coverage analyzers, and test impact analyzers that automate this task. They provide cross-reference reports that associate the test cases with the objects.

TEST CASE/OBJECT MATRIX

OBJECT

TEST CASE	LBC 001	LBP 001	LBM 001	LBR 001	LBS 001	LBD 001	LBB 001	LBX 001
1-1-01	X							X
1-1-02	X							
1-2-01	X							
1-2-02	X							
1-3-01	X							
1-3-02	X							
1-3-03	X							
2-1-01		X						X
2-1-02		X						X
2-1-03		X	X		X			X
2-1-04		X	X					
2-2-01		X						
2-2-02		X						
2-2-03		X	X					

Figure 4.25.   Test case/object matrix.

TEST CASE/OBJECT

2-1-01
   LBP01
   LBX01

2-1-02
   LBP01
   LBX01

2-1-03
   LBP01
   LBM01
   LBS01
   LBX01

2-1-04
   LBP01
   LBM01

Figure 4.26.   Test case/object cross-reference report.

SUMMARY

The design phase of systems testing begins during the design phase of software development. In this phase, the test team executes the approach defined in the planning phase by performing the following:

- Define the test conditions and test cases
- Identify and create the test data required for the tests
- Determine the expected results of each test
- Specify the procedures to conduct each tests
- Determine the test cycles and their sequence
- Prepare command language files to load the test databases
- Prepare command language files to verify the actual results
- Prepare any special command language files required to conduct the tests.

Decision tables are useful in the design and documentation of the test conditions for the systems test.

The Systems Test Specifications is the deliverable from this phase. It is a formal document describing the individual tests in the systems test and the instructions for executing them. It is a permanent document that is stored with the project documentation.

5

The Review

A *review* is a formal analysis of technical work to uncover pertinent information. There are many reviews during the system development life cycle. The system's requirements, design, and coding are reviewed. The Systems Test Specifications are also reviewed.

The review of the Systems Test Specifications for a client/server application is conducted in the same manner as any other systems testing review. However, in a client/server environment, the review should not be considered an optional procedure. It is important to review the Systems Test Specifications before the execution of the tests. Client/server applications have a smaller budget than mainframe-based systems. Any savings realized in the software development of a client/server application will be quickly absorbed by software maintenance costs. Over 50 percent of software bugs are caused by errors in the requirements specifications. These errors should have been discovered during earlier design reviews. However, the Systems Test Specifications review is another opportunity to review the system and its systems testing procedures. This review is primarily concerned with what is being tested and how those features will be tested. The review process should discover any omissions or potential errors with the systems testing procedures.

The staff attending the review for a client/server application may include more end-users than a mainframe-based system. The end-users have more responsibilities in a client/server environment and therefore need to review more procedures during the development of that system. The network administrator is also a key person in all client/server environments and should participate in the review.

PURPOSE

The review ensures the Systems Test Specifications test the system adequately. The reviewers check for omissions, inconsistencies, and inaccuracies.

WHEN SHOULD IT OCCUR?

The review occurs after the design phase of systems testing is completed and the Systems Test Specifications are delivered. Schedule it sufficiently before the systems test execution begins to allow corrections of any issues uncovered in the review.

WHO REQUESTS THE REVIEW?

The test team requests the review. They prepared the Systems Test Specifications and are responsible for the systems test execution.

WHO SHOULD ATTEND?

The entire test team attends. A representative from the following areas should attend:

- Software development
- End-users
- System test review team

The following people may attend:

- The project leader of the application
- The network administrator

- The database administrator
- The auditor
- The security administrator
- Any technical specialists who would add value

SITE

The review should be conducted in a conference area. This area should be removed from the normal work environment so the review will not be interrupted by the normal business activities.

PREPARATION

Distribute the Systems Test Plan and the Systems Test Specifications to the reviewers before the review. These are the only documents the reviewers need to look over before the review. The System Requirements document and any security and auditing policy statements should be available for reference during the review. Appoint a facilitator to conduct the review and a recorder to record any issues uncovered during the review.

Prepare a checklist of questions and issues to address during the review. This ensures a complete and structured coverage of the Systems Test Specifications. The checklist is used by the facilitator to guide the review. It can be saved with the project documentation so it can be used again. Whenever there is a major enhancement to the system, the system must be tested again. The Systems Test Specifications are updated to reflect the enhancements and a new review should be conducted before the systems test is executed.

FORMAT OF THE REVIEW

The review is conducted as a structured walk-through. Present a brief description of the system to provide context for the review. The description should state the following:

- The purpose of the system
- The business area it serves
- The development methodology
- The development tools

- The installation sites and the implementation timetable for each site.

Describe the strategy for systems testing by stating the following:

- The objectives and scope
- The approach
- The testing tools used
- How the test data was created
- The verification procedures

The facilitator reads each question on the checklist in the sequence presented. If any clarification is required, the test team explains the issue. The recorder marks any questions that require clarification. These questions need to be restated for subsequent reviews.

The reviewers listen to the test team present their testing approach for each item. They exchange any ideas they have on the subject and discuss any concerns they have with these issues. Any new or changed requirements should be noted. The reviewers should verify the answers to all questions posed on the checklist. The recorder records any problems revealed by a question. Do not attempt to find solutions. The review is a discovery session, not a design session.

OUTCOME OF THE REVIEW

The test team uses the notes from the review to correct the Systems Test Specifications and prepare the systems test for execution.

THE REVIEW CHECKLIST

The checklist is organized into sections. There is one section for each major objective of the systems test.

QUALITY/STANDARDS COMPLIANCE

This section contains questions and concerns about the systems testing and verifies that the software complies with the quality and standards criteria of the organization. The following issues should be considered in this section:

- Have the key Information Systems standards been identified?
  —Are any standards missing?
  —Are any standards obsolete?
  —Are any standards not applicable to this software?
- What are the risks to not adhering to a standard?
- Have the key quality issues been identified?
  —Are any quality issues missing?
  —Are any quality issues not applicable to this software?
- What are the risks of not identifying poor quality software?
- Have the documentation requirements been identified?
  —Are any documentation requirements missing?
  —Are any documentation requirements no longer required?
  —Are any documentation requirements not applicable to this system?
- Does the compliance testing of documentation verify the security and privacy of the contents?
  —Are the testing procedures adequate?
  —Are the restrictions on the contents (for security and privacy) complete?
  —Are any restrictions on the contents missing?
  —Are any restrictions on the contents no longer required?
- Does the compliance testing of documentation verify the security of the source files?
  —Are the testing procedures adequate?
  —Are the specified security levels accurate?
  —Are any specified security levels missing?
  —Are any specified security levels no longer required?
- Are the procedures to test for security and authorization logic adequate?
  —Are the testing procedures well defined?
  —Are the testing procedures efficient in preparation time?
  —Are the testing procedures efficient in verification time?
  —Are the testing tools used in this procedure adequate?
- Have all the test conditions been identified?
  —Are there any additional quality/standard compliance test conditions that should be included?

—Are any test conditions redundant?
- Are the test procedures to execute the conditions adequate?
  —Are the test procedures well defined?
  —Are the test procedures efficient in preparation time?
  —Are the test procedures efficient in verification time?
  —Are the testing tools used in the test procedures adequate?

TEST CYCLES

This section contains questions on the test cycles and the test procedures to execute them.

- Do the test cycles correspond to the business flow?
  —Is the sequence of execution correct?
  —Are all test cycle dependencies identified?
  —Is the simulation of periodic cycles effective?
- Are the test procedures to execute the test cycles adequate?
  —Are they well defined?
  —Are they efficient in preparation time?
  —Are they efficient in machine-executable time?
  —Are they efficient in verification time?
  —Can the test procedures be restarted?
- Are all manual procedures identified?
  —Are any manual procedures missing?
  —Are any manual procedures no longer required?
  —Are any manual procedures redundant?
- Are the verification procedures adequate?
  —Are the verification procedures well defined?
  —Are the verification procedures efficient?
- Are the systems-expected results defined for each test cycle?
  —Are the systems-expected results accurate?
  —Are the systems-expected results complete?

BUSINESS REQUIREMENTS

This section contains questions on the systems testing that verifies the business requirements. The following issues should be considered in this section.

- Have all the business requirements been identified?
  —Are any business requirements missing?
  —Are any business requirements no longer required?
  —Are any business requirements deferred to the next release?
  —Are any business requirements redundant?

For each business requirement:

- Have all the test conditions been identified?
  —Are any test conditions missing?
  —Are any test conditions no longer required?
  —Are any test conditions redundant?
  —Can any test conditions be combined?
- Are the test cases listed for these conditions adequate?
  —Are any test cases overly complicated?
  —Are any test cases overly simplified?
  —Do the test cases test extremes (maximum commission rate, minimum contract period)?
  —Do the test cases test all the business rules (purchase orders not accepted when credit line exceeded, promotions not allowed until employed three months)?
- Is the security/authorization testing adequate?
  —Is each level of security/authority identified?
  —Are any levels missing?
  —Are there any levels no longer required?
- Is the test data adequate?
  —Is the test data realistic?
  —Is the volume sufficient to test the conditions stated?
- Is the method for generating test data acceptable?
  —Is it efficient in preparation time?
  —Is it efficient in machine-executable time?
  —Does it generate realistic test data?
- Are the test procedures to execute the test cases adequate?
  —Are they well defined?
  —Are they efficient in preparation time?
  —Are they efficient in machine-executable time?
  —Can the test procedures be restarted?
- Are the verification procedures adequate?
  —Are they well defined?
  —Are they efficient?

- Are the expected results defined for each test case?
  —Are they accurate?
  —Are they complete?

PERFORMANCE CAPABILITIES

This section contains questions on the systems tests to verify the performance capabilities of the system. The following issues should be considered in this section:

- Are the performance requirements for the system accurate?
  —Have the requirements changed?
  —Are the requirements complete?
- Are the requirements for system availability accurate?
  —Have the requirements changed?
  —Are the requirements complete?
- If there is batch processing in the system, are the batch window requirements accurate?
  —Have the requirements changed?
  —Are the requirements complete?
  —Are the backups included in this batch window?
  —Do the timings for the backups reflect fully loaded data files?
  —Are database reorganization procedures included in this batch window?
  —Do the timings for the reorganizations reflect fully loaded files?
- Are the estimated transaction volumes accurate?
  —Have they changed?
  —Is there a variation in the workload during the day, week, month, or year?
  —Is the transaction arrival rate accurate?
- Are the response time requirements accurate?
  —Are the requirements complete?
  —Have they changed?
- Have all the test conditions been identified?
  —Are the test conditions accurate?
  —Are any test conditions missing?
  —Are any test conditions redundant?

- Are the test procedures to execute the conditions adequate?
  —Are they well defined?
  —Are they accurate?
  —Are they efficient in preparation time?
  —Are they efficient in verification time?
  —Are the testing tools used in this procedure adequate?
- Are the procedures to execute volume testing adequate?
  —Are the preparation instructions for volume testing adequate?
  —Are all the organizational areas required to perform the volume testing identified?
  —Are all the organizational areas affected by the volume testing identified?
  —Are any areas missing?
  —Are any areas no longer required?
  —Does the execution require special permission or special arrangements?
- Is the volume of data sufficient?
  —Are the procedures to generate volume data acceptable?
  —Are the procedures to extract test data from live files acceptable?
- Do the procedures to extract test data from live files comply with security and privacy policy?
  —Is the security or privacy of the live files compromised by the procedure?
  —Is the security on the extracted data file adequate?
  —Is the security on the documentation that references the live files adequate?
  —Is the security on the actual results from the tests adequate?
- Are the procedures to submit transactions for online volume testing adequate?
  —Are transactions submitted from multiple workstations?
  —Are the transactions simulated from a batch file?

OPERATIONAL CAPABILITIES

This section contains questions on the systems tests to verify the operational capabilities of the system. The following issues should be considered in this section:

- Have all the test conditions been identified?
  —Are any test conditions missing?
  —Are any test conditions redundant?
- Are the test procedures to execute the conditions adequate?
  —Are the test procedures well defined?
  —Are the test procedures accurate?
  —Are the test procedures efficient in preparation time?
  —Are the test procedures efficient in verification time?
  —Are the testing tools used in this procedure adequate?
- Are the procedures to test network security adequate?
- Are the procedures to test data recovery adequate?
  —Are the procedures well defined?
  —Does the execution require special permission or special arrangements?
- Are the procedures to test emergency maintenance adequate?
  —Are all the organizational areas required to perform the testing identified?
  —Are all the organizational areas affected by the testing identified?
  —Are any areas missing?
  —Are any areas no longer required?
  —Does the execution require special permission or special arrangements?
- Are the procedures to test the distribution of the software adequate?
  —Are all the organizational areas required to perform the testing identified?
  —Are all the organizational areas affected by the testing identified?
  —Are any areas missing?
  —Are any areas no longer required?
  —Does the execution require special permission or special arrangements?
- Are the procedures to test physical site security adequate?
  —Are the procedures complete?
- Are the procedures to test the Help Desk adequate?
  —Have requirements been specified for Help Desk availability?
  —Have response turnaround times been defined for resolving questions and issues?

—Have standards been established for logging Help Desk activity?
- Are the procedures to test virus prevention adequate?
  —Have requirements been specified for virus prevention?
  —Are the procedures well defined?
  —Does the execution of these procedures require special permission or special arrangements?
  —Are all the organizational areas affected by the testing identified?
  —Are any areas missing?
  —Are any areas no longer required?
- Are the procedures to test virus recovery adequate?
  —Are the procedures well defined?
  —Have standards been established for logging a virus infection?
  —Does the execution require special permission or special arrangements?
  —Are all the organizational areas affected by the testing identified?
  —Are any areas missing?
  —Are any areas no longer required?

SUMMARY

The Systems Test Specifications should be reviewed to ensure it tests the systems adequately. The review is conducted as a structured walk-through. It verifies the testing procedures for each major objective of the systems test:

- Quality/standards compliance
- Business requirements
- Performance capabilities
- Operational capabilities

6

The Execution Phase

The *execution phase* of systems testing occurs after the review of the Systems Test Specifications. It begins when the software is submitted for systems testing. The purpose of this phase is to do the following:

- Prepare the environment
- Execute the testing
- Record the testing activities
- Verify the results
- Document any inconsistencies
- Summarize testing results to management

The deliverables from this phase include the following:

- Systems-tested software
- Actual results
- Systems Test Activity Log
- Incident Reports generated during the execution
- Incident Log
- Systems Test Summary Report

PREPARATION

The first task is to prepare the environment for the execution of the systems tests. The test team must prepare both the physical and logical environment. The preparation includes the following:

- Obtaining access to the execution environment
- Obtaining the physical resources specified in the Systems Test Plan
- Obtaining disk space for databases and input data files
- Loading the databases with baseline data
- Loading the security and code tables with test data
- Initializing the data files with any control information required
- Creating datasets to simulate input for a test cycle
- Modifying command language files for the execution environment
- Preparing the testing tools for the execution environment
- Migrating the application software and preparing it for execution

Obtaining access to the execution environment

The execution environment was identified in the planning phase. Access to that environment must now be established. When the client/server application is designed for distribution on heterogeneous platforms, systems testing must be conducted on each platform. This can be accomplished by simulating each platform in one environment or executing the tests on each platform. If the latter method is chosen, obtain access to each platform on which the systems testing will execute. For each execution environment perform the following tasks:

- Identify the required network sign-on profiles.
- Submit the forms to have them generated.
- Test each sign-on after it is generated.

Don't wait until the day systems testing execution begins to find out the users do not have authority to access the systems test environment. The users have their normal work to perform. They may want the features of the new system and will participate in its testing. However, it is not their responsibility to verify the systems testing log-ons.

Obtaining the physical resources

The physical resources required for systems testing were identified in the planning phase. Arrangements should have been made to obtain them. Verify that the physical resources are available.

- **Ensure that the workstations are available and ready for use.**
  If the test team is "borrowing" workstations for use in the systems testing execution, verify these workstation are available. If the systems testing will take place during off-hours, make sure the "owner" of the workstation is aware of your schedule.
  On one project we scheduled a systems test for a weekend. We arranged to use the PCs in the Billing Department. Two billing clerks in that department locked their machines each evening. This is an excellent security practice in an open area. However, we were not aware of this practice. We didn't call to remind them to leave the machines unlocked or give us the keys. We had to test with two less machines.
- **If hardcopy output is required, ensure the local printer is available and stocked with sufficient paper.**
  It is important to specifically ask the staff in the testing area if anyone will be using the printers during the systems test execution. There may be sufficient paper for your requirements, but if another group shares that printer and they are producing volumes of reports, there might not be enough to go around.
- **If a remote printer will be used, the output must either be delivered or picked up.**
  Check the delivery schedule to see if it is adequate. If the schedule is inadequate, make special arrangements to pick it up yourself or have another delivery scheduled.

Obtaining disk space

Determine the disk space required for all permanent files. Submit the forms or procedures to allocate this disk space.

Loading the databases

Special programs or utilities may be required to populate the databases with the required test data.

- Execute the jobs to load the databases.
- Verify the results.
- Create a backup of the loaded databases.

Loading the Security and Code tables

The security and code tables used by the application must be initialized with the test data. The Test Specifications indicate the data required for the test cases.

The security table must contain the number and types of profile records to support the testing, for example:

- A supervisor profile is required to access certain features.
- A nonsupervisor profile is required to verify that security prohibits access to supervisor-only features.
- Several profiles are required to verify customized security features where one user cannot update another's data.

The code tables are used to encode/decode data. The tables must contain the records required to support testing. In the client/server environment code tables require special attention. The decoded values must be the same for each site. The records stored at each site may be different. However, they must be a subset of the full set of codes. For example, in the Legal Billing System, the Boston office does not handle environmental matters and therefore does not require the service and disbursements codes associated with environmental matters. Those codes are not loaded in their tables. However, they cannot be used to encode another value. The Systems Test Specifications specify which codes are loaded in each site. If the design allows all codes at each site, the full set of codes should be loaded to the systems test environment. This method would permit the same load procedures to be used in testing each site.

Special programs or utilities may be required to populate the tables with the required test data.

- Create or extract the data required to populate the security and code tables.
- Execute the command language files to populate the tables.
- Verify the results.
- Create a backup of the populated tables.

Initializing data files

All memory files and control tables used by the application must be initialized with the test data. The Test Specifications indicate the initial values required for testing. This may be the initial number used for assigning invoice numbers, accounting periods, or opening balances.

Special programs or utilities must be run to initialize the files with the required test values.

- Execute the command language files to initialize the files.
- Verify the results.
- Create a backup of the files.

Creating datasets to simulate input

The test cycle dependencies and contingencies were identified in the planning phase. Special programs and utilities may be required to simulate input for a test cycle. When input to one test cycle is normally created by a prior test cycle that is not available, the input can be simulated. It must be created before execution begins.

- Execute the command language files that create the input data and verify the results.
- Create a backup of the input data.

Modifying Command Language Files

The systems test environment may not be able to use the exact commands as the production environment. File names, directory names, and disk drive designations may be different. This will require modifications to the command language files.

- Modify the command language files as required, and verify the changes.

Preparing the Testing Tools

The testing tools must be installed or made available to the execution environment. The procedures to execute them must be modified for the execution environment. Any testing tool that extracts or displays data must be tested after the test data is created and before the systems tests are conducted.

- Modify the procedures that execute the testing tools as required.
- Verify the changes.
- Test the procedures. All testing tool procedures must be fully tested before systems test execution begins.

Migrating the application software

The software written for this application and any reusable code it uses must be available to the systems test environment, including the following:

- Application source code
- Screen forms
- Report forms
- Standard queries
- Stored procedures

Always migrate source code into the systems test environment and create executable code. Never move the executable code.

The software developers should turn over their software to the test team when it is ready for systems testing. The turnover procedures should be determined during the planning phase. Management should notify the software developers of these procedures. Any scheduling requirements that must be followed should be published. The following is an example of turnover procedures:

1. Before any software will be accepted for systems testing a Turnover Request form must be submitted to the test team. All software should be unit tested prior to its submission for systems testing. This form can either be delivered in paper format (hand delivered, interoffice mail, or faxed) or submitted to the test team's e-mail box.
2. The test team will log the Turnover Request and review its contents. The date and time of the request are logged so that management can track the software. They can request turnover status reports that list what has been submitted, when the items were submitted, and who submitted items.
3. The test team will move items into the systems test environment twice a day, at 10 A.M. and 3 P.M. Any exceptions to this rule must be approved by a project leader.

Figure 6.1 is a sample Turnover Request form. The Turnover Request lists the name and location of the software to be migrated to the central repository. Each item on that form is described below.

Date
This item is the date the form was prepared by the submitter.

Submitter
This item is the name of the person submitting the test items.

System
This item is the name of the system for which the test items are submitted.

```
FORM TSS01
                    SYSTEMS TEST TURNOVER

Date: 10/30/92
Submitter: Mary Roberts
System: Inventory Control System
```

Test Item	Type	Location	Status
INV002	Code	S:\INV\SRC	Original
INV002.WRD	Specs	S:\INV\DOC	Original
INV002.WRD	Unit Test	S:\INV\UTEST	

Figure 6.1.   Systems Test Turnover Form.

For each item submitted the following must be entered:

Test item

This item identifies the test item submitted. It is the file name or the external title of an item.

Type

This item identifies the type of test item. It can be an object, source code, a memory file, a command language file, a document, a data file, or a backup tape.

Location

This item is the location of the test item. For computer-stored test items specify the fully qualified file name of the item. For other media specify the location and external name of the test item.

Status

This item is the status of the test items. It can be the original test or a subsequent test. For a subsequent test, the Incident Report number should also be listed.

In this example Mary Roberts has submitted three items from the Inventory Control System to be systems tested. These items are source code, program specifications, and an executed unit test plan.

After the test team logs the requests, they verify the contents of the form. All items must be located in the library or site specified. The test team moves source code into the systems test central repository. They use the software inventory list in the systems development documentation to verify that all software has been received. The software inventory list is a list of all software components of the system. This list is maintained by the software developers. All programs, reusable objects, and procedures for the system are listed here. This list should be used as a checklist of the software required to implement the system. It should be an all-inclusive list. If the system is a client/server application that uploads data to the mainframe on a periodic basis, the mainframe interface modules must be included in this list. The test team uses this list to verify all components have been turned over.

The software inventory list can also be used to specify the procedures to generate executable code from the source code. The test team uses these instructions in preparing the systems test version of the application.

Quality/standards compliance testing is the first level of testing that is performed on the software. In the planning phase of systems testing the testing policy was established. The acceptance/rejection criteria was determined. If that policy states that all software must comply with standards before any further systems testing is conducted, then any item that fails is returned at this point. If the code itself does not comply with standards, testing should not continue until the code is modified or management approves the nonstandard code. If documentation is missing or incomplete, the testing of the code could continue. The testing policy should state the actions to be taken. The test team should not have to make these decisions during the execution phase. The following is an example of the testing policy for quality/standard compliance:

- Any development software with missing or incomplete documentation is rejected.

- Any code that fails the quality/standards compliance testing is rejected.
- The software is returned to the software developers for changes. It must be submitted again using the Turnover Request.

ANNOUNCEMENT

There should be a special meeting held to announce the start of systems testing execution.

The project leader schedules this meeting. The entire project team and the systems test reviewers attend. The purpose of this meeting is to accomplish the following:

- Announce systems testing execution will begin soon
- Restate the strategy recorded in the Systems Test Plan
- Reaffirm management's support to systems testing
- Clarify any questions on the systems testing procedures
- Ensure everyone's support

This is the last formal meeting before systems test execution begins. It should be used to communicate. Ask the following questions:

- Is everyone ready?
- Is all the software ready?
- Is the execution environment ready?
- Is the support staff available during this time?
- Are there substitutes for the people who are unavailable?
- Will the test team or supporting staff need access to the premises in off-hours?
- Will they need special arrangements for access? Badges, keys, or security escorts?
- Will the test team or the supporting staff need beepers?
- Will the test team or supporting staff need to borrow laptop or notebook computers to use from home for dial-in support?

CONDUCT SYSTEMS TESTS

The test cycles are executed according the test procedures in the Systems Test Specifications. Each test is logged in the Activity Log. The actual results are reconciled with the expected results.

Any errors are documented. Any items that cause the systems testing to be suspended should be brought to the attention of the project leader immediately.

The test team should hold a status meeting daily during the systems testing execution. This meeting should not last very long. It should be used to inform all test team members of the current status of the testing. The test coordinators for the previous day's testing should give the team a brief overview of what occurred.

THE ACTIVITY LOG

The Activity Log is used to record the systems test execution activity. It provides a chronological record of the details of the testing. It should be saved with the project documentation. The Activity Log can be kept manually or recorded in the computer. The computer document has the following advantages:

- It is legible.
- It can be scanned for key words.
- It can be sorted into any sequence required.
- It can be dynamically expanded by adding entries under the appropriate test cycle at a later date.
- It is accessible.
- It is backed up.
- It is stored in a central location.

A sample Activity Log is shown in Figure 6.2. Each item on that form is described below.

Title

This item contains the title of the document. The title contains the words "Systems Test Activity Log for" followed by the name of the application.

Document locator

This item identifies the location of this document and the procedures to update and print it. It states the LAN or mainframe on which the document is stored and its fully qualified dataset name. It names the software product used to create the document.

ACTIVITY LOG

Systems Test Activity Log for: Executive Information System (EIS)

Document Locator:

This document is stored on the LAN in the Information Services Dept.—Software Development group. It is on the disk pack assigned to the Executive Information System project. The file name is EISAL01.WRP.

Environment:

This systems testing was performed on the LAN in the IS Department—Corporate Division.

Date	Time	Test Cycle	Test Case	Recd By	Description	Outcome
01/12/92	9:30a	2	2-105	CB	Security database does not contain SYSADM ID. John Morris could not log on as Administrator. System didn't recognize SYSADM ID. Must initialize Personnel database with SYSADM entry.	Rejected IR filed Suspended systems testing until the database reloaded
01/12/92	9:50a	2	2-105	CB	Ran OK	P. Mason approved results.

Figure 6.2. Systems Test Activity Log.

Execution environment

This item identifies the platform on which the execution was performed. In the client/server environment the application may be distributed on heterogeneous platforms. The application must be tested on each platform. The Activity Log can be either organized by platform, or a separate log can be maintained for each platform.

Activities

An entry should be recorded in the Activity Log for each execution of a test. It should contain the following details:

Date and time

This item is the date and time the testing occurred. The same test may be attempted several times before it is executed to completion. The time of day is recorded to distinguish test cases that were executed several times in one day. Time is optional and can be omitted when not required for differentiation.

Test cycle number

This item is the test cycle number as specified in the Systems Test Specifications.

Test case number

This item is the test case number as specified in the Systems Test Specifications.

Recorded by

This item is the name of the person who coordinated the test and recorded this entry. When many people are entering data and conducting individual test cases, one person should be responsible for recording the information in the Activity Log. When the Activity Log is maintained as a word processing document, it is easier for one person to access the Activity Log document file. There is more control over the testing activity when the recording is centralized with one person. The test coordinator should not conduct any testing but concentrate on recording information and ensuring all test cases are executed and verified. In the example shown in Figure 6.2, CB are the initials of the person coordinating the testing. John Morris and P. Mason are the persons conducting the tests. The test coordinator entered initials in the column. This person is a member of the Information Systems department and presumably known to the other project members. The test coordinator can be identified by initials, but the test reviewers should be identified by their full names. They are not part of the Informations Systems department and may not be well known by the project members. For large projects or those using outside consultants, a legend could be appended to the document to cross-reference the initials and full names.

Description

This item describes what happened during the execution of the tests. It identifies all personnel involved in this test. It lists the persons who entered the data and the persons who reviewed the results. For abnormal executions, it states what occurred before and after the abnormal event.

In the example, the first test case could not be executed and systems testing was suspended. The Outcome column lists the reason for the suspension, "the Personnel database was missing the SYSADM ID."

In the second entry, the test case executed correctly. No further comments are needed. Do not write extraneous information. The Activity Log is a reference document that must be scanned to find important references. Don't fill it with unnecessary information. If the test executed as expected, the Systems Test Specifications are the source document for the procedures and expected results.

Outcome

This item indicates the user-viewed (observable) results of the test. It states the success or failure of the execution. It answers the following information:

- Did the test run to completion?
- Did the test abort?
- Were error messages generated?
- Did security violations occur?
- Were any inconsistencies noted?
- What action was taken?
- Was an Incident Report filed?
- Was testing suspended?
- Was a test case bypassed?
- Was the test completed successfully?

VERIFY RESULTS

The expected results of each test cycle are described in the Systems Test Specifications. The systems test reviewers compare the actual results with the expected results. Any discrepancies between the two should be documented in an Incident Report. The test team is notified when a discrepancy occurs. They decide whether to suspend or continue testing.

- An error that affects all subsequent testing and renders their results meaningless suspends testing. It must be corrected before testing can resume.
- An error that is isolated to one test case does not suspend testing. The error is recorded and the test case is marked for retesting later.
- An error that affects a path of test cases should not suspend testing. The test cases affected can be bypassed and marked for retesting later.

THE INCIDENT REPORT

Incident Reports are used to notify management of any aspects of the system that require investigation. This can be the system requirements, the design, the code, or the implementation procedures. Any person involved in the system can complete an Incident Report. The team test, test reviewers, users, and operational staff can file Incident Reports.

Incident Reports are used during the execution phase of systems testing to record a problem that occurred while conducting a test case. Whenever an Incident Report is prepared as a result of the testing, the test coordinator should be notified. The Activity Log entry for that test case should indicate an Incident Report was filed. All members of the test team should then be notified of the Incident Report. The software may need to be retested as a result of changes required to resolve the Incident Report. The test team will need to know this to make any adjustments in the systems testing schedule.

All Incident Reports are given to the Incident Report Coordinator, who logs them in the Incident Log. The software developers analyze each Incident Report to determine the cause of the problem and the software changes required to resolve the problem. The project leader assigns a priority to each Incident Report.

The Incident Report should be a form that can be easily filled out and reviewed. The form should be self-documenting. It should ask for the pertinent information and supply choices when appropriate.

A sample Incident Report is shown in Figure 6.3. The form is divided into four sections. Each section is described below. The first section of the form is filled out by the person who reports the incident.

System

This item is the name of the system for which the incident is being reported.

Originator

This item is the name of the person reporting the incident.

Date

This item is the date the person prepared the Incident Report.

Type

This item is the type of incident. The form lists four choices.

- Error—a discrepancy between an actual result and an expected result.
- ABEND—an abnormal termination of a program.
- Enhancement—an addition to the functionality described in the System Requirements document.
- OTHER—indicates the originator has provided a description of type.

The originator checks the appropriate box.

Incident description

This item is a brief description of the incident. It should reference the Activity Log entry of the systems test in which this incident occurred. It describes the impact of this incident on the systems testing and the implementation of the system.

```
FORM SYSD05

                    SYSTEMS INCIDENT REPORT

SYSTEM:

ORIGINATOR:                     DATE:

TYPE: Error _  ABEND _  Enhancement _  Other _

INCIDENT DESCRIPTION:


INCIDENT DETAILS:
```

```
INCIDENT REPORT NUMBER:
STATUS: Logged _ Analyzed _ Assigned _
        Resubmitted _ Closed _ Cancelled _
```

```
ANALYZED BY:                    DATE:
SOFTWARE INVOLVED:


ESTIMATED TIME TO RESOLVE INCIDENT:
```

```
PRIORITY:  A _  B _  C _        ASSIGNED TO:
                                DATE ASSIGNED:
```

Figure 6.3.   Incident Report.

Incident details

This item describes the incident. It includes the following:

- The information that was entered
- The step in the test procedure that was executed
- The screen on which the incident occurred
- The sequence of keystrokes entered

- The error message or condition that occurred
- Any attempts to repeat the incident
- The actual results and the expected results. The actual results should be attached or referenced.

The second section is filled out by the Incident Report coordinator:

Incident Report number

This item is the number assigned to this Incident Report. Numbers are assigned sequentially as the reports are logged.

Status

This item is the status of the Incident Report. The form lists six choices.

- Logged—indicates the Incident Report was logged and assigned a number. It is an open report.
- Analyzed—indicates the Incident Report was analyzed by a software developer. It is an open report.
- Assigned—indicates the Incident Report was assigned to a software developer to resolve. It is an open report.
- Resubmitted for testing—indicates the software involved in the incident was changed and resubmitted for testing. It is an open report.
- Closed—indicates the application was tested again and the incident was resolved. It is a closed report.
- Cancelled—indicates the software developers and the originator have agreed that the incident is no longer an issue. It is a closed report.

The Incident Report coordinator checks the appropriate box. The status changes as the Incident Report is processed. The Incident Report Coordinator tracks the status and updates it accordingly.

The third section is filled out by the software developer who analyzes the Incident Report:

Analyzed by

This item is the name of the software developer who analyzed the Incident Report.

Date
This item is the date the analysis was completed.

Software involved
This item identifies the software that requires changes in order to resolve the incident.

Estimated time to resolve incident
This item is the estimated time required to resolve the incident.

The fourth section is filled out by the project leader:

Priority
This item is the priority of the Incident Report. The form lists three choices.

- Priority A—indicates the resolution of the incident is critical. Systems testing is suspended. The function is an operational necessity.
- Priority B—indicates the resolution of the incident is necessary. Systems testing bypasses all tests that depend on the results.
- Priority C—indicates that the resolution is not an operational necessity. This is an enhancement. Systems testing continues. The system's functionality can be implemented "as is."

The project leader checks the appropriate box. The priority determines the order in which Incident Reports are assigned to software developers for implementing the resolution.

Assigned to
This item is the name of the person assigned to resolving the incident.

Date assigned
This item is the date the person was assigned to the task.

Figure 6.4 is an Incident Report prepared by a test reviewer to report a problem that occurred during the execution of a test case. The actual and expected results were not the same.

This Incident Report was prepared by the test reviewer when the actual results of the Jewelry Pricing System did not match the expected results. It was logged by the Incident Report Coordinator and assigned Incident Report number 027. The Incident Report coordinator assigns the Incident Report numbers sequentially for the project. One of the software developers, A. Edwards, analyzed the report and determined module GEM003 must be changed and the work would require approximately two days to complete. The business requirements were incorrectly implemented. The formula to price the high end of the product line—items costing over $1000—was not specified correctly. This is a basic requirement of the system and therefore must be given immediate attention. The project leader gave this Incident Re-

---

```
FORM SYSD05

                    SYSTEMS INCIDENT REPORT

SYSTEM:  GEM - Jewelry Pricing System

ORIGINATOR: E. Kaplan               DATE: 2/10/93

TYPE: Error X ABEND _ Enhancement _ Other _

INCIDENT DESCRIPTION: All items priced over $1000 are priced
incorrectly.

INCIDENT DETAILS: Item G1004 s/b $2500 was priced at $1495,
Item H506 s/b 1500 was $1125
```

```
INCIDENT REPORT NUMBER: 027
STATUS: Logged X  Analyzed X  Assigned X
        Resubmitted _ Closed _ Cancelled _
```

```
ANALYZED BY: A. Edwards        DATE: 2/10/93
SOFTWARE INVOLVED: GEM005 Mark-Up Module incorrect formula

ESTIMATED TIME TO RESOLVE INCIDENT: 2 days
```

```
PRIORITY:  A X  B _  C _        ASSIGNED TO: J. Gold
                                DATE ASSIGNED: 2/10/93
```

Figure 6.4.   Incident Report—Software Error.

port a high priority, Priority A. It was assigned immediately to J. Gold, one of the programmers. The systems testing can continue, but all test cases for this condition must be retested.

Figure 6.5 is an Incident Report prepared by a user to specify an enhancement to the system. The Incident Report was logged by the Incident Report Coordinator and assigned Incident Report number 032. One of the software developers analyzed the report and determined the software involved was module GEMPRT. This requirement was not specified in the System Requirements

---

```
FORM SYSD05

                 SYSTEMS INCIDENT REPORT

SYSTEM:  GEM - Jewelry Pricing System

ORIGINATOR: I. Chalsom          DATE: 02/11/93

TYPE: Error _ ABEND _ Enhancement X Other _

INCIDENT DESCRIPTION: What-if analysis should be added to
the system. A complete pricing book should be generated and
labelled What-if the cost of X changed. We need to run book
for: Labor changes prior to contract negotiations, Metal
Cost fluctuations, and Stone Cost fluctuations.

INCIDENT DETAILS:
```

```
INCIDENT REPORT NUMBER: 032
STATUS: Logged X Analyzed X Assigned X
        Resubmitted _ Closed _ Cancelled _
```

```
ANALYZED BY: A. Emmet           DATE: 02/12/93
SOFTWARE INVOLVED: GEMPRT modules

ESTIMATED TIME TO RESOLVE INCIDENT: 5 days
```

```
PRIORITY:  A X  B _  C X       ASSIGNED TO: J. Gold
                               DATE ASSIGNED: 2/10/93
```

Figure 6.5.   Incident Report—Enhancement.

document. It is a new requirement that the user would like added to the system. It is not an operational necessity. The system can be implemented without this feature. It can be included in a subsequent release of the system. It was given a low priority, Priority C, and not assigned to a programmer. During the systems testing execution, the software developers must be available to fix errors in the system. Any enhancement work should be deferred until the systems testing is completed.

Figure 6.6 is an Incident Report prepared by the operations support supervisor. The supervisor wrote this Incident Report after reading the operational procedures for backing up the production system.

This Incident Report is categorized as Other. It was logged by the Incident Report Coordinator and assigned Incident Report number 034. A. Edwards analyzed the report and concurred the backup schedule should be changed. He estimated the work would take one day to complete. This task is independent of the others. The change must be made prior to the production implementation but can be deferred, so it was given Priority C. Incident Reports can be used to report changes to operational procedures and performance capabilities. This operations supervisor has been with this company for a number of years and is aware of the cyclical nature of the information processing. The operational support group should be consulted in preparing the operating procedures and backup schedules. The operations staff should attend some of the requirements and design review sessions that discuss this aspect of the system.

INCIDENT LOG

The Incident Log is a summary journal of the Incident Reports. It can be maintained by a spreadsheet or a project management software package. The *Incident Report Coordinator* (IRC) maintains this log. It is used to generate reports that management uses for project control and reporting.

The IRC is the first person to review the Incident Report. The IRC checks the form for completeness and enters key information from the report into the Incident Log. Each Incident Report is assigned the next sequential number from the log. The IRC is responsible for tracking the status of all Incident Reports in the

FORM SYSD05

SYSTEMS INCIDENT REPORT

SYSTEM: GEM - Jewelry Pricing System

ORIGINATOR: L. Martin   DATE: 2/10/93

TYPE: Error _ ABEND _ Enhancement _ Other X

INCIDENT DESCRIPTION: The operational procedures for the
databases backup states the backups will occur each night at
3 A.M. The annual schedule shows heavy volume during June
and July.

INCIDENT DETAILS: The backup schedule is inadequate for the
database changes. Add another backup at noon for June and
July.

INCIDENT REPORT NUMBER: 034
STATUS: Logged X Analyzed X Assigned _
        Resubmitted _ Closed _ Cancelled _

ANALYZED BY: A. Edwards   DATE: 2/12/93
SOFTWARE INVOLVED: Backup schedule and corresponding
procedures

ESTIMATED TIME TO RESOLVE INCIDENT: 1 day

PRIORITY: A _ B _ C X   ASSIGNED TO:
                             DATE ASSIGNED:

Figure 6.6.   Incident Report—Other.

log. The IRC must periodically contact the project members to find out the current status of the reports.

The IRC must be notified when an Incident Report is closed or cancelled so its status can be updated. The Incident Report should no longer be included in management reports listing work-in-progress. A closed Incident Report is one that was analyzed and resolved. If the incident involved software changes, those changes were implemented, retested, and accepted. A cancelled Incident Report is a report that the preparer, the analyst, the IRC, or management decided to cancel. The following conditions would cause an Incident Report to be cancelled:

- **The incident already exists in the log.**
  The IRC cancels any report when the incident described already exists in the log and is an open report. The IRC can scan the log for key words to determine whether the incident was previously submitted. If the incident is logged and currently open, the new report would be cancelled. If the incident is logged but closed (it was supposedly corrected), the incident may be reoccurring. The Incident Report is therefore considered a new incident and would be entered in the log.
- **The incident reported is not an error.**
  The preparer or analyst can cancel a report if they discover the incident is not an error.
- **The proposed enhancement actually is available within the system.**
- **The enhancement is not within the scope of the project.**
- **The enhancement conflicts with the interest of another project.**
- **The solution for the incident is not economically feasible.**
  Management can cancel an Incident Report if the incident is not within the scope of the project, not economically feasible, or conflicts with another project.

Figure 6.7 is an example of an Incident Log. The log contains key information from the Incident Report.

IR#

This is the Incident Report number. The next sequential number in the log is assigned to each Incident Report. The Incident

IR#	DT-PREPD	STATUS	DT-CL/CN	PRTY	DESCRIPTION
			INCIDENT LOG		
005	02/01/93	Closed	02/05/93	A	Round costs. Don't truncate
006	02/02/93	Closed	02/07/93	A	Rounding rule for low-end changed
007	02/02/93	Anlyzd		C	Create labels for samples
008	02/05/93	Anlyzd		B	New report for labor hrs
009	02/02/93	Closed	02/05/93	A	Set costs s/b rounded to whole dollars
010	02/02/93	Cancel	02/05/93	A	Same as IR 005
011	02/04/93	Assgn		B	GemStone table report change

Figure 6.7.   Incident Log.

Reports are assigned numbers in the order in which they are logged, not by the date they were prepared. In Figure 6.7, IR# 011 was prepared on February 4, 1993. It was entered into the log after IR# 008, which was prepared on February 5, 1993. The position of an entry in the log does not determine its position in the work queue. The priority assigned to an Incident Report is the determining factor.

Date prepared

This field is copied from the Incident Report. It is the date the person who prepared the report entered on the form.

Status

This is the current status of the Incident Report. The IRC copies this information from the Incident Report when the report is initially logged. The item is updated when the IRC receives notification of a change in status.

Date closed/cancelled

This field will only contain a date when the Status column indicates the incident was closed or cancelled. The IRC enters the date the Incident Report is closed or cancelled. This information is used in preparing status reports for management. Reports can be generated from the Incident Log listing the number of Incident Reports closed within a specific time-frame or the average number of days it took to close an Incident Report.

Priority

This field is copied from the Incident Report. The project leader assigned each Incident Report a priority. The priority of a report determines the order in which it will be assigned. Management will want to see reports of open Incident Report by priority. The high-priority reports, Priority A, are critical issues and must be resolved as soon as possible.

Summary description

This field is a brief description of the incident. The IRC summarized the statements written in the incident description and incident details section of the report. The IRC is a member of the project and should be familiar with the terminology. When there is only one person performing this function, that person will generally use the same key words and abbreviations in summarizing an incident. This will make the Incident Log easy to scan. Duplicate incidents can be recognized, and similar issues can be grouped together.

The Incident Log can be used to generate reports specifying the following information:

- All Incident Reports listed chronologically by date prepared
- All open Incident Reports listed by priority and date prepared
- Number of open Incident Reports
- Number of open Incident Reports in each priority
- All closed Incident Reports listed by date prepared
- Average number of days to close an Incident Report
- Number of Incident Reports closed within the month
- All cancelled Incident Reports

THE SUMMARY REPORT

The Systems Test Summary Report documents the results of the systems test. It is prepared at the completion of systems testing and is the final deliverable from the systems test activity. It is kept with the project documentation.

The Summary Report provides feedback on both the application that was tested and the testing strategy that was used. The information in the report addresses the following:

- What was tested?
- What was not tested and why?
- What are the results of the tests?
  - What passed?
  - What failed?
  - What are the demonstrated capabilities of the application?
  - What are the demonstrated deficiencies of the application?
- Which Incident Reports are open?
  - What are the risks of not resolving these incidents for this release?
- What is the status of the application?
  - Can it move to the next phase?
- How effective was the testing strategy?
- Were the tests executed as described in the Systems Test Specifications?
  - If not, why?
- What could not be tested effectively?
- Which tests took excessive times to set up or execute?
- What additional documentation is needed?
  - For the testing tools?
  - For the test specifications?
- Were the testing tools effective?
  - Are new ones needed?
- What improvements are needed for the test specifications?
- Were any features insufficiently tested? Why?

Figure 6.8 is a recommended outline for the Systems Test Summary. Each section of the document is described below. Appendix A contains a sample Systems Test Summary Report.

The Summary Report could be set up in the same way as the Systems Test Plan documentation described in an earlier chapter. A

SUMMARY REPORT

Systems Test Summary for:

Date prepared:

Written by:

Submitted to:

Document locator:

Other documents:

General background:

Systems testing dates:

Tests executed:

Tests not executed:

Summary of test results:

Open incident reports:

Status:

Analysis of testing strategy:

Figure 6.8. Systems Test Summary Report.

master document could be created that includes boiler-plate documents and text templates from a general documentation library. The following is a description of each item in the recommended outline.

Title

This section contains the words "Systems Test Summary for," followed by the name of the application.

Date prepared

This section contains the date the summary was prepared.

Written by

This section contains the names and departments of the people who wrote this summary.

Submitted to

This section lists the names and departments of the people to whom the summary was submitted.

Document locator

This section identifies the location of this document and the procedures to update or print it. It states the LAN or mainframe where the document is stored and its fully qualified file name. It specifies the software used to create the document. The information in this section can be created by including a text template and using it as skeleton. The text template can be copied and the appropriate words can be filled in. The following is an example:

This document is stored on the _____ network/ computer. The file name of the master document is: _____. It is written with word processor _____. It was printed using the following attributes: _____.

Other documents

This section lists the name and location of any other relevant documentation available for this system. It serves as a cross-reference. The Systems Test Plan documentation also contains a section listing other documents. In the chapter describing the Systems Test Plan and documentation method, there were several techniques described for cross-referencing the documents. The information in this section can be obtained by referencing or including a master control document that lists all documents for this system. The master document for the Summary Report could contain the following line:

```
Include document name
/* master control list of project documentation */
```

This section could also be created by copying a text template and filling in the appropriate words. The following is an example of this:

> Other documents for this project are stored on the _____ computer/network at_____ (location). They are written with word processor _____.

General background

This section contains a brief description of the application and systems testing execution platform. The information for this section can be created by including a boiler-plate document. The boiler-plate document would have a general description of the system. It could be included in any document that required a system overview. This method has several advantages. It provides a consistent description of the system throughout the project documentation. The author of this document does not have to write another description. If the description needs to change, the boiler-plate document is the only document that requires modification.

Systems testing dates

This section contains the beginning and ending dates of this systems test.

Tests executed

This section lists the test cycles that were executed. The test cycle numbers refer to those specified in the Systems Test Specifications.

Tests not executed

This section lists the test cycles that were not executed. The test cycle numbers refer to those specified in the Systems Test Specifications. A brief explanation is given for why the tests were not executed.

The following is an example of the "Tests executed" and "Tests not executed" sections for the Jewelry Pricing System

Tests executed:

The following test cycles were executed:

Cycle 1   Maintain Product Style information—All test cases

Cycle 2   Maintain Cost Tables—All test cases

Cycle 3   Price Product Line—All test cases

Cycle 4   Delete Discontinued Styles—Test Cases 5-1-101 through 5-1-104 executed (annual purge). See Tests not executed.

Cycle 5   Produce Price/Catalog Lists—All test cases

Cycle 6   Performance Capabilities—All test cases

Cycle 7   Operational Capabilities—All Test Cases

Tests not executed:

The following tests were not executed:

Cycle 4 Delete Discontinued Styles—The annual purge feature was tested and accepted. The Reinstated Style was not tested. We "de-scoped" the project. Management agreed to omit this feature from the initial release. The test cases were designed for this feature. They may be referenced when this feature is implemented.

Summary of test results

This section summarizes the findings of each test cycle that was executed. It lists the location of the actual results of the tests. Reports and data extracts should be stored in a file that is permanently retained. It lists the capabilities and deficiencies of the application as demonstrated in the test.

For quality/standards compliance testing, it states the software that did not comply and notes any items that contain approved variances.

For business requirements testing, it states any limitations or restrictions noted.

For performance capabilities testing, it states the results of the test. It can include the actual measurements recorded. Any information that is restricted should not be included in this document. This document is for general release. Do not include password and network phones in any general release document.

For operational capabilities testing, it states the findings and observations.

The following is an example of the summary of test results for the Jewelry Pricing System.

Summary of test results:

All software, supporting documentation, and procedures complied with quality and standards guidelines.

All business requirements test cases were accepted by the reviewers. Several reviewers submitted Incident Reports for enhancements. Some of the enhancements were included in this release of the system; others were deferred. (See open Incident Reports for more details.)

Performance capabilities were tested and accepted. The measurements are included in the performance and network analysis document. The performance measurements are not for general publication and therefore have not been stated here.

Operational capabilities were tested and accepted. The backup schedule was modified as a result of the testing. It is now performed more frequently during peak season.

The actual results of the tests are stored on the R: drive on the LAN in the Information Services department at corporate headquarters. The reports are stored as files and kept in the same location. The databases were backed up after cycles 1–5.

Open Incident Reports

This section lists the Incident Reports that are open at the completion of systems testing. It states the impact of these Incident Reports on the systems testing. It states the risks of not resolving them for the production release of the application.

The following is an example of the open Incidents section for the Jewelry Pricing System.

Open Incident Reports:

All Incident Reports for software errors and ABEND conditions were closed. The only open Incidents Reports are enhancements. These reports are not necessary for the first release of the system. The following Incident Reports are open:

Incident Report number: 007

Enhancement request to print labels

Incident Report number: 008

Enhancement request to generate a labor hours report

Incident Report number: 032

Enhancement request to do "what-if" analysis

Status

This section contains the status of the systems testing activity. It states the coverage and completeness of the testing. It recommends whether the application can move to the next phase.

The following is an example of the status section for the Jewelry Pricing System.

Status:

The application was fully systems tested. All test cases were accepted. The open Incident Reports are functional enhancements that can be deferred. The application is ready for installation.

Analysis of testing strategy

This section lists any problems encountered in the systems testing. It recommends any changes that would improve the process.

It states any deficiencies noted in the test specifications. It lists any tests that could not be tested as specified. It lists any procedures that took excessive time to prepare or execute. It states any problems encountered with the testing tools. It notes any scheduling problems or missing resources.

The following is an example of the "Analysis of testing strategy" section for the Jewelry Pricing System.

Analysis of testing strategy:

We have inadequate tools to perform the quality/standards compliance testing. We can't check our specific standards. All testing tool products we reviewed check software for general coding verbs. Much of our testing in this area was performed manually and therefore prone to omissions. The risks are minor. If we have software or documentation that is not standardized, the maintenance will be more difficult but the functionality of the system will not be impaired.

We need a better tool for test coverage. We would like a product in which we can specify a test case number and its status will display. The Activity Log and Incident Reports are insufficient for this purpose. There is no single report listing test cases that passed and test cases that failed.

During the initial days of systems testing execution, one Incident Report Coordinator was inadequate. We were not able to log Incident Reports in a timely manner. Programmers were resubmitting items before the Incident Reports were logged. We need more support in logging the Incident Reports.

SUMMARY

The execution phase of systems testing occurs after the review and begins when the software is submitted for systems testing. The purpose of this phase is to do the following:

- Prepare the environment
- Execute the test
- Record the testing activities
- Verify the results
- Document any inconsistencies
- Summarize testing results to management

The following are the deliverables from this phase:

- Systems-tested software
- Actual results
- Systems Test Activity Log
- Incident Reports generated during the execution
- Incident Report Log
- Systems Test Summary Report

7

The Maintenance Phase

The *maintenance phase* of a project begins as soon as the system is implemented. This phase of the System Development Life Cycle is the most difficult phase to control and yet it requires the most control. This paradox arises from the nature of this phase.

CHARACTERISTICS

Maintenance, unlike the other phases, does not have a scheduled completion date. It is the longest phase of the SDLC. The system is maintained until it is replaced by another system or its business functions are no longer performed by the firm.

Maintenance does not have a predefined scope. The overall objectives of the maintenance phase are to support the system in performing the business requirements for which it was designed. The activities in this phase should be limited to correcting or modifying the system so it performs its intended functions. This can include changes in the business requirements and performance capabilities. It does not include redesigning the system architecture or changing functionality. Unfortunately, the number and scope of these changes is unknown at the onset of the phase.

Maintenance tasks are performed as a single activity. The requirements, systems analysis, design, and programming tasks are performed as one activity within a short period of time. Testing does not occur in each phase. There is insufficient time and manpower to perform the design and coding reviews that occurred in the development phases.

Maintenance is not structured. The changes are requested on an as-needed basis. The same business function may be changed many times, and the same module may be changed several times for various functions. There's no way of knowing what the next change will be. Therefore, the changes cannot be organized by functional subsystem or module. Without knowing what is going to change, tasks cannot be grouped.

Maintenance changes are urgent. The changes are required to continue the business functions. They must be implemented promptly.

Maintenance changes are frequent. When the system is initially implemented and enters the maintenance phase, changes can be made two or three times a week. As the system matures, the frequency of the changes will decrease.

Maintenance is performed for a production system. The system is in production. The changes must be accurate.

Maintenance phase staffing is different from development. The original developers may not remain in the group when it moves into the maintenance phase. The size of the staff may be decreased in this phase.

Systems testing is not abandoned when the project moves into the maintenance phase. Its functions continue for the life of the system. Systems testing is a part of the system, and it, too, moves into a maintenance phase. In this phase of systems testing, the test team may be downsized or absorbed by the maintenance staff, but their functions remain the same.

The work in the maintenance phase relies on the foundation built in the prior phases. The documentation from the initial systems testing must be saved. The planning, design, and execution phases of systems testing each produced a set of deliverables that are referenced in the maintenance phase and used as a basis for further testing. When the initial systems test is completed, the test team should review all the deliverables for accuracy and completeness. The deliverables must be updated, so the information stored with the project documentation is current.

The test team should also prepare turnover instructions for accessing and updating the systems testing material. The level of detail in the instructions will vary depending on who maintains the production system. In the mainframe environment, the custodian of the system is the Information Services department.

In the client/server environment, the custodian should have been determined during the planning phase. This decision should be reaffirmed before the system is implemented. If the Information Services department is not the custodian, the test team should arrange a meeting with the designated custodial group to discuss the turnover procedures for systems testing documentation.

Figure 7.1 is a list of the systems test deliverables produced for a Jewelry Pricing System.

Figure 7.2 shows the turnover instructions for those deliverables.

Any change that is made to the system or its supporting environment must be tested before it is implemented in production. The maintenance phase of systems testing benefits from the work of the prior phases. The testing strategy has been established, and the test specifications and test data are available for use. The systems testing in this phase is simplified, but it is not the one-step task of executing the test.

The following tasks must be performed for maintenance phase systems testing:

- Determine the impact of the change on the system.
- Incorporate the change into the systems test.
- Verify that changes comply with standards.
- Execute the test.

The deliverables from this phase may include the following:

SYSTEMS TEST DELIVERABLES: Jewelry Pricing System

The following items are the deliverables from the systems test for the inventory control system:

1. Systems Test Plan
2. Systems Test Specifications
3. Systems Test Activity Log
4. Systems Test Summary
5. Incident Reports
6. Incident Log
7. Test data files
8. Backup files of the test databases
9. Expected results files
10. Actual results files
11. Command language files to execute test cases
12. Software for the testing tools
13. Command language files for the testing tools
14. Users sign-offs

Figure 7.1. Systems test deliverables.

- Systems-tested software
- Actual results
- Activity Log entries
- User verification and approvals
- Updated Systems Test Specifications
- Updated test data
- Updated expected results
- Updated command language files

The test team must be actively involved in the change process. They must be notified of every change that will be made to the system as soon as it is approved. The software developers cannot wait until the software is ready for testing and then merely turn over the items for testing. The test team must have sufficient lead

SYSTEMS TEST TURNOVER INSTRUCTIONS FOR:

Inventory Control System

Documentation
The Systems Test Plan describes the procedures for updating all systems test documents.

Test Data
The test data was created manually using keyboard entry, and the Sort and File Editor programs. The contents of these files can be printed by executing ICTDPRT.BAT in the systems test environment.

Test Databases
The databases for the baseline data and each test cycle were unloaded and stored as ASCII files. They can be restored by executing ICDBLD.BAT.

Expected Results
The expected results of each test case are described in the Systems Test Specifications. All output reports were created as files and stored in the systems test environment.

Actual Results
The final report outputs were saved as files and stored in the systems test environment.

Incident Reports
The Incident Reports are stored in a binder. Open Incident Reports are filed in the first section in Incident Report number sequence. Closed Incident Reports are filed in the second section in Incident Report number sequence.

Incident Log
The Incident Log is maintained as a spreadsheet. The file is stored in the systems test environment. The Incident Report Coordinator must maintain this file adding new Incident Reports and tracking the status of existing Incident Reports.

Testing Tools
The software and related command language files for all testing tools used in this systems test are stored in the systems test environment. The Systems Test Plan contains a description of the software and how it is used on this project.

Figure 7.2.   Systems test turnover instructions.

time to determine the impact this change has on the systems testing. The change to the system may require additional or updated test cases and test data. The expected results and verification procedures may also require changes. The systems testing documentation, unlike the program specifications, cannot be postponed. It must be updated as the system changes. When the Systems Test Specifications do not reflect the current system, it cannot be used for testing, and software that is insufficiently tested will be placed in production.

There are six types of changes that occur in the maintenance phase:

- Configuration changes
- Emergency changes
- Business Requirements changes
- Performance changes
- Operational changes
- Testing Tool changes

Each of these changes must be tested.

CONFIGURATION CHANGES

A configuration change is a change in the network, hardware, or software components. The software components can be the operating system or the supporting software (DBMS, compilers, spreadsheet packages). The changes can include upgrading the hardware or operating systems, adding users to the network, and replacing a supporting software product. There are configuration management software packages available that control the inventory management of the hardware, software, and network and provide cross-references of component usage. These packages do not, however, test the impact of the configuration changes on the individual application systems. Any hardware or software features that change as a result of the configuration change should be published and distributed to all application support groups.

In the mainframe environment, any configuration change is tested by a systems support group. This group is responsible for testing the change and its impact on all application systems.

In the client/server environment, this testing may not be

handled by a systems specialist. If the configuration changes are specific to this application, testing may be the responsibility of the maintenance team. The original systems test can be reexecuted. All test cycles can be run, or only portions of them. This would depend on the type of change that was implemented.

The configuration change is tested using the following approach:

- Determine the impact of the change on the system.
- Incorporate the change into the systems test.
- Execute the test.

Determine the Impact
The test team should identify all test cycles that must be executed.

Incorporate the Change
The test team should make the necessary changes to the systems test documentation, command language files, or test procedures.

Execute the Test
The designated test cycles should be executed and their results should be verified.

EMERGENCY CHANGES

An emergency change is a change to the production system to correct a function that failed and requires immediate resolution. The software developers must analyze the problem, determine the solution, and implement the correction in the minimum amount of time. This time-frame does not permit a formal systems test, and often the staff is unavailable to perform a test. The failure may occur during nonstandard business hours, and the "on-call" systems analyst must resolve the problem independently. The rest of the staff may not be working.

Emergency changes, by definition, cannot be scheduled. However, the procedures for implementing emergency changes should be documented and included in the Operations Guide. These procedures should be tested during the original systems test. Figure

7.3 is an example of Emergency Production Maintenance Procedures for an inventory control system.

In the mainframe environment, the software for the system is executed from one location. The corrected software only needs to be distributed to the production libraries in the mainframe computers. In the client/server environment, the software for the system may be distributed to multiple sites. The failure only occurred at one site, but the error exists in the software at all sites and they must all receive the corrected software. In the example shown in Figure 7.3 the software distribution package manages the distribution. The systems analyst specifies whether the change is distributed immediately to all sites or only first to selective sites and later to the remaining sites.

Although the emergency change is implemented directly to satisfy the user's requirements, this does not close the incident. A follow-up meeting should be scheduled with the test team to inform them of the emergency change. They must conduct a formal systems test of the change that was implemented. In step 4 of the example shown in Figure 7.3, the procedures instruct the on-call analyst to schedule this meeting.

The emergency change is tested using the following approach:

- Determine the impact of the change on the system.
- Incorporate the change into the systems test.
- Verify changes comply with standards.
- Execute the test.

Determine the Impact

The Systems Test Specifications contain several cross-reference matrices: a test case/object matrix, a test case/requirements matrix, and a test case/test cycle matrix. The test case/object matrix is used to determine all test cases in which the corrected software is used. The test case/requirements matrix is used to determine all test cases in which the requirement is tested. The test case/ test cycle matrix is used to determine which test cycles should be executed.

Incorporate the Change

An emergency change can indicate the test cases or test data did not cover all possibilities. Any additional test cases or test data

EMERGENCY PRODUCTION MAINTENANCE

This procedure lists each step in the Emergency Production Maintenance procedures. It describes the action to be performed and the person or area responsible for that action.

1. The on-call systems analyst obtains an emergency maintenance Id from the Information Systems department manager. This Id permits the analyst to access the application software in the production environment.

2. The on-call systems analyst signs on to the production environment using the emergency maintenance Id and selects the "Library Maintenance" feature.

Enter the Program Name.

A. If the program will be replaced by a modified version, select "Modify" and follow the screen directions.

B. If a previous version of the program will be used, select "Prior Version" and follow the screen directions.

Specify the software distribution method.

A. If the new version of the program should be distributed immediately to all computers specified in the Application Distribution table, select "All - Immediate."

B. If the new version of the program should only be distributed to specific computers immediately, select "Specify" and follow the screen directions.

3. The on-call systems analyst enters the date, time, and purpose of the production change in the Emergency Change Log.

4. The on-call systems analyst schedules a meeting with the systems test team to review the emergency change.

5. The on-call systems analyst calls operations and closes the emergency maintenance Id.

6. Operations deletes this Id from the production sign-on table.

Figure 7.3.   Emergency Maintenance to Production Procedures.

required to verify this change must be created and included in the Systems Test Specifications.

Compliance Testing

When the system moves into the maintenance phase, there is a tendency to bypass some of the standards established by the Informations Services department. This is particularly true when an emergency change is implemented. Maintenance phase changes are a permanent part of the system and therefore must adhere to the same quality and standards guidelines as the original system.

The Incident Reports and Turnover Request forms used during the execution phase of systems testing should continue to be used in the maintenance phase. An Incident Report should have been filled out to describe the incident that prompted this emergency change. The on-call systems analyst who resolved the incident should prepare a Turnover form to submit the changed items to the test team. The test team will use this form to move the items to the systems test environment.

The Systems Test Specifications includes a section for quality/standards compliance testing. It contains the test conditions and test procedures for verifying the software and its documentation adhere to standards. The test team should conduct quality/standards compliance testing for all items submitted to them in the maintenance phase of systems testing.

Execute the Test

The test cycles, identified by the impact analysis, must be executed. The user-viewed results and systems results must be verified. The Activity Log, which was used in the execution phase of systems testing, should continue to be used in the maintenance phase. It provides documentation of the testing activity. The following is an example of an emergency change and the approach for testing it.

Emergency Change

The Legal Billing Systems failed to produce the correct date ranges on a bill. The user who generated the bill notified the Help Desk and submitted an Incident Report. The on-call systems analyst resolved the incident by correcting module

```
                    EMERGENCY CHANGE LOG FOR: Legal Billing System
```

Date	Time	By	Description	Resolution
02/25/92	22:35p	RMP	A bill was produced for a matter which included items (Disb & Svc) from last year. The From-date was truncated. See IR# 052	Module LBA003 corrected and moved to prd.

Figure 7.4.   Emergency Change Log.

LBA003 in the Legal Billing System. An emergency production change was performed to implement the changed program and an entry was logged in the Emergency Change Log. Figure 7.4 is the Emergency Change Log entry for the incident.

Impact

The test team receives a copy of the Emergency Change Log entry, the Turnover Request form for program LBA003, and the Incident Report. The Turnover Request form is shown in Figure 7.5, and the Incident Report is shown in Figure 7.6.

```
FORM SYS01            SYSTEMS TEST TURNOVER
Date: 02/25/93

Submitter: R. Perkins

System: Legal Billing System
```

Test Item	Type	Location	Status
LBA003	Code	S:\LB\SRC	IR# 052

Figure 7.5.   Turnover Request form.

FORM SYSD05

SYSTEMS INCIDENT REPORT

SYSTEM: Legal Billing System

ORIGINATOR: K. Gray   DATE: 02/25/93

TYPE: Error X ABEND _ Enhancement _ Other _

INCIDENT DESCRIPTION: Created a billing (see attached copy)
for a matter which was not billed since Nov. 1992 and
therefore had services spanning Nov. 1992 - Feb. 1993. The
Form-To date heading printed incorrectly. Feb. overlaid
1992.

INCIDENT DETAILS:

INCIDENT REPORT NUMBER: 052
STATUS: Logged X Analyzed X Assigned _
        Resubmitted _ Closed _ Cancelled _

ANALYZED BY: R. Perkins   DATE: 2/25/93
SOFTWARE INVOLVED: LBA003

ESTIMATED TIME TO RESOLVE INCIDENT: 2 hours. Emergency
change made 2/25/93

PRIORITY: A X B _ C _   ASSIGNED TO: R. Perkins
                                  DATE ASSIGNED: 2/25/93

Figure 7.6.   Incident Report.

The cross-reference matrices from the Systems Test Specifications are used to determine which test cases must be executed to verify this change. Figure 7.7 is a portion of the test case/object matrix, and Figure 7.8 is a portion of the test case/requirements matrix. Module LBA003 is executed in Test Cases 501–505 and 509–511, and the Produce-a-Bill requirement is executed in test cases 501–511. Although the module that changed, LBA003, is only executed in eight of the test cases that produce bills, all test cases for the requirement must be executed. The systems test verifies the requirement, not the code.

Changes
The Systems Test Specifications must be updated to include a test case that verifies bills can be produced with items that span multiple years. Test case 512 is added to the Systems Test Specifications and test data is created for unbilled services and disbursements from the prior year.

Testing
Module LBA003 is tested for compliance with quality and standards guidelines.

Test cases 501–512 are executed and logged in the Activity Log. Each test case is verified and approved by the reviewers.

TEST CASE	OBJECT LBA003	TEXT CYCLE 5
501	X	X
502	X	X
503	X	X
504	X	X
505	X	X
506	X	
507	X	
508	X	
509	X	X
510	X	X
511	X	X

Figure 7.7.   Legal billing system—test case/object matrix.

TEST CASE	REQUIREMENTS PRODUCE BILL	DATABASES						TEST CYCLE 5
		SVC	DSB	INV	MAT	CLN	CD	
501	X	U	U	U	R	R	R	X
502	X	U	U	U	R	R	R	X
503	X	U	U	U	R	R	R	X
504	X	U	U	U	R	R	R	X
505	X	R	R	R	R	R	R	X
506	X	R	R	R	R	R	R	X
507	X	R	R	R	R	R	R	X
508	X	R	R	R	R	R	R	X
509	X	R	R	R	R	R	R	X
510	X	R	R	R	R	R	R	X
511	X	R	R	R	R	R	R	X

Figure 7.8.   Legal billing system—test case/requirements matrix.

BUSINESS REQUIREMENTS CHANGES

The majority of the systems testing in the maintenance phase is for business requirements changes. Business requirements changes are changes to the production system that add or change the business requirements. These changes are initiated by the users and require software changes. The change requests should be submitted, in a formal request, to the maintenance team. This request can be prepared on the Incident Report or on a separate change request form. The software developers should analyze the request and produce an itemized list of the activities required to satisfy the requirement. The test team should receive a copy of this itemized list to use in preparing the systems testing for the changes. All business requirement changes should be systems tested, no matter how minor the change appears. A business requirement change that appears to affect only one test condition may have downstream effects on other functions.

Requirements changes are tested using the following approach:

- Determine the impact of the change on the system.
- Incorporate the change into the systems test.
- Verify changes comply with standards.
- Execute the test.

Determine the Impact

The test case/requirements matrix is used to determine all test cases that are affected by the changed requirements. The test case/test cycle matrix is used to determine which test cycles should be executed. Any test cycle that executes one of the selected test cases must be executed. The test case/requirements matrix should be updated to include any new test cases and business requirements. The test case/test cycle matrix should be updated to include any new test cases and their assigned test cycle.

Incorporate the Change

The Systems Test Specifications should be updated as required by the impact analysis. Any test cases required to verify the changes should be added or changed. The test data, control totals, and expected results should be updated to support the changes. When a new or different security profile is required to execute the test cases, it should be incorporated in the appropriate files. The test procedures should be updated to include any additional verification procedures. The cross-reference matrices should be updated to include any new test cases or changes in the attributes of existing test cases.

Compliance Testing

When the software developers have completed the changes required to support the business requirement changes, they should use the Turnover Request form to submit the changed items to the test team.

The test team should conduct quality/standards compliance testing for all items submitted on the form. In addition, they should verify all supporting documentation and systems files have been updated. This includes the systems documentation, security rules, auditing instructions, and contextual help.

Execute the Test

The test cycles, identified by the impact analysis, must be executed. The user-viewed results and systems results must be verified. The actual results of each test cycle should be saved. The Activity Log should be used to record the execution of the test.

The following is an example of a business requirements change and the approach for testing it.

Business Requirement Changes

The Legal Billing System is a production system. The users have submitted a request to change the business requirements. The change request is shown in Figure 7.9.

FORM SYSC06

                    SYSTEMS CHANGE REQUEST

SYSTEM: Legal Billing System

REQUESTER: L. Devore   DATE: 11/12/92

TYPE: Change X Enhancement X Other _

DESCRIPTION:
Attorney service hours must =< 16 hours per calendar date.
Change the Service Entry screen to display a message when
total hours exceeds 16 hours per day and prohibit entry. A
new screen must be added to display total service hours per
day of month for a specified attorney. Office Admin. can
display any attorney, other users limited to own hours

CHANGE NUMBER: 023
ASSIGNED TO: H. Novell   DATE: 11/15/92

Figure 7.9.   Change request.

The test team was given the following itemized list of the activities required to satisfy this change:

- Maintain service hours
- Add service hours
- Change service hours
  These functions must verify that the total service hours per calendar day for one attorney does not exceed 16 hours. It must prohibit the addition or change of service hours that would cause the total hours to exceed 16 hours.
- Display service hours
  —For each day of the specified month and year, display the total service hours entered in the system for the specified attorney.
  —This function is available to the office administrator to display service hours for any attorney. All other users are limited to displaying only their own service hours.

Impact

The test team uses this list to determine the impact of this change on the Systems Test Specifications. Figure 7.10 is a combination of portions of the cross-reference matrices from the Systems Test Specifications. It is used to determine the test cases that must be updated and the test cycles that must be executed. The test case/requirements columns indicate test cases 401–408 are used to test the add and change service hours requirements. These test cases and their test procedures must be updated to include the additional validation requirement. The test case/database columns indicate these test cases update the service database and read the personnel matter, security, and codes databases. The baseline data in these databases should be checked to see whether there is sufficient data to support the updated test cases. The test case/test cycle columns indicates Cycle 4 must be executed.

Changes

The Systems Test Specifications must be updated to verify the new requirements for adding, changing, and displaying service hours.

TEST CASE	REQUIREMENTS			DATABASES					TEST CYCLE
	ADD SVC	CHG SVC		SVC	PER	MAT	SEC	CD	1 . . . 4
401	X			R	R	R	R	R	X
402	X			R	R	R	R	R	X
403	X			I	R	R	R	R	X
404	X			I	R	R	R	R	X
405		X		R	R	R	R	R	X
406		X		R	R	R	R	R	X
407		X		U	R	R	R	R	X
408		X		U	R	R	R	R	X

Figure 7.10. Legal Billing System—Business Requirement Changes Cross-Reference Matrices.

Testing

When the software developers turn over the software to the test team, each item is tested for compliance with quality and standards guidelines.

Test Cycle 4 is executed and logged in the Activity Log. Each test case is verified and approved by the reviewers.

PERFORMANCE CHANGES

Performance changes are changes to the production system to improve its performance. These changes must be systems tested to ensure the performance improvements have been realized and the functionality has not been altered.

On one project, a Foreign Exchange Trading and Reconciliation System, one of the customer liability modules was changed to improve its performance. The test team executed all test case for the customer liability requirement. The change did improve performance in the customer liability functions and continued to produce the correct requirements. However, when the module was implemented into the production environment, the module that performed the cables requirements tripled in execution time. The performance change to the customer liability modules updated a database used by the cables modules. The impact of this aspect of the change was not tested. Performance changes in one subsystem can adversely affect another subsystem. In this situation either a full systems test should be performed or minimally all test cases accessing the changed database should be executed.

Performance changes are tested using the following approach:

- Determine the impact of the change on the system.
- Verify changes comply with standards.
- Execute the test.

Determine the Impact

Performance changes can be implemented by changing the application software or changing a supporting software product or feature within that product, such as the database access method.

When the application software is changed, the test case/object matrix should be used to determine all test cases in which the corrected module is used. The test case/requirements matrix should be used to determine all test cases used to test the business requirement in which the performance change was made.

When the supporting software is changed, the impact analysis may be more difficult. If a feature within the DBMS is changed (an index is added, an access method is changed), the test case/database matrix is used to determine all test cases in which that database is used.

The test case/test cycle matrix is then used to determine which test cycles should be executed.

Compliance Testing

The Turnover Request should be used to submit the changed items to the test team.

When the application software is changed, the test team should test the changed software for compliance with the standards and methodology. The changes should be compliance tested as specified by the quality/standards compliance testing procedures in the Systems Test Specifications.

Execute the Test

The Systems Test Specifications contains tests for each major area of systems testing. Performance changes require both business requirements and performance capabilities testing.

The business requirements testing must be conducted first to verify the functionality. The test cycles identified by the impact analysis must be executed and their results must be verified. The performance change should not change the business requirements. The actual results must match the expected results.

The performance capabilities testing is conducted after the business requirements have been verified. The selected test cycles are executed with volume data. Performance measurements must be recorded for all functions within the test cycles. The performance capabilities testing verifies the software operates within the performance measures specified in the System Requirements document. The test team should confirm the changes improved performance in the specified function and it did not increase performance in another function. The Activity Log should be used to record each test.

The following is an example of a performance change and the approach for testing it.

Performance Change

The Legal Billing Systems includes a Global Billing Rates Update function. This function was tested in the original systems test, and it satisfied the specified business and performance requirements. Several changes have been made to the system since it was implemented. The system now maintains two billing rates for each attorney and the number of attorneys in the database has increased. The Global Billing Rates Update function required changes to improve its performance.

Impact

The matrix shown in Figure 7.11 is a portion of the matrices in the Systems Test Specifications for this system. It is used to determine the test cycles that must be executed. The business requirements testing must be executed first. The test case/requirements columns indicate Test Cases 301–303 are used to test the Global Billing Rates Update requirements.

TEST	REQUIREMENTS	DATABASES					TEST CYCLE	
CASE	BILL RATE	SVC	PER	MAT	SEC	CD	3	9
301	X		R		R		X	X
302	X		R		R		X	X
303	X		U		R		X	X
304	X		U		R		X	X

Figure 7.11.   Legal Billing System—Performance Changes Cross-Reference Matrices.

The test case/test cycle columns indicate Cycles 3 and 9 must be executed.

Test Cycle 3 tests the business requirements and Test Cycle 9 tests the performance requirements. The business requirements testing are conducted first, followed by performance requirements.

Testing

The test team should test the software for compliance with quality and standards guidelines. Test Cycle 3 should then be executed and logged in the Activity Log. Each test case must be verified and approved by the reviewers.

Performance capabilities testing requires the databases to be fully loaded. The test case/database columns indicate the test cases access the attorney and security databases. The test procedures for Test Cycle 9 restores the volume data for these databases as its first step. Test Cycle 9 must be executed and logged in the Activity Log. The performance measurements are verified for all test cases in this cycle.

OPERATIONAL CHANGES

Operational changes are changes to the production procedures used to operate the system. These procedures are used to support the operation of the system and include backup, restore, recovery, security, virus detection, and software distribution procedures.

The software that performs the function is generally a commercial software product. The changes that occur are changes to the command language file or the operational instructions for one of these procedures.

The software products executed in these procedures can also change. The product can be upgraded or replaced by another product. In the mainframe environment, a systems support group is responsible for testing changes to software products. In the client/server environment, this testing may not be handled by a systems specialist. It may be the responsibility of the maintenance team.

Operational changes are tested using the following approach:

- Determine the impact of the change on the system.
- Verify changes comply with standards.
- Execute the test.

Determine the Impact

The test team should identify all test cycles that execute the operational procedure.

Compliance Testing

The Turnover form should be used to submit all changed items to the test team.

When command language files or operational instructions are changed, the test team should test the changes for compliance with the standards and methodology. The Systems Test Specifications contain procedures for quality and standards compliance testing of the operational procedures. The changes should be tested as specified by these procedures.

Execute the Test

The test cycles, identified by the impact analysis, must be executed. The systems testing must verify the procedures are manageable and accurate. The operations staff must be able to execute the procedures independently of the software developers. The procedures must produce accurate results. The Activity Log should be used to record each test.

TEST CASE	OBJECT WSARC	REQUIREMENTS ARCHIVES	TEST CYCLE 8
801	X	X	X
802	X	X	X

Figure 7.12.   Legal Billing System Operational Changes Cross-Reference Matrices.

The following is an example of an operational change and the approach for testing it.

Operational Change

The procedures to merge the archival files have been changed.

Impact

The test team receives a Turnover Request for a command language file, WSARC. Figure 7.12 is a portion of the cross-reference matrices used for this system. It is used to determine the test cases that are used to verify the WSARC procedure and the archival function. Test Cases 801 and 802 in Test Cycle 8 must be executed.

Testing

The WSARC command language file and its operating procedures are tested for compliance with standards.

Test Cases 801 and 802 are executed by the operations staff. The test team confirms the procedures can be executed by the operations staff and verifies the systems results. The test is logged in the Activity Log.

TESTING TOOL CHANGES

The test team must be notified when a testing tool is changed, so they can determine whether that tool is used by the systems test to execute a test or verify its results. If a testing tool is replaced with another product, or an in-house tool is modified, the test team should test this change. This step seems obvious, but the test team is often so busy testing the application that it may neglect to test its own software. Any testing tool that is changed or replaced must be tested prior to its use in a systems test.

The testing tools are tested using the following approach:

- Determine the impact of the change on the system.
- Incorporate the change into the systems test.
- Execute the test.

Determine the Impact

The test procedures sections in the Systems Test Specifications specifies any testing tools that are executed in that procedure. The test team should identify all test procedures that execute this testing tool and determine how it is used.

Incorporate the Change

When a testing tool is replaced by another product, all command language files that execute the existing tool must be changed. The test procedure must also be updated to specify the new testing tool.

When an existing testing tool is upgraded or modified, changes to the documentation or command language file may not be required. However, the test procedures should be verified.

Execute the Test

The steps within each test procedure that execute the testing tool should be run, and their results should be verified.

The following is an example of a testing tool change and the approach for testing it.

Testing Tool Change

WSCOMP is an in-house testing tool that compares two files and prints a report of any differences.

COMPFILE is a software product that has been obtained by the firm. This product is faster than the in-house tool and provides additional functionality. The test team changes the systems test to use COMPFILE.

TESTING	TEST CYCLE							
TOOL	1	2	3	4	5	6	7	8
WSCOMP	X	X	X			X		

Figure 7.13. Legal Billing Testing Tool Changes Cross-Reference Matrices.

Impact

The testing tools are not listed in the cross-reference matrices. They are not business requirements and therefore do not require a test case. They are, however, used in preparing and verifying the test cases. The test team can either create a separate matrix listing the testing tool/test procedures relationships or scan the Systems Test Specifications for the testing tool name. Figure 7.13 is a portion of a matrix that lists each testing tool used in systems testing and the test procedures (test case and test cycle procedures) where they are used. WSCOMP was used to verify the systems results in the test procedures for Test Cycles 1, 2, 3, and 6.

Changes

The test team implements the changes by modifying any command language files that execute WSCOMP to use COMPFILE. The test procedures for these cycles are updated to reference the new software product.

Testing

The test procedures for Test Cycles 1, 2, 3, and 6 each contain a step that executes the testing tool. These steps are executed and verified. The testing tool is executed with files that match and files that contain differences.

SUMMARY

The maintenance phase of a project begins when the system is implemented. The systems testing functions continue for the life of the system.

There are six types of changes that occur in the maintenance phase:

- Configuration changes
- Emergency changes
- Business requirements changes
- Performance changes
- Operational changes
- Testing tool changes

The following tasks must be performed for maintenance phase systems testing:

- Determine the impact of the change on the system.
- Incorporate the change into the systems test.
- Verify changes comply with standards.
- Execute the test.

The deliverables from this phase may include the following:

- Systems-tested software
- Actual results
- Activity Log entries
- User verification and approvals
- Updated Systems Test Specifications
- Updated test data
- Updated expected results
- Updated command language files

8

Administration

Systems testing is part of the application project and as such is managed along with the project. Its budget, schedule, and staff are included within the management of the project. The functions within the systems testing, however, require specific administration.

The administration of the systems testing is concerned with directing the technical aspects of systems testing. Management establishes the testing policy and provides direction and support for the test practitioners. The systems test administrator carries out the testing policy established by management.

THE ROLE OF MANAGEMENT

Management must establish policy in the following areas:

- Standards and procedures
- Training programs
- Physical and technical resources
- Security, privacy, and virus prevention

Standards and Procedures

Management establishes the standards and procedures for testing. It determines what is to be tested and when its testing occurs. It specifies the testing requirements and the deliverables for each phase of the system development life cycle. Management not only must issue these standards and procedures, but enforce them. The testing process cannot be successful unless management actively upholds the testing policy.

Training Programs

Management must provide a training program to instruct the staff in its testing methodology. The training program should instruct all software developers on the company's standards and procedures for testing. Management should also offer its test practitioners training in state-of-the-art testing techniques and products. The education and training schedule should include formal classes in testing methodologies.

Physical and Technical Resources

Management must provide the resources required to perform the testing function:

- The staff to perform the testing
- The scheduled time to conduct the testing
- The hardware and software required to execute the testing

Management must ensure there is a trained staff of test practitioners to design the tests and qualified users to verify the results of the tests. It should ensure sufficient machine time is available for the testing effort. Testing tools and computer-assisted software testing (CAST) products are available to assist the test practitioners in performing their jobs. Management must allocate the resources to conduct ongoing research of these products as they become available. It should also provide adequate hardware and software for the test team.

Security, Privacy, and Virus Prevention

Management must establish and enforce procedures and regulations that provide the following:

- Security for the physical premises where the computer equipment resides
- Security for the computer equipment itself at these sites
- Security for the data files stored in these computers
- Privacy for the information within the data files
- A measure of prevention against computer virus infections

Security, privacy, and *virus* prevention are considerations in any information systems applications. In a client/server environment they require more control.

Physical and logical security procedures must exist for each site and each environment (development, testing, and production). In a mainframe environment, the computers are centralized in locked glass rooms. In a client/server environment, the computers are decentralized. They are located throughout the company on desktops in open areas. The security procedures must address this and provide for the servers and the desktop workstations at these sites.

Auditing procedures should exist for the security files used to access the network and to grant authorization within the applications. The procedures should ensure passwords are changed frequently. They should verify security records do not exist for personnel who have left the area. Whenever personnel leave an area, their security records should be deleted from the table promptly. Many companies leave the records in the table and only change the associated passwords. This procedure is inadequate and dangerous. The security is based on the existence of the record in the table and its corresponding password. When the record is left in the table, half the security is missing. An intruder only needs to identify the new password.

Computer viruses are a serious problem in all computing environments. In a client/server environment, where software resides on the users' desktop computers, a virus prevention policy is essential.

A virus is a segment of code that exists within a host program. The host program performs a legitimate function; the virus does not. The virus is not directly executed by the users. The user does not even know the code exists within the system. It's hidden inside the host program and executes whenever the host program is invoked. It can self-replicate by searching for another executable program and modifying it to include a copy of itself. The virus can infect an application program, an operating system component, the disk boot sector, and the hard disk partition table. The designer of the virus determines the number of times the virus can self-replicate and the action that virus will perform. Some viruses only display a message while others perform more serious actions including altering data and erasing the entire contents of the hard drive. The virus designer also determines when the virus will perform its action by including a logic bomb or time bomb within the virus.

> A *logic bomb* is code that specifies the conditions under which the damaging program will activate. When the conditions are satisfied, the code begins its destructive actions. The condition could be generalized one, such as hitting a sequence of keystrokes, typing a specific word on the screen, or executing a specific program. The condition could also be specific to the company such as when an account balance falls below $100 or when an employee is fired.

> A *time bomb* is code that specifies when a damaging program will activate. When the specific date or time occurs, the code begins its destructive actions. There are known viruses that activate on Friday the 13th, March 6 (Michelangelo's birthday), October 12 (Columbus Day), and April 1 (April Fool's Day).

Viruses used to be confined to college computer centers where the students coded them as practical jokes. This is no longer the case. The Michelangelo Virus, which infected desktop computers in many major corporations, clearly indicates all companies, large and small, are vulnerable.

A few years ago, a manager of an end-user department thought someone was stealing memory chips from the computers in his area. Some of the computers were unable to run the client/server application we had installed. There was insufficient memory to load the software. Their hardware technicians assured them that all the memory chips were in the computers. It seems they occasionally saw a bouncing ball appear on the screen, but they ignored it. The users were unaware that a virus had infected their system. This particular virus did not erase any files, but it did replicate. Each time a host program was invoked, it searched for another target program and attached itself. The virus also contained a bug in its code that caused it to not recognize a program that was already infected. Therefore it continued to copy itself into the same programs until it increased the size of the programs to a point where the software could no longer run. Today, users are more aware of viruses, but they are still not educated about preventing a viral infection and are therefore careless in their computing practices.

A virus can enter a computer from an infected disk or by being downloaded from a network. The designer of the virus wants the virus to enter as many computer systems as possible. One way to do this is to hide the virus code in a Trojan Horse. A *Trojan Horse* is a term used to describe a program that seems to perform a useful function but actually has damaging code hidden inside of it. The Trojan Horse is an attractive program, a game, or a utility program that people will want to use. The designer camouflages the virus in the Trojan Horse and places it on a bulletin board knowing people will download it and bring it to the office. As soon as the program is executed on another system the virus attaches itself to one of the programs in that system. The virus has now entered the company's computer system. If the program to which it attaches itself accesses the file server, that virus can infect all systems on that network.

These are some of the ways in which a virus can be introduced into a system:

- A user brings to work a computer game that is infected with a virus to play at lunchtime.
- A shareware or freeware program that contains a virus is installed on the system.
- A pirated copy of a commercial product that contains a virus is installed on the system.
- An infected demo disk is used to evaluate a software product.
- A user from another area uses the computer and runs a program from an infected disk.

- A user works at home on a home computer that has a virus. When the work is brought back, so is the virus.
- A user rents a PC during a business trip to prepare some reports. The rented PC has a virus that infects the user's disk.
- A hardware technician uses an infected diagnostic disk in servicing a machine.
- Deliberately! A disgruntled employee or an outsider may want to cause problems for the company.

Management must establish a virus prevention policy before any client/server applications are implemented. The practices and procedures in this policy must be incorporated in the software development and systems testing of that application. The policy should cover the following three items:

- Education
- Prevention
- Recovery

Education

All personnel who use computers—Information Systems personnel as well as endusers—should receive some form of education on computer viruses. They should become familiar with computer viruses, how it enters a computer system, how it spreads to other computer systems, and what kind of damage it can cause. They should be educated on the actions of known viruses. They should also be informed about antiviral programs, their functions, what types exist, and the effects they have on viruses. The education program should to be just that—education. It should not frighten the staff about using the system or make them feel they will be blamed if their computer becomes infected. It should make the staff aware of computer viruses and teach them to recognize changes in the operation of their system that may indicate a viral infection. They should be trained to be alert for the following items:

- Undocumented error messages displayed on the screen
- Unusual and unexpected screen graphics

- An increase in the time for a program to load
- An increase in the size of a program
- A decrease in the available memory on their system
- Any programs that have been deleted
- Any new programs that have been added
- Programs accessing disk drives that should not be using them

The education program should be ongoing. The staff should receive updated information on any new viruses that have been discovered and new *antiviral programs* for that strain. The education program should include sessions that explain the company's policy on virus prevention and virus recovery. Any updates to this policy should be immediately conveyed to all staff members.

Prevention

A virus prevention program should be a combination of three elements: education, physical security measures, and computing procedures. The education program (just discussed) is the first element. All personnel using computers must be educated on computer viruses.

Physical security is the second element. The security procedures for the physical premises should be reviewed to consider safeguarding the computer equipment from computer viruses. Security is generally concerned with theft and vandalism of the physical equipment. A virus does not generally damage the hardware; its target is the software and the data. The hardware costs are relatively cheap compared to the cost of recovering the data and the disruption of computing services. The physical security should examine the accessibility of the file server and database server. These computers store files that are shared by other computers. If a computer virus is placed in one of these computers, it can spread throughout the local area network and, depending on the communications architecture, throughout the company (all branches).

The computing practices of the staff are the single most important element in virus prevention. Management must establish set guidelines to follow for safe computing practices. The following are some key suggestions. It is by no means a complete list of considerations. A virus prevention policy should be carefully drafted by the technical staff or outside specialists. The completed guidelines should then be distributed at a meeting where they can be explained and the staff can ask questions.

1. **Attend all virus education programs, and read all related materials.**
   Users should read all messages and bulletins informing them about the latest viruses and antiviral programs.

2. **Monitor the activity of the system.**
   Users should be familiar with their system and trained to look for indications of a viral infection.

3. **Adhere to the physical security regulations established by management.**

4. **Never use pirated software.**
   Pirated software is not only illegal, it is a prime source of computer viruses. The guidelines must stress the importance of only installing licensed original software on any workstations.

5. **Only use software purchased and authorized by the company.**
   The staff should not bring in their own disks with products they got from a friend or downloaded from a bulletin board. This includes the latest nude, lewd, and humorous graphics programs. Pornographic software is bait. The designers of the virus put these programs on a bulletin board knowing people will download them, bring them to the office, and share them with their coworkers.

6. **A write-protection tab should be affixed to all original disks. The disks should then be stored in a physically secured site.**
   The original disks should not be given to the users. They should be stored for use in a recovery procedure.

7. **Authorized Information Systems personnel and hardware technicians should be the only staff permitted to install or execute programs on computers in another department.**
   Don't allow unauthorized people to use the computers. When the Information Systems department's software support staff needs to install or execute software in the user's area, they should make an appointment or show identification. The users should only permit authorized hardware technicians with

scheduled appointments to execute programs on their computers.

8. **"Trapdoors" should be removed from all application software before it is installed in the production environment.**
A *trapdoor* is a segment of code within a program that allows someone to bypass the normal security. This code was written by the programmer during the software development phase. It was used by that programmer to access the system without supplying a password or having a security record in the authorization table. The programmer used the trapdoor to easily access the system for monitoring and testing purposes. This trapdoor code is often left in the program. The user doesn't know it exists. The original programmer may no longer work at the company. Yet the code exists and someone will find it. The trapdoor may be useful during emergency maintenance of the application. Management must decide whether it is worth the risk. The trapdoor is an open door, not only to that application, but to the entire company's computer system. If management bans trapdoor code from production systems, the systems testing should verify this standard. The quality/standards compliance testing should verify source code does not contain any trapdoors.

9. **Back up the computers on a regular basis.**
Write-protect any backed up disks.
Use external labels on all backed up tapes and disks listing the date and time of the backup.
Store backups in a secure site.
The file servers and database server are probably backed up frequently by the operational staff, with the backups stored in a secured site. The users should also back up their desktop computers and store those backups in a secured place, a locked drawer at least.

If a computer virus is not detected immediately, the backup files may also contain the computer virus. One way to provide additional security is to keep multiple generations of backups. The backups should be externally labelled with the date and time the backup was taken. If a virus is detected and the date of its infection can be approximated, any backups created prior to that date are safe. Any backups created after that date will contain the infection. The external label should be used to identify the "clean" backups. The backup should not be inserted in the computer and read to determine its backup date. This could cause the virus to reenter the computer. After a recovery from a virus, all storage media (disks and tapes) must be checked and only clean copies can be saved. All others must be thrown away or reformatted. Destroy any disks that contain a copy (not the original manufacturer's version) of the operating system. These disks could contain boot sector viruses. They should be destroyed, not just tossed into a wastebasket. Someone could pick it up and reuse it. The virus can be reintroduced by using a disk that contains the virus.

On one project, the computers seemed to be getting infected every other month. Actually, they were not being infected with a new virus. The users were putting the same virus back into their computers. After they recovered from the first virus infection, they did not check the backups. Two users had backup disks in their desks that were created after the initial viral infection and therefore were also contaminated. Whenever one of these users had to restore a file, a backup disk from the desk drawer was used. The virus was on the disk, imbedded in an executable program. The computer virus would enter the computer's hard drive, and the pattern started all over again.

10. **Use caution when using someone else's PC, either a rental or a system from another area.**
    Don't use any disks on other computers unless the write-protection tab is set. If the data must be updated on the other machine, only bring the data files to that machine. Do not store executable programs on that same disk. Currently computer viruses can only attach themselves to executable code. They do not infect data files, so the data files are "clean."

11. **Don't execute any programs from an unidentified disk.**
    The users should put a volume label on all disks and include an external label. Never accept software from unauthorized personnel. Disks that contain self-expanding files are particularly dangerous. The files contain multiple files stored in one compressed file. The user can't readily see the contents of the disk.

12. **Don't allow users from other areas to execute their programs on your computer.**
   Personnel from other areas should not be permitted to bring their disks into your area to run programs. The other department may not be following the company's virus prevention guidelines, and their disks could contain a computer virus. When two departments need to exchange information, only the data should be exchanged. Executable programs should not be included on the disks being exchanged. Each department should have the application software required to access that data.

13. **Don't download programs from an unknown bulletin board.**
   Verify that the SysOp of the bulletin board tests and approves all files that are uploaded. The SysOp should validate all users who upload software and not accept files from unknown sources. If you don't know the practices followed by the SysOp, don't use that BBS.

14. **Don't use any shareware or freeware from unidentified authors or distribution sources.**
   A freeware or shareware program should not be executed on a business computer without knowing its purpose and its author. Shareware authors want users to register their copy of the product and therefore include their name and address in the external and internal product description. Some *shareware* authors are members of the Association of Shareware Professionals and therefore can be contacted directly or through the organization. This verification is one precaution. The software may be a legitimate product, but it could have been infected by a virus during its distribution. The products are distributed in various ways. They can be downloaded from a bulletin board, copied from another computer, ordered from a distributor, or ordered directly from the author. The latter two methods are preferable. When ordering software from distributors, verify the procedures used by the distributors. They should know the purpose of the program and if possible the name, address, and background of the author. The distributors should verify the software by executing a virus detection program before accepting the product for distribution. Shareware authors can be contacted directly, and they will send you a registered copy of the product. If you want to try out the product, they may send you

a demo copy. There are excellent freeware and shareware products available today, and they should not be avoided for fear of viruses. However, it is wise to use precautions. The products could be installed but kept isolated by either placing them in a separate directory or on a standalone computer.

15. **Establish a separate group that certifies all noncommercial software before it can be installed on other computers.**
This group could verify the software using antiviral programs on a standalone computer before it is released to anyone in the company.

16. **Select and install antiviral programs.**
There are several types of antiviral programs: virus detection programs, virus prevention products, and virus removal programs. Each type has a different purpose, and the individual products vary in effectiveness.

Virus detection programs detect a virus infection *after* it occurs. They scan the system for any changes in executable programs and alert the user of a possible virus infection. These programs can be executed on request or executed automatically after each power-on.

Virus prevention products are hardware and software products that prevent viruses from entering the system.

Virus removal programs identify the specific type of virus and remove it. These products are generally one step behind the latest virus. It is only after a virus is discovered that the antiviral program can be written.

17. **Establish virus reporting and investigation procedures.**
All users should know how to report a possible virus infection. Each report must be investigated. Management should receive a summary of all reported viruses and the outcome of the investigations.

18. **Conduct periodic audits of the software installed on the computers.**
The audits will reveal any unauthorized software which is installed on the computers. It will not, however, reveal any unauthorized software which is not installed on a hard disk but stored on disks. This software is generally games and

personal programs kept in the desk drawer and executed from disk. It has a higher probability of containing viruses but unfortunately it will not be detected in a audit.

19. **Establish virus recovery procedures.**
The procedure to recovery from a virus should be documented and practiced.

Recovery

Management must develop and publish virus recovery procedures. All personnel should receive copies of these procedures. They must know what to do if they believe their computer has been infected. The recovery procedures should be a checklist that can be posted at each workstation or in a highly visible section within in each area. The checklist should inform the users what to do, whom to notify, and where to get help. It should include a hot-line phone number, accessible 24 hours a day, that can be used to report the virus and seek technical help. Figure 8.1 is a sample virus reporting checklist.

Items 2, 3, and 4 on the checklist are concerned with isolating any disks that were used during this session and, therefore, may contain the virus. Item 5 asks the user to write down what hap-

---

Virus Reporting Checklist

1. Power off the computer.
2. Remove any disks from the drives.
3. Put these disks and any others used in this session in a manila envelope.
4. Seal the envelope and label it "infected disks." Sign your name, the date, and the time on the envelope.
5. Write down what happened. Use form SYSV01 or a blank sheet of paper.
6. Call hot-line number 555-8888, and follow instructions of support personnel.

Figure 8.1.   Virus reporting checklist.

SYSV01   Virus Reporting Form

Name: Date:

1. Write down what you observed
   A. Any unusual screen activity (bouncing ball, falling letters)?
   B. Any unusual music or sounds (computer played "Yankee Doodle")?
   C. Any unusual messages displayed on the screen (Your computer is now stoned, Sorry for any inconvenience)?
   D. Unable to load a program, longer to load?
   E. Files disappeared, renamed?
   F. Programs increased in size?
   G. Available memory decreased?
   H. Disk drive light went on unexpectedly?

2. Who was using the computer when you noticed these items? Who used your computer today?

3. List all files accessed in this session. Did you access any servers?

4. Are you connected to a LAN? To the mainframe?

5. Do you have a modem? Did you use it today? Did you set it on auto-answer?

6. Did you receive data from another area today? From whom? How was it sent? Disk? Tape? Downloaded from a network?

7. Did you send data to another area today? To whom? How was it sent? Disk? Tape? Uploaded to a network?

8. What is the date of your last backup? Is this a backup of the entire system? Just data files?

9. Was the hardware recently serviced?

10. Was any new software recently installed on this computer?

11. What type of work is done on this computer? Programming? Administration (word processing, spreadsheet)? User applications? Training sessions?

Figure 8.2.   Virus reporting form.

pened. Users should do this immediately when all the information is fresh in their minds. This item is listed before calling the hot-line phone number so the users can review the information that must be given to the support personnel. Figure 8.2 is an example of form SYSV01, the virus reporting form.

The support personnel must diagnose the scope of problems and include this information in their findings. The time and costs involved in virus recovery depend on the following:

- The type of virus
- The amount of time the virus has been in the system
- The number of computers it has infected
- The types of computers it has infected

A virus infection on the file server or database server is far more serious than one on a standalone system without any communications. The recovery procedure must include identifying all infected storage media. All disks and tapes created from the infected computers must be checked. Any infected disk or tape must be destroyed or the virus will reappear as soon as that item is used again. A disk that contains a copy of the operating system programs should not be placed in the drives without a write protection tab.

THE ROLE OF THE SYSTEMS TEST ADMINISTRATOR

Systems test administration directs the following:

- The systems test environment
- The systems test design
- The systems test execution
- The maintenance phase monitoring

Administrating The Systems Test Environment

The systems test environment must be controlled and maintained. In the mainframe environment, a central systems group generally administers the systems test environment and investigates system products such as testing tools.

In the client/server environment, this task may be the responsibility of the project and therefore part of systems testing administration. The administration tasks include the following:

- **Ensuring that the systems test environment has proper security**
  The test team and authorized test reviewers should be the only personnel allowed to update the contents of the systems test environment. The software developers should only be permitted to read the information in this environment.
- **Ensuring that the systems test environment has sufficient resources**
  The systems test administrator ensures that the test team has sufficient disk space, backup disks, and tapes.
- **Ensuring that the systems test environment has the proper versions of the software to perform the testing**
  The software involved includes the operating system, the network operating system, and the software development products.
- **Providing backup and restore capabilities for the central repository, the test databases, test data, control procedures, and documentation files**
- **Ensuring that the systems test environment has a virus-detection program**
- **Ensuring that the computing practices in the systems test environment adhere to the company's virus prevention policy**
- **Reporting any virus infection to management and assisting in the virus recovery procedures**
- **Evaluating, selecting, and upgrading the testing tools**
  In the client/server environment, new testing tools are released each month. The evaluation of new testing tools is an ongoing task. The test practitioner must be kept informed on new technology to determine its potentials for the project.

Administrating The Systems Test Design

The systems test administrator must control the design phase of systems testing. The administration tasks include the following:

- Ensuring that the Systems Test Specifications, test data, and required command language files are created and comply with the testing policy.
- Ensuring that requirement changes are incorporated into the systems test design.

Change Control

Change control is a process that occurs after the System Requirements document is delivered. Its purpose is to process any requests for changes to the published System Requirements. In an ideal situation the requirements are "frozen" when they are published, so the software developers can design a system to implement these requirements. This never happens, nor should it. Although the software developers would have an easier time implementing a system from frozen requirements, the purpose of a system is to satisfy the user's requirements. When the "frozen" requirements are incomplete, so is the system. The requirements must be allowed to change in order to capture the user's needs. The change control process is the mechanism for incorporating changes to the requirements into the ongoing design.

The systems test administrator monitors the change control process to ensure that the test team is kept aware of any changes in the requirements or the design that affect the test cases. The test team should be actively involved in all reviews of the System Requirements and design. They should be informed of any changes so they can incorporate them in the systems test design and modify any test specifications already prepared.

All system changes that have been approved and will be incorporated in the current release of the system must be recorded in a document that is available to all project members. One way to record this information is in a change control log. Figure 8.3 is an example of this log.

The following is a description of each column in the change control log:

Date

This is the date the change was approved.

Type

This is the type of change. The changes can be made to the requirements, the system design, or the code. On this log the first entry is a change to requirements. The second and third entries are changes to the system design.

Incident Report

This column contains the Incident Report number when applicable. Incident Reports can be used throughout the system development life cycle. They can be used in the design and maintenance phase of the project to request changes, corrections, and enhancements to the system. The Incident Report number is listed as a cross-reference. On this log the third entry contains an Incident Report number referencing a report prepared by a user during a design review. This design change is an enhancement that was approved for implementation in this release.

By

This column identifies the department or person that requested this changed. On this log, the first entry was requested by the personnel department (identified by "Per").

Change Control Log
For Job Search System

Date	Type	Incident Report #	By	Changed Item	Summary
02/01/93	Req		Per	LST database New Screen	Add Total Dept Size Open/Dept screen
02/17/93	Desgn		MJB	Open Positions	Screen Design changed
03/17/93	Desgn	028	MJB	Highlight End Date	5 days prior to End Date

Figure 8.3. Change control log.

The second and third entries were requested by a user (identified by the initials MJB).

Changed Item

This column lists the items that change. This can be the design of a database, the layout of a screen, or the business rules in processing the information.

Summary

This column should be a brief description of what is changing. The information in this log should only be key words so that project personnel reading the log can scan for items that may affect their work. If they need further information, they can check with the project leader or the person who requested the change.

Administrating The Systems Test Execution

The execution phase of systems testing requires direction and control. The tasks include the following:

- Ensuring that the tests are executed according to the specifications
- Ensuring that the test results are verified
- Ensuring that the tests are recorded in the Activity Log
- Ensuring that the systems test documentation is updated as required
- Ensuring that the test cases that were accepted have user sign-offs
- Ensuring that the test cases that were rejected have Incident Reports filed for them
- Ensuring that the corrected software is retested properly
- Ensuring that the Incident Reports are assigned a priority and logged in the Incident Log
- Controlling the program source versions
- Reporting the status of systems testing execution to management
- Ensuring that the Systems Test Summary contains accurate and complete information
- Presenting the Systems Test Summary to management

Controlling the Program Source Versions

This task is part of the overall functions of software asset management. Software asset management is a term that describes the management procedures for software distribution, software auditing, and version control.

Software distribution is the process of distributing software products and their upgrades to the required computers. In a client/server environment, the computers may be located in multiple branches spanning several time zone. The distribution process must be fast, controlled, and documented. It should occur during non-business hours so that the upgraded system is available for the start of business. Records should be kept, listing the date and time each computer received the software or upgrade.

Software auditing is the process of recording what software is installed in each computer at each site. It should report the software products with their respective versions. The software audit not only informs management of what software the company owns and where it is installed, it also reveals any additional products the users may have installed on their computers. This information is useful in tracking requirements for computer licensing agreements and providing a measure of control in virus prevention. The unlicensed or unauthorized products can be a violation of software licensing agreements and a potential virus threat. This audit will assist the company in identifying and removing these products from the computers.

Version control is the process of tracking the software versions in each computer. Software versions must be tracked for licensed software and custom applications. Licensed software are system component products (the operating system and the network operating system) and supporting applications (word processors and spreadsheets). Custom applications are software written specifically for the company by either the in-house Information Systems department or an outside consulting firm. The software versions of all installed software must be recorded, tracked, and ideally maintained at the same level throughout the company. This information is used by the software developers, test practitioners, and Help Desk personnel in their respective functions (design, testing, and support of computing systems).

There are packages available that automate the software asset management tasks. They provide the following features:

- Distribution of the software and their upgrades
- Reports listing all computers that received the software distributions
- Reports listing all computers that did not receive the software distributions
- Reports listing the date and time each computer received the software distributions
- Reports listing the date and time any unsuccessful attempts were made to distribute the software to a computer
- Auditing of the hard drives on all computers
- Reports listing the software on each computer (the products and their respective versions)
- Reports listing the total number of installed copies of each software product
- Version control of the software
- Reports listing the programs with their version in each computing environment (development, testing, and production)

These reports provide valuable control information to the applications and operations support staff. The software distribution and version control reports would have been useful to the Help Desk on one project.

The Help Desk provided the users with support for their custom applications. One particular user would call the Help Desk periodically with the same problem. The data entry screens would reject all input. The user would enter apparently valid information and receive error messages. The Help Desk would investigate the problem and discover the user's computer did not contain the latest version of the client/server application software. They assumed this computer did not receive the latest upgrade and therefore the new data was rejected by the old version of the software. They would upgrade the software on the computer and close the incident. They did not uncover the actual cause of the problem. The software in this computer had been upgraded successfully. There were no software distribution logs listing when each computer received a software upgrade and, more importantly, which computers did not receive the upgrade. This user backed up the contents of the hard disk on a weekly basis, a commendable act. However, any time there was a problem with a file, the user restored all files from the backup. Any upgrades distributed after the backup was taken were lost. The user didn't realize the restore process caused the problem and never mentioned it to the Help Desk. The Help Desk didn't ask any questions that would reveal this. This situation would have gone undetected if a software developer had not been in the area and noticed the user restoring the entire contents of the hard drive.

Software asset management is a major concern in all computing environments. In the mainframe environment, where the software is centralized in mainframe computers, this task is the responsibility of the Information Services department. A specialized group within the IS department installs and upgrades all software. They maintain an inventory of the software products installed on each computer, verify the software versions are consistent throughout the company, and ensure that the software upgrades are compatible with the existing products.

In the client/server environment, it is not always clear which area is responsible for these tasks. When the client/server environment utilizes distributed processing, the software resides in desktop computers in multiple sites. This requires the software distribution, software auditing, and version control functions to be effectively managed. The software developers and the test team must know the software versions of all supporting software in the production environment.

The test team is also responsible for controlling the source code for the programs within the systems test environment. The software developers submit test items to the test team for systems testing. There is generally a Turnover Request form used to process this request. The test team must control the programs they receive to ensure they have the current version of each module. Items submitted for testing may be rejected and require several testing iterations before they are approved.

There are software products that control software versions and produce reports listing the programs' version number and date

					Qual/Std	Bus Req		
Source	Submitted			Moved	Test	Test		
Program	By	Date	By	Date	Date	Status	Date	Status
INV002	MJC	02/18/93	RMP	02/19/93	02/19/93	OK	02/20/93	Rej
INV003	MJC	02/18/93	RMP	02/19/93	02/19/93	OK	02/20/93	OK

Source Control Log
Inventory Control System

Figure 8.4. Source Control log.

last updated. However, the test team must manage the turnover process. One way to do this is to maintain a log. Figure 8.4 is an example of a Turnover log. The following is a description of each column on that log.

Source Program

This column identifies the source program. In this log program INV002 and INV003 were submitted to the systems test team.

Submitted

By
This column identifies the department or person that submitted the source program. On this log, the entries were submitted by a software developer identified by the initials MJC.

Date
This column is the date the program was submitted.

Moved

By
This column identifies the person who moved the source program into the systems test environment.

Date
This column is the date the move occurred.

Qual/Std Test

Date
This column is the date the quality/standard compliance testing was performed for this program.

Status
This column is the status of the testing. The program can be accepted or rejected. In Figure 8.4, the Status column contains "OK" for both entries, indicating they were accepted.

Bus Req Test

Date
This column is the date the business requirements testing was performed for this program.

Status
This column is the status of the testing. The program can be accepted or rejected. In Figure 8.4, the first entry contains "Rej," indicating the program was rejected. This program must be corrected and resubmitted. The second entry contains "OK," indicating it was accepted.

Reporting Systems Test Status

During the execution phase of systems testing, management is concerned about progress. They want to know the status of the testing and will request frequent reports on what has been tested and what has been rejected. Depending on management style and critical business function, status reports will be required weekly or daily.

Systems test administration must provide management with execution tracking reports that summarize the testing status. Graphic charts are effective presentation tools and should be used where applicable.

The reports should highlight the following:

- Percentage of testing that is complete
- Projected completion dates

- Number of Incident Reports filed
- Any hardware, network, or software problems

Figure 8.5 is an example of an execution tracking report. This report shows the total number of test cycles, the number of cycles that passed, and the number that failed. It uses a pie chart to show tested cycles as a percentage of overall test cycles.

Figure 8.6 shows the progress of the systems testing. It tracks the number of test cycles completed by days. It uses a line graph to show the planned versus actual number of test cycles completed by each test day.

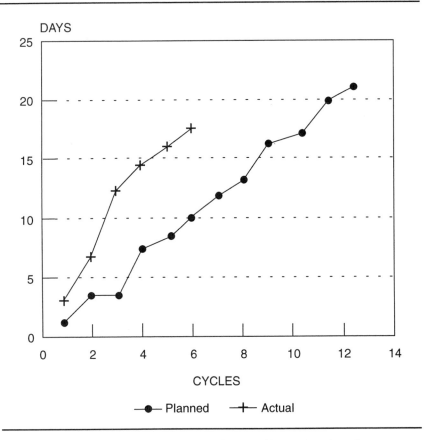

Figure 8.5.   Execution Tracking—System Progress of testing.

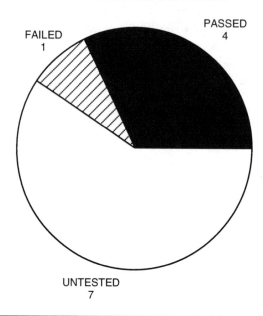

**TEST CYCLES
LEGAL BILLING SYSTEM**

Figure 8.6. Execution Tracking—Test cycles tested.

The progress of the Incident Reports has a direct bearing on the systems testing. Accordingly, management will require reports on their status. The Incident Log can be used to generate summary and statistical reports on the Incident Reports.

Figure 8.7 shows the status of the Incident Reports. It uses a bar chart to show the number of open, closed, and total Incident Reports in each priority group.

Administrating the Maintenance Phase

During the maintenance phase of systems testing, the systems test administrator should review the effectiveness of testing techniques used in the original systems testing in addition to monitoring the systems testing of the ongoing changes. The tasks for administrating the maintenance phase include the following:

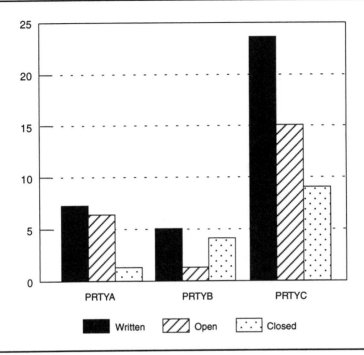

Figure 8.7.   Execution Tracking—Progress of incident reports.

- Ensuring that the Systems Test Specifications and test data are updated as systems changes are made
- Ensuring that the test cases are not rebuilt when already available
- Monitoring the testing of changes
- Monitoring the Help Desk reports
- Monitoring the emergency changes
- Monitoring configuration changes and operating system changes

Monitoring The Help Desk

This task provides feedback on the testing process. It should categorize the questions and problems handled by the Help Desk to determine whether the quality/standards compliance testing techniques are adequate. When the Help Desk receives many questions on the same feature, the test team should investigate the documentation of that feature. If the documentation itself is inadequate, they should notify management. A review of the documentation standards may be required. If the standards are adequate, they should verify the documentation compliance-testing procedures to see if any improvements can be made.

Monitoring The Emergency Changes

This task provides feedback on the testing process. It should analyze the cause for the emergency change to determine which test conditions would have tested this feature.

Monitoring Configuration Changes

The purpose of this task is to keep the test team informed of configuration changes at the production sites. It should identify the hardware and software installed at each production site. It should also identify the number of users connected to the system at each site. The test team uses this information to determine whether any modifications to the systems test environment or the performance capabilities testing are required.

SUMMARY

Systems testing carries out the testing policy established by management. It requires direction and support from management in the following areas:

- Standards and procedures
- Training programs
- Physical and technical resources
- Security, privacy, and virus prevention

Systems Testing Administration directs the following:

- The systems test environment
- The systems test design
- The systems test execution
- The maintenance phase monitoring

Sample Systems Test Documentation

This appendix contains samples of the following systems testing documentation:

- Systems Test Plan
- Systems Test Specifications
- Systems Test Summary Report
- Systems Test Activity Log
- Incident Report
- Incident Log

The sample documentation is based on a system designed for a client/server environment. The application is a Real Estate Residential Listings System. A brief description of that system precedes the sample.

REAL ESTATE RESIDENTIAL LISTING SYSTEM

This system is a sales support application using a client/server architecture. It was written by the Information Services Department—Corporate Division. They are responsible for the systems testing and installation of the system.

These are the major functions of the application:

- Maintain sales associates/broker personnel information
- Maintain open listings for residential real estate
- Search the open listings and select those that meet specified criteria
- Delete expired listings
- Transfer sold listings to the mainframe sold property database

The application will be distributed to four branch offices. Each office has multiple PC workstations on a local area network (LAN). A communication server handles access to the mainframe and the other LAN servers.

Office automation is supported with word processor, spreadsheet, calendar, and e-mail software. This is the first custom-written application to execute on the LANs. Each office will have a copy of the same application software. Each branch office will only enter and maintain information for their branch region. They can access the information in the other three branch regions. They will each have the same software, but the data will be different.

A second release of this application is scheduled for January 1994. It will add electronic document management, so photographs of the residential real estate can be stored and displayed.

Systems Test Plan for
Real Estate Residential Listings System

Preferred Properties Realty Company Inc.
Proprietary Information may not be copied or reproduced
without permission

Prepared by: **Ken Davis**
                   Cynthia Morgan

Information Services Department—Corporate Division

Date written: September 10, 1992
Modification Date: Original issue

1. IDENTIFICATION

1.1 Title

Systems Test Plan for: Real Estate Residential Listings System

1.2 Application

The Real Estate Residential Listings System is a data entry and retrieval application. It is part of the corporate Sales Support Systems used by the residential sales associates and brokers. It belongs to the Preferred Properties Realty Company Corporate Division. It was developed by the Information Services Department—Corporate Division.

It was designed using a client/server architecture. The application functions are shared between the workstations and other servers. The workstations provide data entry, system navigation, selection specification, and data display. The servers provide communications services, file services, database retrieval, and print services. The application will be distributed to four branch offices. Each office has multiple workstations connected by a local area network (LAN). The network software provides communication within and between branch offices.

This system provides the user with the following capabilities:

- Maintain (add, change, delete) the sales associate/broker personnel information.
- Maintain (add, change, delete, close) listings for residential real estate.
- Search residential listings for specific criteria and display those that meet the criteria.
- Transfer sold listings to the mainframe sold property database.
- Provide security authorizations for access to the network and within the application.

1.3 Document Locator

This document is stored on the LAN in the Information Services Department—Corporate Division. It is on the disk pack assigned to the Residential Listing System developers. It is written with word processor XYZ Release 3.3.

1.4 Other Documents

Other documents for the Real Estate Residential Listing System are stored in the same location as this document. They are all written with word processor XYZ Release 3.3.

Document	File Name
System Requirements	RELRD01.DOC
Software Inventory	RELSI01.DOC
Design Document	RELDD01.DOC

2. SYSTEMS TEST ENVIRONMENT

2.1 Site

Systems testing will be conducted on the LAN in the Corporate Division Information Services Department in Greenwich, Connecticut. The software developers also use this network. The test team will use two PC workstations on this network. This network has a communications server and a print server that will be used for systems testing. The communications server accesses the mainframe and the Greenwich Branch Office LAN. This is sufficient for this release of the system. The test cases that verify the transfer of the sold listings to the sold property database must access the mainframe. The test cases that verify the search facility must access a listing database at a remote branch office. The Greenwich Branch Office can be set up as the remote branch office. After the application is installed at the Greenwich Branch Office, the test procedures must be changed to access another remote database.

The software development tools and the testing tools are stored on the LAN and can be accessed by the test team. Any reusable objects included in this application must be available to the systems test environment. The test team moves the software to be tested to the systems test central repository. They use the same software development tools as the software developers to generate the systems test version of the application. There is a LAN license for these development tools. Only executable code will be distributed to the production sites. The production sites will not require run-time licenses.

The disk pack allocated to systems testing will store the following:

- The application source code
- Test data to load the personnel and listings databases
- Test files to load the codes databases
- Command language files to execute the testing tools
- Output from the test cycles
- Backups of the test databases after each test cycle

2.2 Security

Access to the systems test environment is restricted to the test team members. The network administrator will set up security so that the test team will be the only personnel authorized to update files on the systems test disk pack.

2.3 Submitting Test Items

Form TSS01 Systems Test Turnover is used to submit test items to the test team. This form is described in the *Systems Development Standards Manual*. It is stored in the Information Systems forms library on the "S" drive. It can be printed or copied to a personal disk. The form must be filled out and sent to the test team. It can be sent in paper format or transmitted to the test team by e-mail or fax transmission.

The test team moves the test items from their location in the development environment to the systems test central repository. The test team uses the same software tools as the developers to generate the systems test version of the application.

2.4 The Libraries and Directories

The network administrator will allocate a disk pack to the systems test team. This disk pack will be used for the central repository, the test databases, and the output from the tests.

2.5 Backup/Restore Procedure

The files on the LAN are backed up nightly. The network administrator provides the procedures to do this. In addition, the test team will back up the test databases during the execution of the test cycles.

3. OBJECTIVES AND SCOPE

3.1 Objectives of this Systems Test

The systems test verifies the Real Estate Residential Listings System performs the business requirements. It also verifies the reliability and operational capabilities of the system.

3.2 Scope of this Systems Test

Features Being Tested

The following business requirements are being tested:

- Add, change, and delete sales associate and broker Personnel information
- Reassign the open listings of a sales associate or broker who leaves the company to the Office account
- Add, change, and delete a listing
- Automatically remove expired listings
- Close a sold listing and transfer the information to the mainframe sold property database
- Search the listings and display those that satisfy the specified criteria
- Print a specified listing

Performance capabilities will be tested for adherence to the requirements specified in the System Requirements document.
The following operational capabilities will be tested:

- Restore the systems databases from a backup
- Upgrade the application software

Features not Being Tested

The initial loading of the codes database is not part of the systems test. The Transition Project is responsible for extracting the data from the mainframe files and loading it to the database. They will load the codes database for the initial installation. The codes data is static. If the data is ever updated, these same procedures will be used: the database will be initialized and loaded with the data extracted from the mainframe files.

Restrictions

The printers in the systems test environment are the same as those in the sales offices with one exception. The Darien Branch Office has an additional printer that is not available at the corporate office.

3.3 Prior Testing

The users and software developers must review the System Requirements and the supporting design.

The software developers and network administrator must review the anticipated network traffic generated by this application.

The software developers must unit test the code before submitting it to the test team.

4. APPROACH

4.1 Test Design

The users identify the business requirements and their respective test conditions. The test team creates test cases for these conditions. The test team prepares the test specifications and test data. The users and test team jointly identify and record the expected results for each test case. The test team prepares any special procedures required to verify the tests. This includes procedures to display the actual results and compare them with the expected results.

4.2 Cycles and Sequence

The business requirements are divided into test cycles. Test data is prepared so each test cycle can be tested independently. For example, the test data for the listings will contain closed listings in addition to the baseline listings required for the maintenance and query feature. This will allow the test cases that verify the transfer of closed listings to be executed independently of the tests to verify the maintenance of the listings.

4.3 Acceptance/Rejection Criteria

The expected results for each test case are described in the Systems Test Specifications document. The actual results must agree with the expected results. Designated users and test team members will serve as systems test reviewers during the execution of the tests. The users verify the user-viewed results (graphical user interfaces and reports). The test team members verify the systems results (database records, transfer files, and mainframe interfaces). If the reviewers detect a difference between the expected results and the actual results, they must fill out an Incident Report and notify the test team coordinator. The Incident Report is then submitted to the Incident Report Coordinator, who logs the report.

4.4 Suspending/Resuming the Systems Test

Systems testing will bypass any test cases that fail. The software will be sent back to the developers for changes. The test cases are reexecuted when the changed test item is resubmitted. The test data is created so that each cycle is independent. The test team can change command language files, control data, testing tool procedures, and test data. However, any changes to the application code must be returned to the software developers.

4.5 Reporting Changes and Corrections

Any changes or corrections to the application must be reported using form SYSD05, Systems Incident Report. This form is stored in the Information Systems forms library on the "S" drive. The form can be printed from this library or copied onto a personal library. The form must be filled out and sent to the test team. It can be submitted in paper format, sent with e-mail, or transmitted by fax. This form is described in the *Systems Development Stan-*

dards Manual. Incident Reports are tracked and reported using the Incident Log. The log is a spreadsheet that lists information on all Incident Reports (their Incident Report number, a brief description of the incident, and their status). The Incident Log is described in the *Systems Development Standards Manual.*

4.6 Support

The systems test reviewers must be available during the execution of the systems tests to verify the test cases. The software developers must be available to change or correct any software as noted by the systems test reviewers.

4.7 Levels

Systems testing will be conducted in two levels. The first level tests the business requirements including security and the operational capabilities of the system. This level uses controlled test data and verifies functionality. The second level tests the system's performance. It uses fully loaded databases and measures performance capabilities.

5. STAFFING

5.1 Systems Test Responsibilities

Systems Test Team
- Obtain security access for the network.
- Maintain the systems test disk space.
- Maintain a systems test central repository for source code.
- Migrate test items to the systems test environment.
- Obtain or write backup and restore procedures for snapshot images.
- Ensure backup and restore facilities are available when needed for the systems test environment.
- Maintain the status of test items—submitted, accepted, rejected, not available.
- Create test specifications and test data.
- Prepare expected results.
- Determine the testing tools required.

- Evaluate testing tools available.
- Install testing tools and prepare any command language files and data required for them.
- Write utilities, command language files, and queries to assist systems test reviewers to verify the actual results.
- Coordinate the execution of the systems test.
- Maintain an Activity Log for the execution phase.
- Ensure that all test cases are verified and reported.
- Document the status of the testing.
- Prepare a Summary Report for management.

Systems Test Reviewers

- Review the actual results of each test case.
- Compare the actual results with the expected results described in the Systems Test Specifications.
- Identify and report any exceptions.
- Submit an Incident Report on each exception.

Software Development Team

- Submit unit-tested items to test team with form TSS01 Systems Test Turnover.
- Analyze Incident Reports to determine the cause of the problem.
- Determine software changes required to resolve Incident Reports and change accordingly.
- Support the test team during the execution phase.

Project Leader

- Coordinate systems testing.
- Ensure proper security is maintained for the systems test environment.
- Ensure availability of the network for the systems test execution.
- Ensure availability of the hardware for the systems test execution.
- Review and approve any requests for testing tools.
- Assign priorities to Incident Reports.
- Ensure Incident Reports are logged.

- Track the progress of Incident Reports.
- Ensure that the software and the software changes are completed on schedule.
- Ensure that the software submitted meets quality and standards requirements.

Incident Report Coordinator

- Log Incident Reports.
- Update the Incident Reports as their status changes.
- Provide reports to management on the Incident Reports.

5.2 Systems Test Assignment List

The personnel assignments for the initial systems test follows.

Systems Test Team

Cynthia Morgan—Information Services Department—September 10, 1992

Systems Review Team

Peter Mason—Sales Department—September 10, 1992
TBN another user—Sales Department by October 31, 1992

Software Development Team

Mary Ferrer—Information Services Department—September 10, 1992

Ken Davis—Information Services Department—September 10, 1992

Project Leader

Barbara Harris—Information Services Department—September 10, 1992

Incident Report Coordinator

Susan Cannon—Information Services Department—September 12, 1992

6. HARDWARE, SOFTWARE, AND NETWORK REQUIREMENTS

The hardware, software, and network requirements for systems testing are the same as those for the production environment. See the Real Estate Residential Listings System Architecture document RELAD01 for the mainframe and sales offices configurations.

7. TESTING TOOLS

7.1 Testing Tools Evaluated

Source:	Market
Product:	AAA Capture and Replay
Release:	3.1
Vendor:	ZZZ Systems Group
Description:	This product captures online input (including keystrokes and mouse clicks) and stores them in a file for replay later.
Price:	$$$$ per single users. LAN and site prices higher.
Licensing Agreements:	The product can be purchased with either a single machine, LAN, or site license.
Date Investigated:	May 1992
Decision:	Not selected
Reason:	Management wants to wait until other projects begin development. The tools will be reevaluated at that time, so any products selected would also meet their needs.

Source:	In-house
Product:	DB Select
Release:	Not applicable
Vendor/Author:	Sales MIS Project
Description:	Selects specified records and prints or displays them.
Price:	Not applicable. It is available to all corporate projects.
Date	

Investigated: April 1992
Decision: Selected
Reason: The test team is familiar with its use. It has
                 excellent documentation and meets our needs.

7.2 Testing Tools being used

DB Select : In-house product

Documentation is available in the systems library. The test team must write command language files to execute the product for the systems test databases. It verifies the database updates performed by the test cases.

Fast Backup / Restore - Market product

Documentation is available in the system library. Procedures to execute the product are available on the system library. It backs up the mainframe sold property database.

File Formatter - To be written by the test team.

This testing tool will execute on the mainframe. It reformats input data into a Sold Listings transfer file. This file can be used to test the mainframe test cycle independently. It will be written using existing objects. The code, documentation, and execution procedures will be stored in the systems test environment.

8. SYSTEMS TEST DELIVERABLES

The following are the deliverables for the design phase:

- Systems Test Specifications
- Test data
- Expected results
- Command language files to confirm the actual results

The following are the deliverables for the execution phase:

- Systems-tested software
- Actual results
- Systems Test Activity Log

- Incident Reports generated during the execution
- Incident Log
- Systems Test Summary Report

The Systems Test Specifications is a document that specifies the tests to be executed. It contains a description of the test cases, the expected results, and instructions to perform the tests and verify the results.

The test data are files that contain the data required by the test cases. The files are used as input to procedures that either load the systems test databases or create input transactions.

The Expected Results are files that contain the expected outputs. The files can contain reports or images of updated databases. They can be used as input to a program that compares expected and actual results.

The command language files execute programs or queries that assist the reviewers in verifying the actual results of the tests.

The systems-tested software refers to the source code submitted by the developers and stored in the systems test central repository.

The actual results are files that contain the actual outputs. The files can contain reports or images of the updated databases.

The Systems Test Activity Log is a document that contains a record of the details of each test case execution.

The Incident Reports are forms. They are used by the reviewers to report any inconsistencies or omissions in the actual results of the tests.

The Incident Log is a spreadsheet used to track the status of Incident Reports.

The Summary Report is a document that contains a summary of the results of the systems test.

9. SYSTEMS TEST TASKS

The Project Management directory contains a complete list of the tasks for this project. The systems testing tasks are included in that list. The list is updated weekly with the status of each task. It contains the scheduled and actual completion dates of each task with the persons assigned to the task.

The following list is only the tasks that must be accomplished in the remaining phases of systems testing.

1. Identify test conditions for each systems testing objective.
2. Create test cases for each test condition.
3. Prepare test data for each test case.
4. Determine expected results for each test case.
5. Prepare test procedures to execute each test case.
6. Divide testing into test cycles and determine their execution sequence.
7. Document all test cases in the Systems Test Specifications document.
8. Schedule a formal review of the Systems Test Specifications.
9. Review the Systems Test Specifications in a review session.
10. Modify the Systems Test Specifications as required by the findings of the review.
11. Generate test data.
12. Write any utilities or command language files required to load the test data.
13. Write any utilities or command language files required to execute the test cases and review actual results.
14. Write any utilities or command language files required to verify the actual results of the tests (file compares, unloads, reports, queries).
15. Write any utilities or command language files required to back up and restore the test databases.
16. Test all utilities and command language files written for this systems test.
17. Verify the delivery schedule of software to be tested with software developers.
18. Revise test cycle sequences and schedule as required by revised software delivery dates.
19. Create any data files required to simulate input for a test cycle.
20. Obtain disk space or tapes required to save actual results.
21. Obtain network logon Ids for all systems test reviewers.
22. Verify that logon Ids have been set up and work properly.
23. Load test databases with baseline data.
24. Load security and code tables with test data.

25. Initialize data files with any control information required.
26. Arrange systems test execution schedule with network administrator and other departments.
27. Order or arrange for extra stock paper for the systems testing reports.
28. Make special arrangements for access to physical premises after normal business hours.
29. Make any special arrangements required for physical premise facilities (arrange for heat or air conditioning to be turned on during the off-hours testing periods).
30. Verify that all test items required for systems testing have been submitted to the test team.
31. Move application software to systems test environment and prepare it for execution.
32. Set up Activity Log document.
33. Review procedures for entering information into Activity Log with all test team participants.
34. Designate a systems test coordinator for each shift during the execution of the systems testing. This person is responsible for logging all test cases in the Activity Log.
35. Conduct quality/standards compliance testing.
36. Retest any items that were rejected in the quality/standards compliance testing.
37. Schedule and conduct a systems test execution announcement meeting.
38. Resolve any issues uncovered in the announcement meeting.
39. Conduct systems testing for business requirements and operational capabilities test cycles.
40. Verify actual results.
41. Resolve any critical Incident Reports generated during systems testing.
42. Conduct performance capabilities testing.
43. Resolve Incident Reports generated during systems testing.
44. Repeat tests until all required Incident Reports have been resolved.
45. Write Summary Report for management.
46. Modify any systems testing methods and procedures that were inadequate.

47. Modify any systems test cases that were incorrect or inadequate.
48. Update the Systems Test Specifications accordingly.
49. Turn over systems test deliverables to management.
50. Prepare for the maintenance phase of systems testing.

SYSTEMS TEST SPECIFICATIONS FOR REAL ESTATE RESIDENTIAL LISTINGS SYSTEM

Contents

1. IDENTIFICATION

Systems Test Specifications for: Real Estate Residential Listings System

1.1 Prepared by:

Ken Davis—Information Services Department
Cynthia Morgan—Information Services Department

1.2 Date written: October 14, 1992

1.3 Modification Date: Original issue

1.4 Document Locator:

This document is stored on the LAN in the Information Services Department—Corporate Division. It is on the disk pack assigned to the Real Estate Residential Listings System development project. It is written with word processor XYZ Release 3.3.

1.5 Other Documents

Other documents for the Real Estate Residential Listings System are stored in the same location as this document. They are all written with word processor XYZ Release 3.3.

Document	File Name
System Requirements	RELRD01.DOC
Software Inventory	RELSI01.DOC
Design Document	RELDD01.DOC
Systems Test Plan	RELTP01.DOC

2. TEST CYCLES

2.1 Test Cycle Descriptions

The following list contains the name and description of the test cycles for the systems test.

Cycle Number	Name	Description
1	Maintain Personnel	Add, change, and delete the sales associate and broker personnel information in the personnel database.
2	Maintain Listings	Add, change, and delete the residential listing information in the listings database.
3	Search Listings	Display listings that meet specified criteria.
4	Delete Expired Listings	Notify listing agents of expired listings.

		Automatically delete expired listings.
5	Close Sold Listings	Change status of listing to sold. Enter sold price and sold date. Listings are migrated to sold property database.
6	Measure System Performance	Volume data is entered into the network for a combination of transactions. Response time is measured.
7	Verify Operational Procedures	Restore databases. Upgrade software.

2.2 Test Cycle Sequence

The following list contains the sequence of execution of the test cycles. The sequence ensures the output from prior cycles can be used in subsequent cycles. Test cycles with the same sequence number can be executed concurrently.

Sequence	Cycle Number	Name
01	1	Maintain Personnel
02	2	Maintain Listings
03	3	Search Listings
03	4	Delete Expired Listings
03	5	Close Sold Listings
05	6	Measure Performance
04	7	Verify Operational Procedures

2.3 Test Cycle Procedures and Expected Results

The following is the test procedure for one of the test cycles in this system, Test Cycle 2 Maintain Listing.

2.3.2 Test Cycle 2 : Maintain Listings Test Procedures and Expected Results

1. Log-on to the systems test environment using the identifier and password assigned to you.
2. Execute INCY2.BAT
   This procedure restores the databases to the state after Test Cycle 1 has completed. The files being restored are either the backups taken after Test Cycle 1 was executed or the files prepared by the test team to initialize this cycle.
3. Log the restore in the Systems Test Activity Log.
4. Execute the test cases for Test Cycle 2 Maintain Listings.
   The test cases are listed in the test case/test cycle matrix. Each test case is described in the Business Requirements Section, Subsection 3.2—Maintain Listings. It contains the Test Condition—Test Cases and the Test Procedures and Expected Results for each test case that will be executed in this cycle. The test cases should be executed in the order listed in the matrix.
5. Log the results of each test case in the Systems Test Activity Log. Prepare an Incident Report for any items that fail the test or require investigation.
6. Execute TT001.BAT.
   This procedure prints the contents of the databases at the end of Test Cycle 2. It produces a report for each database, listing all records in the databases in ASCII format.
7. Execute TT003.BAT.
   The expected results were created as a file. This procedure executes a testing tool that prints the expected results.
8. Execute TT002.BAT.
   This procedure executes a testing tool that compares the actual results with the expected results and prints a report with any differences. The systems analyst assigned to reviewing this test cycle should assist in verifying the output of this step. An Incident Report should be prepared to report any differences in the files.
9. Log the verification in the Systems Test Activity Log.
10. Execute BKCY2.BAT
    This procedure backs up the databases after Test Cycle 2 test cases are completed.
11. Log the back up in the Systems Test Activity Log.

3. BUSINESS REQUIREMENTS

The systems test verifies the following business requirements:

1. Maintain Personnel
2. Maintain Listings
3. Search Listings
4. Delete Expired Listings
5. Close Sold Listings

3.1

The Test Conditions—Test Cases and Test and Test Procedures—Expected Results section for the Maintain Listing requirements are included. There is one section for the following functions within this requirement:

- Add a listing
- Change a listing
- Delete a Listing

3.2 Maintain Listings

3.2.1 Add a Listing

3.2.1.1 Test Conditions—Test Cases

1. Is the signed-on user either the listing sales associate or the office administrator?
   These are the only types of users with authority to add a listing. Sales associates can add only their own listings. The Office Administrator can add any listing.
2. Is the sales associate for this listing an active staff member of the company?
   Sales associates must be active to have their listings entered in the database.
3. Is the sales associate a member of the Multiple Listing Service (MLS) that will list the property?
   The sales associate is required to be a member of the MLS that lists the property.

2-001 Add a Listing

	1	2	3	4
1. Is the signed-on user the listing sales associate?	Y	Y	Y	N
2. Is the sales associate's personnel status active?	Y	Y	N	Y
3. Is the sales associate a member of the respective MLS?	Y	N	Y	Y

	1	2	3	4
Add listing	X			
Don't add listing		X	X	
Go to Table 2-002				X

Figure A.1. Add a Listing Decision Table 2-001.

2-002 Add Listing—entered by Office Administrator

	1	2	3	4
1. Is the signed-on user the office administrator?	Y	Y	Y	N
2. Is the sales associate's personnel status active?	Y	Y	N	Y
3. Is the sales associate a member of the respective MLS?	Y	N	Y	Y

	1	2	3	4
Add listing	X			
Don't add Listing		X	X	X

Figure A.2. Add a Listing Decision Table 2-002.

Test Cases

2-001-1	The signed-on user is the listing sales associate 001, whose personnel status is active and is a member of the MLS for area 01.	Listing No. G1004 is added for sales associate 001
2-001-2	The signed-on user is the listing sales associate 002 whose personnel status is active but is not a member of the MLS for area 01.	Listing No. G1001 not added for sales associate 002.
2-001-3	The signed-on user is the listing sales associate 003 who is a member of the MLS for Area 01 but does not have a personnel status of active.	Listing No. G3002 not added for sales associate 003.
2-001-4	The signed-on user is the office administrator.	See 2-002-1.
2-002-1	The signed-on user is the office administrator. The listing sales associate 001 has a personnel status of active and is a member of the MLS for area 01.	List No. G1002 for sales associate 001 is added.
2-002-2	The signed-on user is the office administrator. The listing sales associate 002 has a personnel status of active but is not a member of MLS for area 01.	Listing No. G1001 not added for sales associate 002.
2-002-3	The signed-on user is the office administrator. The listing sales associate 003 is a member of the MLS for area 01 but does not have a personnel status of active.	Listing No. G3002 not added for sales associate 003.
2-002-4	The signed-on user is sales associate 005. The listing sales associate is 001 whose personnel status is active and is a member of the MLS for area 01.	Listing No. G1003 not added.

3.2.1.2 *Test Procedures and Expected Results*

Test Case: 2-001-1 Add a listing

1. Log on to the systems test environment and access the Real Estate Residential Listings System with the log-on Id for sales associate 001.
2. Select Maintain Listing option from the menu bar.
3. Type Listing No. G1004 in Listing No. field that appears in the dialogue box. Leave default MLS as area 01.
4. A listing screen should appear with only Listing No. G1004 and Listing Agent 001 filled in. Enter the following information:

LISTING NO:	G1004	START DT:	July 15, 1992
LISTING AGENT:	001	EXPIRATION DT:	Oct 15, 1992
STATUS:	Open	PRICE:	269,900
CONT/CLOSE DT:		DT PRICE CHG:	
PROPERTY TYPE:	Single-Family	STYLE:	Raised Ranch
ADDRESS:	125 Maple Avenue	YR BUILT:	1978
TAXES		HEAT:	

BR:4 BATH:3 GAR:2 LR:1 DR:1 FR:1 EIK:1 FP:1 AC: POOL: SCHOOL D:

B OPEN HOUSE DT:

REMARKS:

SOLD PRICE: SOLD DT:

Figure A.3.   Listing Screen—Add Listing G1004.

5. Listing should be added.
6. Log Test Case 2-001-1 in the Systems Test Activity Log.
7. Log off the Real Estate Residential Listings System.

Test Case: 2-001-2 Add a listing

1. Log on to the systems test environment and access the Real Estate Residential Listings System with the log-on Id for sales associate 002.
2. Select Maintain Listing option from the menu bar.
3. Enter Listing G1001 in the Listing No. Field in the dialogue box. Leave default MLS as area 01.
4. Error message should appear stating sales associate 002 is not a member of MLS area 01.
5. Log Test Case 2-001-2 in the Systems Test Activity Log.
6. Log off the Real Estate Residential Listings System.

Test Case: 2-001-3 Add a listing

1. Log on to the systems test environment and access the Real Estate Residential Listings System with the log-on Id for sales associate 003.
2. Select Maintain Listing option from the menu bar.
3. Enter Listing G1001 in the Listing No. Field in the dialogue box. Leave default MLS as area 01.
4. An error message should appear stating sales associate 003 is not an active staff member.
5. Log Test Case 2-001-3 in the Systems Test Activity Log.
6. Log off the Real Estate Residential Listings System.

Test Case: 2-002-1 Add a listing

1. Log on to the systems test environment and access the Real Estate Residential Listings System with the log-on Id for the office administrator.
2. Select Maintain Listing option from the menu bar.
3. Enter Listing G1002 in the Listing No. field in the dialogue box. Leave default MLS as area 01.
4. A Listing screen should appear with only Listing No. G1002 and no Listing Agent filled in.

Enter the following information:

LISTING NO:	G1002	START DT:	Aug. 15, 1992
LISTING AGENT:	001	EXPIRATION DT:	Nov. 15, 1992
STATUS:	Open	PRICE:	189,900
CONT/CLOSE DT:		DT PRICE CHG:	
PROPERTY TYPE:	Single-Family	STYLE:	Raised Ranch
ADDRESS:	29 Oak Place	YR BUILT:	1968
TAXES		HEAT:	

BR:3 BATH:1.5 GAR:2 LR:1 DR:1 FR:1 EIK:1 FP: AC: POOL: SCHOOL D: Rox.
B OPEN HOUSE DT:

REMARKS:

SOLD PRICE: SOLD DT:

Figure A.4.   Listing Screen—Add Listing G1002.

5. Listing should be added.
6. Log Test Case 2-002-1 in the Systems Test Activity Log.

Test Case : 2-002-2 Add a listing

You are still logged on to the Residential Listings System as the office administrator.

7. Select Maintain Listing option from the menu bar.
8. Enter Listing G1001 in the Listing No. Field in the dialogue box. Leave default MLS as area 01.
9. A Listing screen should appear with only Listing No. G1001 and no listing agent filled in.
10. Enter the Listing Agent as 002
An error message should appear stating sales associate 002 is not a member of MLS for area 01.
11. Log Test Case 2-002-2 in the Systems Test Activity Log.

Test Case : 2-002-3 Add a listing

12. Enter the Listing Agent as 003
An error message should appear stating sales associate 003 is not an active staff member.
13. Log Test Case 2-002-3 in the Systems Test Activity Log. Log off the Real Estate Residential Listings System.

Test Case : 2-002-4 Add a listing

1. Log on to the systems test environment and access the Real Estate Residential Listings System with the log-on Id for sales associate 005.
2. Select Maintain Listing option from the menu bar.
3. Enter G1003 in the Listing No. field in the dialogue box. Leave default MLS as area 01.
4. A Listing data entry screen displays with listing agent as 005.
5. Attempt to override the listing agent to another agent. The system should prohibit this from happening. Do not complete the data entry process.
6. Log Test Case 2-002-4 in the Systems Test Activity Log.
7. Log off the Real Estate Residential Listings System.

3.2.2 Change a Listing

3.2.2.1 Test Conditions—Test Cases

1. Is the signed-on user either the listing sales associate or the office administrator?
   These are the only users with authority to change a listing. Sales associates can only change their own listings. The office administrator can change any listing.
2. Is the status of the listing other than closed (open, binder, or contract)?
   A closed listing cannot be changed by this function.
3. Does the listing agent have a personnel status of active?
   Only active staff members can add or change listings.
4. Is the listing agent a member of the respective MLS?
   Only listing agents who are members of the respective MLS can add or change listings on the MLS.
5. Is the new price > $0?
   A listing price must be greater than $0.
6. For listing that is changed to a closed status
   Is the sold price > $0?
   Is the sold date > listing start date?

   When the listing status is changed to closed, sold price and sold date must be entered and validated.

Test Cases

2-3-01	Sales associate 001 changes own listing, Listing No. G1004 which is under contract.	Listing agent 001 changes Listing No. G1004
2-3-02	Sales associate cannot change a closed listing.	Listing agent 001 cannot change closed Listing No. G1001.
2-3-03	Office administrator changes Listing No. G1002. Change the listing agent to 004.	Listing agent is changed on Listing No. G1002.
2-3-04	Office administrator cannot change listing agent on Listing No. G1005 to Listing agent 003 who is not a member of MLS.	Listing No. G1005 not changed.
2-3-05	Office administrator cannot change listing agent on Listing No. G1005 to Listing Agent 002 who is not an active personnel	Listing No. G1005 not changed.
2-3-06	Office administrator cannot change closed Listing No. G1001	Listing No. G1001 not changed.
2-3-07	Sales associate can change price on Listing No. G3002.	Listing No. G3002 changed.
2-3-08	Sales associate cannot change price on Listing No. G1005 to $0.	Listing No. G1005 not changed.
2-3-09	Sales associate cannot change Listing No. G1001; Status is Closed.	Listing No. G1001 not changed.
2-3-10	Sales associate cannot change Listing No. G1005 to Status of Closed; Sold Price = $0.	Listing No. G1005 not changed.
2-3-11	Sales associate cannot change Listing No. G1005 to Status of Closed; Sold Date less than Listing Start Date.	Listing No. G1005 not changed.

2-003 Change a Listing

	1	2	3
1. Is the signed-on user the listing sales associate?	Y	Y	N
2. Is the listing status not = closed?	Y	N	Y

Go to 2-005 Validate	X		
Go to 2-004 Office Administrator			X
Reject		X	

2-004 Change Listing—Office Administrator

	1	2	3	4	5
3. Is the signed-on user the office administrator?	Y	Y	Y	Y	N
4. Is the listing status not = closed?	Y	Y	Y	N	Y
5. Does the listing agent have a personnel status of active?	Y	Y	N	Y	Y
6. Is the listing agent a member of the respective MLS?	Y	N	Y	Y	Y

Go to 2-005 Validate	X				
Reject		X	X	X	X

2-005 Change Listing—Validate

	1	2	3
7. Is the price > $0?	Y	Y	N
8. Is the changed status = closed?	Y	N	Y

Go to 2-006 Close	X		
Change Listing		X	
Reject			X

Figure A.5.   Change Listing Decision Tables 2-003.

2-006 Change Listing—Close

	1	2	3	4
9. Is the sold price > $0	Y	Y	N	
10. Is the sold date > listing start date?	Y	N	Y	
Change Listing	X			
Reject		X	X	

Figure A.6.   Change Listing Decision Table 2-006.

3.2.2.2 *Test Procedures and Expected Results*

Test Case: 2-3-01 Change Listing by Sales Associate

1. Log on to the systems test environment and access the Real Estate Residential Listings System with the log-on Id for Sales associate 001. This test case requires the user to be signed on as a sales associate.
2. Select Maintain Listing option from the menu bar.
3. Select Listing No. G1004 from the list which appears in the dialogue box.
   The listing should display with the information shown in Figure A.7.

```
LISTING NO:        G1004                START DT:        July 15, 1992
LISTING AGENT:     001                  EXPIRATION DT:   Oct 15, 1992
STATUS:            Contract Signed      PRICE:           259,900
CONT/CLOSE DT:     Oct 10, 1992         DT PRICE CHG:    Aug 15, 1992
PROPERTY TYPE:     Single-Family        STYLE:           Raised Ranch
ADDRESS:           125 Maple Avenue     YR BUILT:        1978
TAXES                                   HEAT:
BR:4 BATH:3 GAR:2 LR:1 DR:1 FR:1 EIK:1 FP:1 AC: POOL: SCHOOL D:
B OPEN HOUSE DT:
REMARKS:
SOLD PRICE:                             SOLD DT:
```

Figure A.7.   Listing Screen—Maintain Listing G1004.

4. Change the Status to Closed, enter Sold Price of $245,000 and Sold Date of October 10, 1992.
5. Change should be accepted and the Listing should be updated.
6. Log the test case in the Systems Test Activity Log.

3.2.3 *Delete a Listing*

3.2.3.1 Test Conditions—Test Cases

1. Is the signed-on user the office administrator?
   The office administrator is the only user authorized to delete a listing.
2. Is the status of the listing open?
   Only listings with an open status can be deleted by this function.

2-007 Delete a Listing

	1	2	3
1. Is the signed-on user the office administrator?	Y	Y	N
2. Is the listing status = open?	Y	N	Y
Delete Listing	X		
Don't Delete Listing		X	X

Figure A.8.   Delete a Listing Decision Table 2-007.

Test Cases

2-4-01	Office administrator is signed on. Listing No. G1009 Status is Open.	Listing No. G1009 is deleted.
2-4-02	Office administrator is signed on. Listing No. G1003 Status is Contract.	Listing No. G1003 not deleted.
2-4-03	Sales Associate 001 is signed on.	Listing No. G3003 is not deleted.

3.2.3.2 Test Procedures and Expected Results

Test Case : 2-4-01 Delete a Listing

1. Log on to the systems test environment and access the Real Estate Residential Listings System with the log-on Id for the office administrator.
2. Select Maintain Listing option from the menu bar.
3. Select Listing No. G1009 from the list that appears in the dialogue box.
4. Select the Delete button in the dialogue box.
5. Delete should be accepted and the Listing No. should disappear from the list.
6. Log the test case in the Systems Test Activity Log.
   Do not log off. Continue with Test Case 2-4-02 signed on as the office administrator.

Test Case: 2-4-02 Delete a listing

7. Select Maintain Listing option from the menu bar.
8. Select Listing No. G1003 from the list that appears in the dialogue box.
9. The Delete button should not be accessible.
   This listing is under contact, and therefore can't be deleted.
10. Log the test case in the Systems Test Activity Log.
11. Log off the Real Estate Residential Listings System as the office administrator.

Test Case: 2-4-03 Delete a listing

1. Log on to the systems test environment and access the Real Estate Residential Listings System with the log-on Id for sales associate 001.
2. Select Maintain Listing option from the menu bar.
3. Select Listing No. G3003 from the list that appears in the dialogue box.
4. The Delete button should not be accessible.
   A sales associate cannot delete listings.
5. Log the test case in the Systems Test Activity Log.
6. Log off the Real Estate Residential Listings System.

4. PERFORMANCE CAPABILITIES

The systems test verifies the following performance capabilities:

Perform business functions within response times specified in System Requirements document with volume transactions.

4.1 Test Conditions

The test conditions for the performance capabilities of the system would be described in this section.

4.2 Test Procedures and Expected Results

The test procedures and expected results for each test case that verifies the performance capabilities of the system would be described in this section.

5. OPERATIONAL CAPABILITIES

The systems test verifies the following operational capabilities:

Perform database backup and restore procedures.
Upgrade system software.

5.1.1 Back Up and Restore Databases

5.1.1.1 Test Conditions

1. Do operational procedures exist for backing up and restoring the databases for each site?
2. Are those operational procedures complete, accurate, and in compliance with the guidelines in the *Standards Manual*?
3. Can the operations staff use the procedures without any assistance from the software developers?
4. Can the databases be restored from a backup file?

5.1.2 Test Procedures and Expected Results

1. Verify that operational procedures exist to back up and restore the databases for each site.
   If not, the procedure fails the test case.

7-101 Back Up / Restore Databases

	1	2	3	4	5
1.1 Do operational procedures exist to back up and restore database for each site?	Y	Y	Y	Y	N
1.2 Are the operational procedures complete, accurate, and in compliance with the guidelines in the *Standards Manual*?	Y	Y	Y	N	
1.3 Can the operations staff use those procedures without any assistance from the software developers?	Y	Y	N		
1.4 Can the databases be restored from backup files?	Y	N			
Approve Procedures	X				
Reject Procedures		X	X	X	X

Figure A.9.   Back Up/Restore Database Decision Table.

2. Verify operational procedures are complete and comply with standards.
   If not, the procedure fails the test case.
3. Observe operations staff as they back up the files.
   If procedures do not execute properly, they fail the test case.
4. Observe operations staff as they restore the files.
   If procedures do not execute properly, they fail the test case.
5. Verify restored files are accessible by executing TSPRT.BAT.
   Database records should print accurately.
6. Log test case in Systems Test Activity Log.

5.2 Upgrade System Software

5.2.1 *Test Conditions*

1. Do operational procedures exist for upgrading system software?

7-102 Upgrade System Software

		1	2	3	4	5
1.1	Do operational procedures exist to upgrade system software?	Y	Y	Y	Y	N
1.2	Are the operational procedures complete, accurate, and in compliance with the guidelines in the Standards Manual?	Y	Y	Y	N	
1.3	Can the operations staff use those procedures without any assistance from the software developers?	Y	Y	N		
1.4	Can the system software be upgraded using these procedures?	Y	N			

Approve Procedures	X				
Reject Procedures		X	X	X	X

Figure A.10.   Upgrade System Software Decision Table.

2.   Are those operational procedures complete, accurate, and in compliance with the guidelines in the *Standards Manual*?
3.   Can the operations staff use the procedures without any assistance from the software developers?
4.   Can the system software be upgraded using these procedures?

5.2.2 *Test Procedures and Expected Results*

1.   Verify that operational procedures exist to upgrade system software.
     If not, the procedures fail the test case.
2.   Verify operational procedures are complete and comply with standards.
     If not, the procedures fail the test case.
3.   Observe operations staff as they perform procedures.
     If procedures do not execute properly, they fail the test case.

4. Verify upgraded software by logging on to system.
   System should be accessible.
5. Log test case in Systems Test Activity Log.

6. BASELINE DATA

This section lists the baseline data in each database. The baseline data must be loaded into its respective database before the systems test cases can be executed.

The following procedures are used in processing the baseline data.

1. LOADST.BAT loads the databases from the baseline data files. This procedure must be executed prior to the execution phase of systems testing.
2. STPRTBD.BAT prints the contents of the baseline file in ASCII format.
3. TSPRTDB.BAT prints the contents of the databases in ASCII format.

6.1 Personnel Database

Personnel No.	001	002	003
Last Name	Griffin	Elliot	Simon
First name	Jane	Diane	Lenore
M.I.		M.	
R.E. License No.	S23000	B12000	S24000
Branch Office	G	G	G
MLS Branch G	Y	Y	Y
MLS Branch S			
MLS Branch D		Y	
MLS Branch W			
Home Phone No.	555-9999	555-7777	555-4444

Figure A.11. Personnel Database Test Data.

6.2 Listings Database

The contents of the listings database can be printed by running LSTPRT from the systems test environment /STDATA directory. This procedure executes a utility that prints all information in the test listing database. The information in this database has changed several times during the design phase, and thus it was decided to not include a copy of this document. The LSTPRT procedure should be used. It will create a report that is current and accurate.

6.3 Codes Database

The codes database is maintained by the Transition Project. The contents of that database can by accessed by running TRANCD from the /TRANS directory.

6.4 Security Database

This file contains the log-on Ids and passwords for the personnel used in the systems test environment for the test cases. See the test team coordinator for information on this file. It is not listed in this document. This is a general distribution document and the contents of this database are restricted.

7. CROSS-REFERENCES

7.1 File Location

File Location	
File Name	**Location**
Command Language Files	
RETC01.BAT	All command files
RETC02.BAT	are stored on
RETC03.BAT	S:\REALE\SYSTST\BAT\
RETC04.BAT	
RETC05.BAT	
RETC06.BAT	
RETC07.BAT	
Test Data Files	
REDTPER.DAT	All test data files are
REDTLST.DAT	stored on
REDTSEC.DAT	S:\REALE\SYSTST\TSD
REDTCLS.DAT	
Expected Results Files	
REER01C.DAT	All expected results
REER02X.DAT	files are stored on
REER03X.DAT	S:\REALE\SYSTST\EXPCT
REER04X.DAT	
Actual Results Files	
	All actual results files are
	stored on S:\REALE\SYSTST\ACT
Backup Files	
REBKINIT.BAT	All backup files are stored
REBK01.BAT	on S:\REALE\SYSTST\BKUP\
REBK02.BAT	

7.2 Test Case/Requirements Matrix

	TEST CASE/REQUIREMENTS MATRIX				
	REQUIREMENT				
	1	2	3	4	5
TEST CASE	PER	LSTG	SRCH	DEL	CLSE
1-001-01	X				
1-001-02	X				
1-002-01	X				
1-002-02	X				
1-003-01	X				
1-003-02	X				
1-003-03	X				
2-001-01		X			
2-001-02		X			
2-001-03		X			
2-002-01		X			
2-002-02		X			
2-002-03		X			
2-002-04		X			
2-003-01		X			
2-003-02		X			
2-003-03		X			
2-003-04		X			
. . . . .					
3-001-01			X		
3-001-02			X		
3-001-03			X		
4-001-01				X	
4-001-02				X	
4-001-03				X	
5-001-01					X
5-001-02					X
5-001-03					X

Figure A.12. Test case/Requirements Matrix.

7.3 Test Case/Database Matrix

TEST CASE	PERS	LIST	DATABASES CODES	SEC	SOLD
1-001-01	I		R	R	
1-001-02	R		R	R	
1-002-01	U		R	R	
1-002-02	R		R	R	
1-003-01	D	R	R	R	
1-003-02	R		R	R	
1-003-03	D	U	R	R	
2-001-01	R	I	R	R	
2-001-02	R	R	R	R	
2-001-03	R	R	R	R	
2-001-04	R	R		R	
2-002-01	R	I	R	R	
2-002-02	R	R		R	
2-002-03	R	R		R	
2-002-04	R	R	R	R	
2-003-01	R	U	R	R	
2-003-02	R	R	R	R	
2-003-03	R	R		R	
2-004-01		D		R	
2-004-02		R		R	
3-001-01		R			
3-001-02		R			
3-001-03		R			
3-001-04		R			
3-001-05		R			
3-001-06		R	R		
4-001-01		R			
4-002-01		D			
5-001-01		D			I
5-001-02		D			I
5-001-03		R			

Figure A.13. Test case/Database Matrix.

7.4 Test Case/Test Cycle Matrix

TEST CASE/TEST CYCLE MATRIX

TEST CASE	TEST CYCLE						
	1	2	3	4	5	6	7
1-001-01	X					X	
1-001-02	X					X	
1-002-01	X					X	
1-002-02	X					X	
1-003-01	X					X	
1-003-02	X					X	
1-003-03	X					X	
2-001-01		X				X	
2-001-02		X				X	
2-001-03		X				X	
2-001-04		X				X	
2-002-01		X				X	
2-002-02		X				X	
2-002-03		X				X	
. . . .							
3-001-01			X			X	
3-001-02			X			X	
3-001-03			X			X	
3-001-04			X			X	
3-001-05			X			X	
3-001-06			X			X	
4-001-01				X		X	
4-002-01				X		X	
5-001-01					X	X	
5-001-02					X	X	
5-001-03					X	X	
. . . .							

Figure A.14. Test case/Test cycle Matrix.

SYSTEMS TEST SUMMARY REPORT FOR REAL ESTATE RESIDENTIAL LISTINGS SYSTEM

Date Prepared: November 30, 1992

Written By: Cynthia Morgan

Submitted to:

K. Davis—Information Services Department
E. Kaplan—Information Services Department

Document Locator:

This document is stored on the LAN in the Information Services Department—Corporate Division. It is on the disk pack assigned to the Real Estate Residential Listings system development project. It is written with word processor XYZ Release 3.3.

Other Documents

Other documents for the Real Estate Residential Listings System are stored in the same location as this document. They are all written with word processor XYZ Release 3.3.

Document	File Name
System Requirements	RELRD01.DOC
Software Inventory	RELSI01.DOC
Design Document	RELDD01.DOC
Systems Test Plan	RELTP01.DOC
Systems Test Specifications	RELTS01.DOC
Systems Test Activity Log	RELAL01.DOC

General Background:

The Real Estate Residential Listings System is a sales support application that was designed using a client/server architecture. It will be distributed to four branch offices. Each office has the same platform and will have the same software. The data will be different.

The application will be installed in phases. The Greenwich Branch will be the first installation. The remaining branch offices will be installed within four months of that installation.

The application was tested on the LAN in the Information Services Department—Corporate Division. This LAN is configured the same as those in the branch offices. The communication software used to access to mainframe and the remote branch office's databases is the same as that used by branch offices. The systems test environment was set up to access the test databases installed on the LAN in the Greenwich branch office.

Systems Testing Dates:

Systems testing execution

Started: November 3, 1992
Ended: November 10, 1992.

Tests Executed:

The following tests were executed:

Cycle 1 Maintain Personnel Information—All test cases

Cycle 2 Maintain Listings—All test cases

Cycle 3 Search Listings—All test cases but not all printers. See Tests not executed.

Cycle 4 Delete Expired Listings—All test cases

Cycle 5 Close Sold Listings—All test cases

Cycle 6 Performance Capabilities—All test cases

Cycle 7 Operational Capabilities - Test Cases 7-1-001 through 7-3-011 were executed for the Greenwich Branch Office only. See Tests not executed.

Tests Not Executed:

The following tests were not executed:

Cycle 3 Search Listings—Did not print listings on the printer used in the Stamford Branch office. All printers used in the Greenwich office were tested.

Cycle 7 Operational Capabilities—Test Cases 7-4-001 through 7-6-009 were not executed.

The software distribution and emergency maintenance procedures were only tested for the Greenwich Branch office.

The Help Desk is not set up and therefore could not be tested. The Information Services department will be the primary help contact for this initial installation. A Help Desk facility will be set up within three months.

The only site that was tested for compliance with physical security and premise guidelines and regulations was the Greenwich Branch Office.

Summary of Test Results:

After correcting some minor errors, all the test cases were accepted by the reviewers.

The actual results of the tests are stored on the LAN in the Information Services Department - Corporate Division. All reports are stored as files. The databases were backed up after Cycles 1, 2, 4, and 5.

Open Incident Reports:

The following Incident Reports are open:

Incident Report Number: 023

Listings contain a Broker Open House Date. This field contains the date the listed property is held open for brokers to preview. It is used as search field to display all broker open houses for a specified date. There is no provision to store the hours the property is held open. This information was entered in the Remarks field. The Remarks field does not display on the Broker Open House display.

This Incident Report is a change in requirements. The Greenwich Office holds all broker open houses on Tuesdays. Single-family homes are held open from 10:00 A.M. to 12:30 P.M. Condominiums are held open from 1:00 P.M. to 3:00 P.M. Property Type is displayed on the Broker Open House screen and they can determine the hours from this data. The resolution of this incident can be deferred.

Incident Report Number: 027

Send a message to the mailbox of the listing agent on the following conditions:

A listing with a status of Binder has its contingency date past due

A listing with a status of Contract has its closing date past due

A listing is due to expire within the next 7 days

This Incident Report is an enhancement to the system. It can be deferred to the next release.

Status:
The application was fully systems-tested. The results of all test cases were accepted. The open Incident Reports are functional enhancements or changes that can be deferred. The application is ready for installation at the Greenwich Branch Office.

Analysis of Testing Strategy:
The tools to verify that software adheres to the quality and standards requirements is inadequate. We need a product that enables us to specify our standards. The product we used only checks that the code followed general coding guidelines. We had to manually scan the code for violations of the standard to use reusable objects when available. This technique was haphazard. Although the risks to the system are minor, we may have missed some violations.

We need a better method to record the status of each test case. The Activity Log and Incident Reports are insufficient. We have no concise report that says a test case passed or failed. A spreadsheet should be set up that lists each test case number. We could record the status next to each test case along with the Incident Report number when applicable.

We fell behind in recording the results. We need more clerical support in logging the Incident Reports and the test cases.

SYSTEMS TEST ACTIVITY LOG FOR:

Real Estate Residential Listings System

Document Locator:

This document is stored on the LAN in the Information Services Department—Corporate Division. It is on the disk pack assigned to the Residential Listing Systems development project. It is written with word processor XYZ Release 3.3.

Environment:

This systems testing was performed on the LAN in the IS Department—Corporate Division.

DATE	TIME	TEST CYCLE	RECD BY	DESCRIPTION
11/03/92	9:30a	1	CM	Ran all test cases for cycle. Ran OK.
	11:40a	2	KD	Ran all test cases for cycle. Ran OK Incident Reports filed for enhancements.
11/04/92	8:30a	4	CM	Expired Listing which was under contract was deleted. Incident Report filed.
	10:30	3	CM	All test cases were executed. System can't display listing when multiple page description, dropped last two lines. Incident Report filed.

INCIDENT REPORT

Real Estate Residential Listings System

PREFERRED PROPERTIES REALTY COMPANY INC.
INCIDENT REPORT

INCIDENT #: 037

ORIGINATOR: J. Yale   DATE: 12/05/92

SYSTEM: Residential Listings

TYPE: Error _ ABEND _ Enhancement X Other _

PROBLEM DESCRIPTION: Renewed Listings

Provide facility to report all listings that were renewed.
List the following data:

    Original Listing Date, Original Expiration Date,
    Original Selling Price, History of price changes for
    this listing.

EXPECTED RESULTS:

ANALYZED BY: CM   DATE: 12/06/92

SOURCE CATEGORY: Req. X Design _ Code _ Implement. _

MODULES AFFECTED: Reporting RPT010, Closing LCL190

ESTIMATED TIME TO RESOLVE INCIDENT: 5 days, requires
database changes

PRIORITY: A _ B _ C X   ASSIGNED TO: TBN

                                DATE ASSIGNED:

INCIDENT
STATUS: Logged X Analyzed X Assigned _ Resubmitted _
        Closed _ Cancelled _

INCIDENT LOG

Real Estate Residential Listings System

IR#	DT-PREPD	STATUS	DT-CL/CN	PRTY	DESCRIPTION
030	12/01/92	Closed	02/05/93	A	Truncate cents in Price
031	12/02/92	Closed	02/07/93	A	Price range should be inclusive of high and low prices
032	12/03/92	Anlyzd		C	New screen school district/listing
033	12/05/92	Anlyzd		B	Set up separate code for pool/spa
034	12/02/92	Closed	02/05/93	A	Carry Commission Rate with 2 decimals
035	12/02/92	Closed	02/05/93	A	Display Selling Agent % on screens
036	12/02/92	Cancel	02/05/93	C	Same as IR 027
037	12/05/92	Anlyzd		B	Reporting all renewed Listings

Glossary

acceptance testing Testing performed by the users to provide them with assurance that a new software system is ready for production use.

Activity Log A chronological log containing details about the execution of the systems testing.

actual results The values and conditions generated by a software system during execution. Actual results are compared with expected results to verify the reliability of the system.

antiviral programs Antiviral programs are programs that are used as part of a computer virus-prevention policy. There are several types of antiviral programs: virus detection programs, virus prevention programs, and virus removal programs. Virus detection programs detect virus infections after they occur. Virus prevention programs prevent viruses from entering a system. Virus removal programs identify and remove specific viruses.

BBS Bulletin Board System

Beta test site The second level of testing performed on new computer software where the product is used by the customer, in the customer's environment, with actual conditions.

boiler-plate text Text that is copied into each document or section of a document. It provides consistency and saves writing time.

business requirements testing Tests to verify that the system performs the business requirements specified in the System Requirements document.

cascading windows An arrangement of windows where the windows overlap each other. The title bar of each window remains visible.

CASE Computer Aided Software Engineering. CASE tools are used to develop and maintain software systems.

CAST Computer Aided Software Testing. CAST tools used to develop and manage software testing.

change control A method used for incorporating changes to the requirements into the ongoing design.

check box A GUI control element used to select items from a list. Check boxes appear as small square boxes next to each item in a list. When an item is selected, its check box is marked with a check, an "X", or a color.

client The client is a desktop computer with its own operating system, capable of executing desktop software and custom application software. It provides user interface and presentation functions for the application and requests services from a server computer.

client/server A system architecture in which a client computer cooperates with a server over a network to perform the information processing.

CLIST Command List. A file containing TSO commands and logic, which operates in the MVS/TSO environment.

communications server A server that provides WAN communications services.

concurrency Multiple users accessing the data at the same time.

contextual help Help information for a specific area of the screen. When the user requests help, help information is displayed for the area of the screen where the pointer is positioned.

custodian A person or group responsible for the operational maintenance of a system.

DASD Direct Access Storage Device

database server A server that provides database access for the system. It services the data requests of the client.

DBMS Database Management System. DBMS software that organizes, maintains, and provides access to a database.

debugging The process of locating and removing coding mistakes in a computer program.

debugging tool A testing tool used during unit testing to assist the developer in debugging the program.

deliverable An output from a process or phase of the System Development Life Cycle (SDLC) that must be turned over (delivered) to another group at the completion of that process or phase.

dialogue box A window that pops up in the center of the screen and is used to ask the user questions and accept the responses.

downsize To move a software system from a large computer to a smaller, less costly computer.

drop-down menu See pull-down menu.

emergency change A change to production software that has failed and must be implemented immediately.

error A discrepancy between the actual values or conditions generated by the computer software and the expected values or specified conditions.

expected results The predetermined conditions and values that the system is expected to produce. This includes screen images, reports, and updates files.

failure The inability of the software system to continue performing its specified functions.

fax server A server that provides fax services. It sends and receives fax transmissions for the users of that system.

file comparators A testing tool used to compare two files and report the differences. It can be used to compare the actual results of a test execution with prepared expected results.

file server A server that supports the data storage and retrieval for files other than the database. The file server is generally the computer that runs the network operating system software and is considered the central node of the LAN.

freeware Software that is not copyrighted. It has been placed in the public domain and may be copied and used freely.

GUI Graphical User Interface. A user interface in which graphics and characters are used on the screens to communicate with the user.

I-CASE Integrated Computer Aided Software Engineering. I-CASE tools are used in software development. They attempt to integrate Upper and Lower CASE tools and address the design, coding, and testing of a system. See Lower CASE tools, Upper CASE tools.

icon A miniature picture displayed on the screen and used to represent a function available to the user. When the icon is selected, the function is initiated and its screen is displayed.

impact analysis The process of determining which components of a system are affected by a change to the software or hardware that the system utilizes.

Incident Report A form or report used to document an issue arising from the execution of a test and requiring further investigation.

JCL Job Control Language. A computer language used to define a job and its resource requirements to the operating system.

LAN Local Area Network

LAN-user license A license that permits multiple users on a LAN to use a software product.

logic bomb A logic bomb is computer code that specifies the conditions under which a damaging program will activate. When the conditions are satisfied, the code begins its destructive actions. Logic bombs are often contained within a virus program.

Lower CASE tools Software development tools used in coding and debugging a system.

maintenance The tasks associated with the modification of production software to continue its ability to perform the required functions.

menu A list of choices from which the user can select.

menu bar A bar along the top of a screen that contains a series of words representing choices from which the user can select.

monitor A monitor is a testing tool used to measure and report system performance. See performance monitor

mouse A device used to move the pointer around on the computer screen. It contains a ball mounted in the bottom of the device. When the device is moved across a flat surface, the pointer moves in that direction.

navigation A method of moving through an online system.

network A system that connects computers and allows them to share software and peripherals.

network operating system Software that resides in a file server and controls the operation of a local area network (LAN). It is considered the central node of the LAN.

operating system Software that supervises and controls the operation of a computer.

operational capabilities testing Tests to verify that the system can be operated by the designated staff using the system's procedures and instructions.

performance capabilities testing Tests used to verify that the software operates within the performance measures specified in the System Requirements document.

performance monitor A testing tool used to measure the performance levels delivered by a software product.

pointer A character on the screen that is controlled by a pointing device and used to make selections. It can have various shapes such as an arrow or a blinking box.

pointing device A device, such as a mouse or a track ball, that is used to move the pointer on the screen.

pop-up menu A menu that appears when the user selects an item on the screen that requires selection and is designed to invoke a menu. The menu displays (pops up) in the main screen area near the item selected.

print server A server that provides printing services for the system.

process Specific activities that must be performed to accomplish a function.

public domain software See freeware.

pull-down menu A menu that appears when the user selects a choice from the menu bar. The menu pulls down into the main screen area.

quality/standards compliance testing Tests to verify that the system adheres to the guidelines specified by the Informations Systems department.

radio button A GUI control element used to accept input from the user. Radio buttons are small circles that appear next to each item in a list. When the user selects the item, the radio button is highlighted.

RDBMS Relational Database Management System

redlining A revision technique in which a bar line is printed next to the text that has been updated since the last version. Redlining makes it easy to see additions, deletions, and changes in the document.

regression testing Tests used to verify a previously tested system whenever that system is modified. It verifies the modification and its impact on the existing functions.

review A testing tool used to analyze a technical work. The review can be conducted for the system design, database design, program design, code, test specifications, and operational procedures.

RPC Remote Procedure Call

screen capture/replay A testing tool used to test online (user-interface) programs. It captures user input in a file, which can then be analyzed, edited, or replayed.

scroll Move through a window, either vertically or horizontally, in order to view information that does not fit in the display area.

scroll bar A GUI element used to control the scrolling.

SDLC System Development Life Cycle

server The server is a computer on a local area network (LAN) that provides services to other computers.

shareware A method of software distribution where the author maintains the copyright on the software but allows users to copy and share the software freely. The users try the software to decide whether they like it. If they continue to use the software, they must register it with the author.

simulator A testing tool used to simulate a system configuration or environment. It provides a means of systems testing an application without having to acquire the hardware or software used on the target environment.

single-user license A license that permits a single user to copy and use a software product.

site license A license that permits an unrestricted number of users at one site or one organization to copy and use a software product.

sliders A GUI control element used to set a value when the choices consist of a continual range of values rather than a set of discrete ones. A slider is an empty track with a slider button inside. The button can be dragged from one end to the other using the pointer, and the setting continually changes in that direction.

software license The right to use a software product. A license authorizes the holder to make a specified number of copies. The license fee varies depending on type. A license can be for a single user, multiple users on a LAN, or unrestricted users at a site. See single-user license, LAN-user license, site license.

SQL Structured Query Language

systems testing The functional testing of an application system to verify that it performs the business functions specified in the System Requirements document within the required performance limits.

test coverage A measure of the portion of the program or system under test that is, in fact, tested ("covered") by the testing process.

test coverage analyzer A testing tool that provides reports showing the features of the system covered by the test cases.

test cycle A set of ordered test conditions that will test a logical and complete portion of the system.

test data Data used to test a program or a system. Expected results are associated with the test data so that the program or system being tested can be validated.

test data generator A testing tool used to generate test data.

test design generator A testing tool that generates test cases from the business requirements specifications.

test driver A program that directs the operation of another program.

test impact analyzer A testing tool that provides reports showing the systems test features that are impacted by a change.

test library manager A testing tool used to manage the source library for systems testing. It tracks and reports information on the programs such as version level, turnover date, and testing status.

test practitioner Person who tests software.

test supervisor A testing tool that automates the execution of the systems test. It automatically submits the test procedures, logs the tests, verifies results, and reports discrepancies.

testing tool A manual procedure or software used for testing parts of a software system.

text template A template that contains text that can be copied and used as a skeleton in writing new documents of the same type.

tiled windows An arrangement of windows where the windows do not overlap each other. Each window takes up a separate portion of the screen.

time bomb A time bomb is computer code that specifies when a damaging program will activate. When the specific date or time occurs, the code begins its destructive actions. Time bombs are often contained within a virus program.

toggle To turn a program function on and off by pressing a key or selecting a screen button.

track ball A device used to move the pointer around on the computer screen. It contains a ball mounted in the upper portion of a box. When the ball is rotated, the pointer moves in that direction.

trapdoor A trapdoor is a concealed entry point in a program that allows someone to enter the system bypassing normal security procedures.

Trojan Horse A Trojan Horse is a term used to describe a program that seems to perform a useful function but actually has damaging code hidden inside of it.

unit testing Testing performed on individual programs to verify that the program performs its required functions as specified in the program specifications and executes the code correctly.

Upper CASE tools Software development tools used to design a system.

version control Procedures to track the version of the software stored in a computer or software library file.

virus A segment of code that attaches itself to another program (an application program or an operating system component). It can self-replicate and enter new computers. The designer of the virus determines the number of times the virus can self-replicate and the action that virus will perform. The action performed by the virus can vary in seriousness from displaying a message to erasing the entire contents of the hard drive.

walk-through A testing tool used to analyze a technical work. A walk-through is a type of review in which the software developer leads the group through the work being reviewed. A walk-through can be conducted for the system design, database design, program design, code, and test design.

WAN Wide Area Network

window A rectangle on a screen that presents information.

Index